DIRTY
TRUTHS

By Michael Parenti

Against Empire (1995)
Democracy for the Few (6th edition, 1995)
Land of Idols: Political Mythology in America (1994)
Inventing Reality: The Politics of News Media (2nd edition, 1993)
Make-Believe Media: The Politics of Entertainment (1992)
The Sword and the Dollar (1989)
Power and the Powerless (1978)
Ethnic and Political Attitudes (1975)
Trends and Tragedies in American Foreign Policy (1971)
The Anti-Communist Impulse (1969)

DIRTY
TRUTHS

Reflections on Politics, Media, Ideology,
Conspiracy, Ethnic Life and Class Power

Michael
Parenti

CITY LIGHTS BOOKS
SAN FRANCISCO

Cover design: John Miller, Big Fish Books
Book design: Nancy J. Peters
Typography: Harvest Graphics

Library of Congress Cataloging-in-Publication Data

Parenti, Michael, 1933–
        Dirty truths / Michael Parenti
            p.   cm.
        Includes index.
        ISBN 0-87286-318-2 (cloth). — ISBN 0-87286-317-4 (pbk.)
        1. Social problems.   2. World politics—1989–   3. Social
history—1970–   I. Title.
        HN27.P35   1996
        361.1—dc20   96–1716
                                                                              CIP

City Lights Books are available to bookstores through our primary
distributor: Subterranean Company, P.O. Box 160, 265 S. 5th St.,
Monroe, OR 97456. 541-847-5274. Toll-free orders 800-274-7826.
FAX 541-847-6018. Our books are also available through library jobbers
and regional distributors. For personal orders and catalogs, please write
to City Lights Books, 261 Columbus Avenue, San Francisco, CA 94133.

CITY LIGHTS BOOKS are edited by Lawrence Ferlinghetti and
Nancy J. Peters and published at the City Lights Bookstore,
261 Columbus Avenue, San Francisco, CA 94133.

ACKNOWLEDGMENTS

Many thanks to my valued friend Sally Soriano for the assistance and unswerving support she has furnished in the writing of this book. Also an expression of appreciation to Jane Scantlebury for suggesting useful changes in the manuscript.

I owe a special debt to Peggy Noton who encouraged me to embark upon this project and helped to organize the initial undertaking. She also painstakingly edited the entire manuscript, bringing needed improvements to it. In addition, she co-authored one of the articles.

Over the years, Kathleen Lipscomb has offered critical comments on earlier versions of a number of the selections herein and for this she has my gratitude.

Once again I had the benefit of working with Nancy J. Peters, editor at City Lights Books. My thanks to her and other members of the City Lights staff who helped produce the final product.

CONTENTS

INTRODUCTION

I call these writings *Dirty Truths* because they deal with the kind of undiluted information and ideas largely excluded from our corporate-dominated media, schools, and mainstream political life, views that are studiously ignored or strenuously denounced, so much so as to take on the appearance of something improper. They are not merely dissident but "dirty," as it were, lacking the unexamined repetition and aura of respectability that are bestowed upon more conventional opinions.

Some truths are considered so dirty as to reflect poorly on those who utter them. The propagators of iconoclastic thoughts risk being shunned by persons of the Right and Center and even by many who profess to be of the egalitarian Left; that is, who claim to be critical of exploitative wealth and undemocratic power.

Thus forewarned, the reader should proceed with caution yet without fear of being sullied, for truths no matter how uncomfortable are better than the imprisonment of lies we endure whenever ordained leaders and pundits open their mouths. An exposure to the information and ideas herein will, I hope, prove to be a refreshing departure from the predominating ideological pap that is fed to us time and again about such things as poverty and wealth, fascism and free markets, media and culture, consciousness and class power.

Many of these selections have been written especially for this book and are presented here for the first time. Most of the articles that appeared earlier have been subjected to sufficient rewriting and rethinking as to be considered new versions. These selections cover a wide range of ideas and experience, moving from the political to the personal in an attempt to show the links between social forces and individual experience. In pursuit of that, I have included two previously published autobiographical accounts. Also included are three poems, an indulgence my editor did not have the heart to deny me.

— *Michael Parenti*

1 POLITICS AND ISSUES

HIDDEN HOLOCAUST, USA

"I've had grown men wet this floor with tears, begging for a job. We have to pray with some to keep them from killing themselves. So many say they just want to die," says Charlie Tarrance, a director of a private social agency. His task is to deal with growing lines of despairing people looking for jobs, housing, and food. The place is Gadsden, Alabama, but it could be anywhere in the United States.

It could be Washington, D.C., at a Safeway supermarket a mile or so from the White House where an elderly man is crying and holding a can of dog food. When asked what's wrong, he says, "I'm hungry. I'm hungry."

It could be New York City, where a woman begins screaming at the landlord who evicts her and her several children. The Bureau of Child Welfare takes her children, which distresses her all the more. She herself is transported to a New York mental hospital crying angrily—only to be diagnosed and committed by the all-knowing psychiatrists as a "paranoid schizophrenic."

There is misery and cruelty in the land. As U.S. leaders move determinedly toward their free-market Final Solution, stories abound of hunger, pain, and desperation. Such things have existed for a long time. Social pathology is as much a part of this society as crime and capitalism. But life is getting ever more difficult for many.

Some Grim Statistics

Conservatives are fond of telling us what a wonderful, happy, prosperous nation this is. The only thing that matches their love of country is the remarkable indifference they show toward the people who live in it. To their ears the anguished cries of the dispossessed sound like the peevish whines of malcontents. They denounce as "bleeding hearts" those of us who criticize existing conditions, who show some concern for our fellow citizens. But the dirty truth is that there exists a startling amount of hardship, abuse, affliction, illness, violence, and pathology in this country. The figures reveal a casualty list that runs into many millions. Consider the following estimates. In any one year

- 27,000 Americans commit suicide.
- 5,000 attempt suicide; some estimates are higher.
- 26,000 die from fatal accidents in the home.
- 23,000 are murdered.
- 85,000 are wounded by firearms.
- 38,000 of these die, including 2,600 children.
- 13,000,000 are victims of crimes including assault, rape, armed robbery, burglary, larceny, and arson.
- 135,000 children take guns to school.
- 5,500,000 people are arrested for all offenses (not including traffic violations).
- 125,000 die prematurely of alcohol abuse.

- 473,000 die prematurely from tobacco-related illnesses; 53,000 of these are nonsmokers victimized by secondary smoke inhalation.
- 6,500,000 use heroin, crack, speed, PCP, cocaine, or some other hard drug on a regular basis.
- 5,000-plus die from illicit drug use. Thousands suffer serious debilitations.
- 1,000-plus die from sniffing household substances found under the kitchen sink. About 20 percent of all eighth graders have "huffed" toxic substances. Thousands suffer permanent neurological damage.
- 31,450,000 use marijuana, 3,000,000 of whom are heavy users.
- 37,000,000, or one out of every six Americans, *regularly* use emotion-controlling medical drugs. The users are mostly women. The pushers are doctors; the suppliers are pharmaceutical companies; the profits are stupendous.
- 2,000,000 nonhospitalized persons are given powerful mind-control drugs, sometimes described as "chemical straitjackets."
- 5,000 die from psychoactive drug treatments.
- 200,000 are subjected to electric shock treatments that are injurious to the brain and nervous system.
- 600 to 1,000, mostly women, are lobotomized.
- 25,000,000, or one out of every 10 Americans, seek help from psychiatric, psychotherapeutic, or medical sources for mental and emotional problems, at a cost of over $4 billion annually.
- 6,800,000 turn to nonmedical services, such as ministers, welfare agencies, and social counselors for help with emotional troubles. In all, nearly 80,000,000 have sought some kind of psychological counseling in their lifetimes.
- 1,300,000 suffer some kind of injury related to treatment at hospitals.

- 2,000,000 undergo unnecessary surgical operations; 10,000 of whom die from the surgery.
- 180,000 die from adverse reactions to all medical treatments, more than are killed by airline and automobile accidents combined.
- 14,000-plus die from overdoses of legal prescription drugs.
- 45,000 are killed in auto accidents. Yet more cars and highways are being built while funding for safer forms of mass transportation is reduced.
- 1,800,000 sustain nonfatal injuries from auto accidents; but 150,000 of these auto injury victims suffer permanent impairments.
- 126,000 children are born with a major birth defect, mostly due to insufficient prenatal care, nutritional deficiency, environmental toxicity, or maternal drug addiction.
- 2,900,000 children are reportedly subjected to serious neglect or abuse, including physical torture and deliberate starvation.
- 5,000 children are killed by parents or grandparents.
- 30,000 or more children are left permanently physically disabled from abuse and neglect. Child abuse in the United States afflicts more children each year than leukemia, automobile accidents, and infectious diseases combined. With growing unemployment, incidents of abuse by jobless parents is increasing dramatically.
- 1,000,000 children run away from home, mostly because of abusive treatment, including sexual abuse, from parents and other adults. Of the many sexually abused children among runaways, 83 percent come from white families.
- 150,000 children are reported missing.
- 50,000 of these simply vanish. Their ages range from one year to mid-teens. According to the *New York Times*, "Some

of these are dead, perhaps half of the John and Jane Does annually buried in this country are unidentified kids."
- 900,000 children, some as young as seven years old, are engaged in child labor in the United States, serving as underpaid farm hands, dishwashers, laundry workers, and domestics for as long as ten hours a day in violation of child labor laws.
- 2,000,000 to 4,000,00 women are battered. Domestic violence is the single largest cause of injury and second largest cause of death to U.S. women.
- 700,000 women are raped, one every 45 seconds.
- 5,000,000 workers are injured on the job, 150,000 of whom suffer permanent work-related disabilities, including maiming, paralysis, impaired vision, damaged hearing, and sterility.
- 100,000 become seriously ill from work-related diseases, including black lung, brown lung, cancer, and tuberculosis.
- 14,000 are killed on the job; about 90 percent are men.
- 100,000 die prematurely from work-related diseases.
- 60,000 are killed by toxic environmental pollutants or contaminants in food, water, or air.
- 4,000 die from eating contaminated meat.
- 20,000 others suffer from poisoning by *E.coli* 0157-H7, the mutant bacteria found in contaminated meat that generally leads to lifelong physical and mental health problems. A more thorough meat inspection with new technologies could eliminate most instances of contamination—so would vegetarianism.

At present
- 5,100,000 are behind bars or on probation or parole; 2,700,000 of these are either locked up in county, state, or federal prisons or under legal supervision. Each week 1,600 more people go to jail than leave. The prison population has

skyrocketed over 200 percent since 1980. Over 40 percent of inmates are jailed on nonviolent drug related crimes. African Americans constitute 13 percent of drug users but 35 percent of drug arrests, 55 percent of drug convictions and 74 percent of prison sentences. For nondrug offenses, African Americans get prison terms that average about 10 percent longer than Caucasians for similar crimes.

- 15,000-plus have tuberculosis, with the numbers growing rapidly; 10,000,000 or more carry the tuberculosis bacilli, with large numbers among the economically deprived or addicted.
- 10,000,000 people have serious drinking problems; alcoholism is on the rise.
- 16,000,000 have diabetes, up from 11,000,000 in 1983 as Americans get more sedentary and sugar addicted. Left untreated, diabetes can lead to blindness, kidney failure, and nerve damage.
- 160,000 will die from diabetes this year.
- 280,000 are institutionalized for mental illness or mental retardation. Many of these are forced into taking heavy doses of mind-control drugs.
- 255,000 mentally ill or retarded have been summarily released in recent years. Many of the "deinstitutionalized" are now in flophouses or wandering the streets.
- 3,000,000 or more suffer cerebral and physical handicaps including paralysis, deafness, blindness, and lesser disabilities. A disproportionate number of them are poor. Many of these disabilities could have been corrected with early treatment or prevented with better living conditions.
- 2,400,000 million suffer from some variety of seriously incapacitating chronic fatigue syndrome.

- 10,000,000-plus suffer from symptomatic asthma, an increase of 145 percent from 1990 to 1995, largely due to the increasingly polluted quality of the air we breathe.
- 40,000,000 or more are without health insurance or protection from catastrophic illness.
- 1,800,000 elderly who live with their families are subjected to serious abuse such as forced confinement, underfeeding, and beatings. The mistreatment of elderly people by their children and other close relatives grows dramatically as economic conditions worsen.
- 1,126,000 of the elderly live in nursing homes. A large but undetermined number endure conditions of extreme neglect, filth, and abuse in homes that are run with an eye to extracting the highest possible profit.
- 1,000,000 or more children are kept in orphanages, reformatories, and adult prisons. Most have been arrested for minor transgressions or have committed no crime at all and are jailed without due process. Most are from impoverished backgrounds. Many are subjected to beatings, sexual assault, prolonged solitary confinement, mind-control drugs, and, in some cases, psychosurgery.
- 1,000,000 are estimated to have AIDS as of 1996; over 250,000 have died of that disease.
- 950,000 school children are treated with powerful mind control drugs for "hyperactivity" every year—with side effects like weight loss, growth retardation, and acute psychosis.
- 4,000,000 children are growing up with unattended learning disabilities.
- 4,500,000-plus children, or more than half of the 9,000,000 children on welfare, suffer from malnutrition. Many of these suffer brain damage caused by prenatal and infant malnourishment.

- 40,000,000 persons, or one of every four women and more than one of every ten men, are estimated to have been sexually molested as children, most often between the ages of nine and twelve, usually by close relatives or family acquaintances. Such abuse almost always extends into their early teens and is a part of their continual memory and not a product of memory retrieval in therapy.
- 7,000,000 to 12,000,000 are unemployed; numbers vary with the business cycle. Increasing numbers of the chronically unemployed show signs of stress and emotional depression.
- 6,000,000 are in "contingent" jobs, or jobs structured to last only temporarily. About 60 percent of these would prefer permanent employment.
- 15,000,000 or more are part-time or reduced-time "contract" workers who need full-time jobs and who work without benefits.
- 3,000,000 additional workers are unemployed but uncounted because their unemployment benefits have run out, or they never qualified for benefits, or they have given up looking for work, or they joined the armed forces because they were unable to find work.
- 80,000,000 live on incomes estimated by the U.S. Department of Labor as below a "comfortable adequacy"; 35,000,000 of these live below the poverty level.
- 12,000,000 of those at poverty's rock bottom suffer from chronic hunger and malnutrition. The majority of the people living at or below the poverty level experience hunger during some portion of the year.
- 2,000,000 or more are homeless, forced to live on the streets or in makeshift shelters.
- 160,000,000-plus are members of households that are in debt,

a sharp increase from the 100 million of less than a decadago. A majority indicate they have borrowed money not for luxuries but for necessities. Mounting debts threaten a financial crack-up in more and more families.[1]

A Happy Nation?

Obviously these estimates include massive duplications. Many of the 20 million unemployed are among the 35 million below the poverty level. Many of the malnourished children are also among those listed as growing up with untreated learning disabilities and almost all are among the 35 million poor. Many of the 37 million regular users of mind-control drugs also number among the 25 million who seek psychiatric help.

Some of these deprivations and afflictions are not as serious as others. The 80 million living below the "comfortably adequate" income level may compose too vague and inclusive a category for some observers (who themselves enjoy a greater distance from the poverty line). The 40 million who are without health insurance are not afflicted by an actual catastrophe but face only a potential one (though the absence of health insurance often leads to a lack of care and eventually a serious health crisis). We might not want

---

[1] All the above figures are gleaned from the U.S. Census Bureau *Statistical Abstract of the United States* (1975, 1992, 1994.); FBI Crime Reports; U.S. Department of Justice, Bureau of Justice Statistics; U.S. Bureau of Mortality Statistics; *World Almanac;* SCAN/INFO April 1995; and *Journal of the American Medical Association;* also reports provided by National Institute of Health Statistics; House Select Committee on Aging; U.S. Center for Disease Control; U.S. Public Health Service; and University of California, Berkeley, School of Public Health; and studies summarized in *Science* magazine, the *Washington Post, Los Angeles Times, New York Times, San Francisco Examiner,* and numerous monographs and books on poverty, suicide, crime, child abuse, and the aged, and studies of mental and medical institutions and occupational safety. For many of these specific citations see my *Democracy for the Few,* 6th ed. (New York: St. Martin's Press, 1995), pp. 24-32, 106-111, 130-132.

to consider the 5.5 million arrested as having endured a serious affliction, but what of the 1.5 million who are serving time and what of their victims? We might want to count only the 150,000 who suffer a serious job-related disability rather than the five million on-the-job injuries, only half of the 20 million unemployed and underemployed so as not to duplicate poverty figures, only 10 percent of the 1.1 million institutionalized elderly as mistreated (although the number is probably higher), only 10 per cent of the 37 million regular users of medically prescribed psychogenic drugs as seriously troubled, only 5 per cent of the 160 million living in indebted families as seriously indebted (although the number is probably higher).

If we consider only those who have endured physical or sexual abuse, or have been afflicted with a serious disability, or a serious deprivation such as malnutrition and homelessness, only those who face untimely deaths due to suicide, murder, battering, drug and alcohol abuse, industrial and motor vehicle accidents, medical (mis)treatment, occupational illness, and sexually transmitted diseases, we are still left with a staggering figure of over 19,000,000 victims. To put the matter in some perspective, in the twelve years that saw 58,000 Americans killed in Vietnam, several million died prematurely within the United States from unnatural and often violent causes.

Official bromides to the contrary, we are faced with a hidden holocaust, a social pathology of staggering dimensions. Furthermore, the above figures do not tell the whole story. In almost every category an unknown number of persons go unreported. For instance, the official tabulation of 35 million living in poverty is based on census data that undercount transients, homeless people, and those living in remote rural and crowded inner-city areas. Also, the designated poverty line is set at an unrealistically low income level and takes insufficient account of how inflation especially affects the basics of food, fuel, housing, and health care that consume such a disproportionate chunk of lower incomes. Some economists estimate that actually as many as 46 million live in conditions of acute economic want.

Left uncounted are the more than two thousand yearly deaths in the U.S. military due to training and transportation accidents, and the many murders and suicides in civilian life that are incorrectly judged as deaths from natural causes, along with the premature deaths from cancer caused by radioactive and other carcinogenic materials in the environment. Almost all cancer deaths are now thought to be from human-made causes.

Fatality figures do not include the people who are incapacitated and sickened from the 1,000 potentially toxic additional chemicals that industry releases into the environment each year, and who die years later but still prematurely. At present there are at least 51,000 industrial toxic dump sites across the country that pose potentially serious health hazards to communities, farmlands, water tables, and livestock. One government study has concluded that the air we breathe, the water we drink, and the food we eat are now perhaps the leading causes of death in the United States.

None of these figures include the unhappiness, bereavement, and long-term emotional wounds inflicted upon the many millions of loved ones, friends, and family members who are close to the victims.

Public Policy, Personal Pain

If things are so bad, why then has the U.S. mortality rate been declining? The decline over the last half-century has been due largely to the dramatic reduction in infant mortality and the containment of many contagious diseases, largely through improvement in public health standards. Furthermore, years of industrial struggle by working people, especially in the twentieth century, brought a palpable betterment in certain conditions. In other words, as bad as things are now, in earlier times some things were even worse. For example, about 14,000 persons are killed on the job annually, but in 1916 the toll was 35,000, with the labor force less than half what it is today.

The growth in health consciousness that has led millions to quit smoking, exercise more regularly, and have healthier diets also has reduced mortality rates, especially among those over 40. The 55-mile-per-hour speed limit and the crackdown on drunken driving contributed by cutting into highway fatalities. But the cancer death rate and other pathologies and life-diminishing conditions continue in an upward direction. Small wonder the climb in life expectancy has leveled off to a barely perceptible crawl in recent years.

When compared to other nations, we discover we are not as Number One-ish as we might think. The U.S. infant mortality rate is higher than in thirteen other countries. And in life expectancy, twenty-year-old U.S. males rank thirty-sixth among the world's nations, and twenty-year-old females are twenty-first. The additional tragedy of these statistics is that most of the casualties are not inevitable products of the human condition, but are due mostly to the social and material conditions created by our profits-before-people corporate system. Consider a few examples.

First, it may be that industrial production will always carry some kind of risk, but the present rate of attrition can be largely ascribed to inadequate safety standards, speedup, and lax enforcement of safety codes. Better policies *can* make a difference. In the chemical industry alone, regulations put out by the Occupational

Safety and Health Administration (OSHA)—at a yearly cost to industry of $140 per worker—brought a 23 percent drop in accidents and sickness, averting some 90,000 illnesses and injuries.

OSHA's resources are pathetically inadequate. It has only enough inspectors to visit each workplace once every eighty years. Workplace standards to control the tens of thousands of toxic substances are issued at the rate of less than three a year. Even this feeble effort has been more than business could tolerate. Under the Reagan and Bush administrations, OSHA began removing protections, exempting most firms from routine safety inspections, and weakening the cotton dust, cancer, and lead safety standards, and a worker's right to see company medical records.

Second, it may be that in any society some children will sicken and die. But better nutrition and health care make a difference. The Women, Infants, and Children nutrition program (WIC) did cut down on starvation and hunger. On the other hand, years after passing a law making some thirteen million children eligible for medical examination and treatment, Congress discovered that almost 85 percent of the youngsters had been left unexamined, causing, in the words of a House subcommittee report, "unnecessary crippling, retardation, or even death of thousands of children."

Third, it may be that medical treatment will always have its hazards, but given the way health care is organized in the United States, money often makes the difference between life and death. Many sick people die simply because they receive insufficient care or are treated too late. Health-insurance premiums have risen astronomically and hospital bills have grown five times faster than the overall cost of living. Yet it is almost universally agreed that people are not receiving better care, only more expensive care, and in some areas the quality of care has deteriorated.

Some physicians have cheated Medicaid and Medicare of hundreds of millions of dollars by consistently overcharging for services and tests; fraudulently billing for nonexistent patients or for services not rendered; charging for unneeded treatments, tests, and hospital admissions—and most unforgivable of all—performing unnecessary surgery. Meanwhile, private health insurance companies make profits by raising premiums and withholding care. So people are paying more than ever for health insurance while getting less than ever.

Fourth, it may be that automobile accidents are unavoidable in any society with millions of motor vehicles, but why have we become increasingly dependent on this costly, dangerous, and ecologically disastrous form of transportation? In transporting people, one railroad or subway car can do the work of fifty automobiles. Railroads consume a sixth of the energy used by trucks to transport goods.

These very efficiencies are what make railroads so undesirable to the oil and auto lobbies. For over a half-century, giant corporations like General Motors, Standard Oil of California, and Firestone Tires bought up most of the nation's clean and safe electric streetcar networks, dismantled them, and cut back on all public transportation, thereby forcing people to rely more and more on private cars. The monorail in Japan, a commuter train that travels much faster than any train, has transported some three billion passengers without an injury or fatality. The big oil and auto companies in the U.S. have successfully blocked the construction of monorails here.

In ways not yet mentioned corporate and public policies gravely affect private lives. Birth deformities, for instance, are not just a quirk of nature, as the heartbroken parents of Love Canal or the thalidomide children can testify. Many such defects are caused by fast-buck companies that treat our environment like a septic tank. Unsafe products are another cause; there are hundreds of hair dyes, food additives, cosmetics, and medicines marketed for quick profits that have been linked to cancer, birth defects, and other illnesses.

The food industry, seeking to maximize profits, offers ever-increasing amounts of highly processed, chemicalized, low-nutrition foods. Bombarded by junk-food advertising over the last thirty years, TV viewers, especially younger ones, have changed their eating habits dramatically. Per capita consumption of vegetables and fruits is down 20 to 25 per cent while consumption of cakes, pastry, soft drinks, and other snacks is up 70 to 80 per cent. According to a U.S. Senate report, the increased consumption of junk foods "may be as damaging to the nation's health as the widespread contagious diseases of the early part of the century." All this may start showing up on the actuarial charts when greater numbers of the younger junk-food generation move into middle age.

In 1995-96, a Republican-controlled Congress pushed for further cuts in environmental and consumer safety standards and in the regulation of industry, cuts in various public health programs, and cuts in nutritional programs for children and pregnant women. State and local governments are also cutting back on public protection programs and human services in order to pay the enormous sums owed to the banks and to compensate for reductions in federal aid. Thus New York City took such "economy measures" as closing all of its venereal disease clinics and most of its drug rehabilitation and health centers.

We are told that wife-beating, child abuse, alcoholism, drug abuse, and other such pathologies know no class boundaries and are found at all income levels. This is true but misleading. The impression left is that these pathologies are randomly distributed across the social spectrum and are purely a matter of individual pathology. Actually, many of them are skewed heavily toward the low-income, the unemployed, and the dispossessed. As economic conditions worsen, so afflictions increase. Behind many of these statistics is the story of class, racial, sexual, and age oppressions that have long been among the legacies of our social order, oppressions that are seldom discussed in any depth by political leaders, news media, or educators.

In addition, more and more middle-income people are hurting from the Third Worldization of America, suffering from acute stress, alcoholism, job insecurity, insufficient income, high rents, heavy mortgage payments, high taxes, and crushing educational and medical costs. And almost all of us eat the pesticide-ridden foods, breathe the chemicalized air, and risk drinking the toxic water and being exposed to the contaminating wastes of our increasingly chemicalized, putrefied environment. I say "almost all of us" because the favored few live on country estates, ranches, seashore mansions, and summer hideaways where the air is relatively fresh. And, like President Reagan, they eat only the freshest food and meat derived from organically fed steers that are kept free of chemical hormones—while telling the rest of us not to get hysterical about pesticides and herbicides and chemical additives.

All this explains why many of us find little cause for rejoicing about America the Beautiful. It is not that we don't love our country, but that we do. We love not just an abstraction called "the USA" but the people who live in it. And we believe that the pride of a nation should not be used to hide the social and economic disorder that is its shame. The American dream is becoming a nightmare for many. A concern for collective betterment, for ending the abuses of free-market plunder, is of the utmost importance. "People before profits" is not just a slogan, it is our only hope.

CREATING THE POOR

We are taught to think of poverty as an unfortunate but inevitable condition visited upon some portion of the population. And we tend to think of the poor as a breed apart who, if not exactly deserving of their situation, are an unfortunately predictable component of the social landscape. This view is as old as antiquity. In Matthew 26:11 (and similarly in Mark 14:7), when a woman anoints Jesus' head, the apostles protest, "for this ointment might have sold for much and given to the poor." But Jesus praises the woman for her "good work" in tending to him and assures the apostles that "ye have the poor always with you," suggesting that since poverty is so persistent, there is no compelling need to trouble ourselves about it.

Indifference to indigence has incurred the ire of those compassionate people who, like the apostles, believe that poverty is a matter of some urgency. I recall how Martin Luther King Jr. soundly castigated the rich and powerful for their lack of concern for the needy. More recently I have come to the conclusion that the rich and powerful are anything but indifferent. They always "look to the poor" as both a troublesome lot and an essential adjunct to the accumulation of wealth. And they have a real if seldom articulated concern that the mass of working poor do not become too successful or elevated in their collective class condition. Indeed, the owning class sees such a development as threatening to its own vital interests.

Blaming the Poor

Throughout the ages, the affluent have argued that the poor are the authors of their own poverty, that indigence is caused by the profligate and demoralized ways of the indigent. In seventeenth-century England, impoverished people were thought to be not the victims of circumstances but of their own "idle, irregular and wicked courses." Little has changed since then. In 1995, in the time-honored manner of all reactionary elites, right-wing Republican leader Newt Gingrich reduced poverty to a matter of personal inclination: "I am prepared to say to the poor, 'You have to learn new habits. The habits of being poor don't work.'"

Meanwhile Gingrich tirelessly pursued policies to enlarge the ranks of the poor. As House Speaker he fought to shift still more of the tax burden onto low- and middle-income people; he fought to eliminate the minimum wage, to cut spending for public housing, and to abolish school lunches, food stamps, and aid to families with dependent children (welfare). He supported enormous tax cuts for the corporate rich, for deregulating business activities, downgrading jobs, downsizing workforces, and breaking unions—all policies that have led to both deeper and more widespread poverty and more concentrated accumulations of wealth.

For affluent persons, the poor are less than human; they are demoralized creatures who seem to prefer squalor and misery, freeloaders who live off the rest of us. When they do work, they want to be paid too much for too little effort. And when they organize into unions, they become troublesome encumbrances to productivity and prosperity. All this we hear again and again.

Some persons of modest means embrace the denigrating opinions about the poor circulated by political leaders and opinion makers. Yet, during the 1995 budget debate, there was no mass support for the mean-spirited cuts imposed by a Republican Congress. A survey by the Center for the Study of Policy Attitudes (Washington, D.C., December 1994) found that 80 percent of respondents felt that society and government have a moral obligation to alleviate poverty. About the same number reject the right-wing argument that poverty is the outcome of inferior culture among the impoverished rather than material economic causes. But thanks to conservative disinformationists like Rush Limbaugh, who claims that 90 percent of government anti-poverty funds fail to reach the poor, respondents thought the programs were poorly administered with much waste. In fact, as economist Doug Henwood notes, the exact opposite is true. Only about 10 percent of the funds are spent on administrative costs with the rest going to recipients.

Another bit of conservative disinformation frequently mouthed by right-wing members of Congress and other commentators is that "$5.3 trillion has been spent on welfare in the past thirty years," a bit of fiction that is seldom challenged by their poorly informed media hosts or liberal adversaries. In fact, the actual figure is less than a tenth of that, about $400 billion, or what the Pentagon spends in a year and a half.

In contrast to right-wing Republicans, those of more liberal bent see poverty as a problem created by hard times, a tight job market, substandard schools and housing, deteriorating neighborhoods, a lack of much needed public programs, broken families, crime, and drugs. While well-meaning enough, this view sometimes confuses effect with cause, for most of the aforementioned conditions are really just symptoms. Substandard housing, crime, drugs, and deteriorating neighborhoods do not cause poverty but are part of its results. (This is not to deny that such effects can themselves have a demoralizing impact upon deprived people.) The question remains, what in the system brings about such results?

The liberal view tends to treat poverty as an outcome of impersonal forces. The differences between rich and poor are accepted as a natural given, a reflection of happenstance and circumstance. This view fails to recognize that poverty and wealth do not just coexist but are causally linked to each other. The notion propagated by conservatives and some liberals is that the more wealth accumulates in society, the better it is for all of us: as the pie gets bigger, we all get more. Supposedly it is not a zero-sum system. In fact, for most working people it is. More for one interest usually does mean less for another. What matters is not only the size of the pie but how it is sliced.

Wealth as the Cause of Poverty

Does wealth cause poverty? Certainly the converse is true. Throughout history, in societies where no great amount of wealth was accumulated by the few, there was no great poverty. Most hunting and food-gathering societies and early horticultural communities lived modestly under a rough social equality. When the herds disappeared and the crops failed, everyone bore the brunt of the deprivation.

During normal times, most of these societies enjoyed levels of consumption, health standards, and longevity rates that would compare favorably to their descendants in the present era. The diseases of "advanced" societies, such as cancer, typhoid, heart ailments, bubonic plague, tuberculosis, smallpox, diabetes, diptheria, syphilis, and gonorrhea were nonexistent or relatively rare—as were the combined conditions of poverty, poor sanitation, and overcrowding that produced them. Nor did the people work from dawn to dusk, as is popularly thought. Modern research has revealed that there was a great deal of free time for recreation and community gatherings.

The poverty of so much of the Third World is not an original historic condition. It was created by the expropriation of European and North American colonizers who stole the people's land and enslaved their labor, driving them into destitution. Thus under British imperial rule, the per capita income level in India plummeted 65 percent between 1830 and 1900. As the colonizing leaders grew richer, the colonized grew poorer.

If land and resources were used for social need instead of private greed, there would be enough for everyone in just about every society. Every country in the world has sufficient land to feed its population. Many poor ones export more agricultural products than they import. In India, the number of hungry people is conservatively estimated at 300 million, more than any other nation. Yet India's wheat and rice surplus in 1991 was about fourteen million tons, mostly in the hands of big producers and exporters. A fairly modest portion of this surplus would be a sufficient supplement for that nation's malnourished millions. The problem is not supply but distribution.

The dirty truth is that the rich are the great cause of poverty. When large surpluses are accumulated by the few, then want and deprivation will be endured by the many who have created the surplus. Slaveholders lived in luxury and opulence because slaves toiled from dawn to dusk creating the slaveholder's wealth while consuming but a meager portion for subsistence. Lords and ladies lived in great castles amidst splendid finery with tables laden with food because there were servants and serfs laboring endless hours to sustain them in the style to which they were accustomed.

Today, wherever there are great landholdings and latifundios, so there will be landless, destitute peasants crowded onto the dusty infertile hills, forced to work the agribusiness fields for something close to starvation wages—when work is to be had. Wherever there are rich factory owners and bankers who extract enormous profits from production and investment, so are there workers who put in long hours while paid but a small fraction of the value they produce.

The correlation is not a mere coincidence. How else is wealth accumulated save from the labor of those who produce far more than they are allowed to consume? Did the slaveholders or feudal lords, who spent their days hunting, riding, fighting, feasting, and drinking, create the abundance they enjoyed? Do the big shareholders, who spend their time boating, traveling, partying, attending charity balls, or running for public office, create the fortunes that accumulate from their investments? In reality, class systems of accumulation *are* zero-sum.

Those who toil at the lower rungs of the social ladder are not "neglected" or "overlooked." They are harnessed into the toughest, meanest, least-rewarding, lowest-paying work. In the early 1960s we heard that the residents of Appalachia, one of the poorest regions in the United States, were a forgotten people left behind by history. In fact, Appalachia is a rich region, having produced vast fortunes for the Mellons, Morgans, and Rockefellers. Only its people are poor. But their poverty is not an accidental condition. It is directly linked to the wealth extracted from their land and labor. The people of Appalachia were driven from the choice lands by the coal companies. They were overworked and underpaid; thousands were killed or maimed in the mines or broken in health by harsh occupational conditions. Their unions were threatened and attacked and their lives put at risk by company gun thugs, Pinkertons, state militia, police, and the U.S. Army. Their community needs were regularly betrayed by local, state, and federal politicos and courts in the service of the big coal companies.

The Appalachian poor are not "forgotten" by history. They long have been the focus of keen ruling-class attentions, of strenuous deception, repression, and exploitation. Their poverty is not a natural or inevitable condition nor a reflection of their own lack of effort. When masses of people labor so hard and end up with so little at such a cost to their own well-being, while so much is accumulated by a privileged few, then it is time to stop blaming the poor and direct our critical attention to the politico-economic powers that systematically impoverish them.

Wealth and Labor

By now it should be clear that when talking about wealth, we should also talk about labor, for the two are interrelated. Where does wealth come from? First of all, from the natural resources of our planet: the land, minerals, forests, and seas, which offer valuable life-sustaining materials. The other source of wealth is the human labor that extracts and transmutes these materials into marketable products. What transforms a tree into a salable commodity like timber is the labor that goes into harvesting it. Human labor also transforms the timber into lumber, another commodity, then into salable furniture.

Of itself, capital cannot create anything. It is the thing created by labor, the value accumulated by the living process of labor. It can only increase by being mixed with more labor. This is what is meant when people say they are "putting their money to work." The value accumulated is preserved in the form of money, gold, stocks, and bonds. Of themselves, all these forms of wealth could not produce the book you now are reading; only human labor can do that. But what of productive capital such as machinery and technology, do they not produce value? Marx would argue that machines only transfer value that is created by living labor. To be sure, it is human labor that creates, maintains, and operates machinery and other such productive capital. The ruling powers present themselves as the creators of wealth, to whom we are beholden. They would have us think they produce the milk when all they do is skim the cream.

Labor is the ultimate source of all commodity value. Adam Smith, one of capitalism's founding theorists, wrote in 1776: "Labor is alone the ultimate and real standard by which the value of all commodities at all times and places can be estimated and compared. It is their real price, money is their nominal price only." The first Republican president, Abraham Lincoln, said: "Labor is prior to and independent of capital. Capital is only the fruit of labor and could not have existed had not labor first existed. Labor is the superior of capital and deserves much the higher consideration."

All of humanity can be categorized into three groups. Group A consists of that tiny portion of people who usually do not work because they do not have to. The people in group A receive the bulk of their money from dividends on stock investments; interest payments on bonds and securities; the sale of appreciated holdings in commodity futures, real estate, and other ventures;

rents on income property; payments on privately financed loans or mortgage notes that they hold as creditors; government business subsidies and other giveaways; royalties from oil and other mineral deposits; and various other investments. Some prominent tycoons who preside over vast financial empires may work, but they do so out of personal choice, not economic necessity. And the workday they put in does not explain the source of their immense wealth nor the pace at which it accumulates. The far greater portion of their fortune comes from the ownership of assets that directly or indirectly engage the labor of others.

Most of humanity, group B, consists of those who live principally off wages, salaries, bonuses, fees, commissions, and pensions. To be sure, group B includes a wide income spread, from affluent professionals who have to work because they cannot live exclusively off their investment earnings, to working poor who have no net assets and endure real deprivations. Generally what the people in groups A and B have in common is that they both live principally off the labor of the people in group B.

Group C comprises the most desperate millions throughout the world who have been forced off the labor market and who live in absolute destitution. Their political function is to be castigated and scapegoated as social parasites. Their economic function is to provide a surplus of needy workers at home and abroad who help glut the labor market and depress wages. They make up what Marx called, "the reserve army of labor."

Two studies conducted in 1995 respectively by the Rand Corporation and the Brookings Institution do their best to muddy our understanding of wealth in the United States. They find that individuals typically achieve affluence not from inheritance but by maintaining their health and working hard. Most of their savings comes from earnings and has nothing to do with inherited wealth, the researchers conclude.

In typical social science fashion, the investigators prefigure their findings by limiting the scope of their data. Both studies fail to note that the capacity to achieve a high income is itself in large part due to inherited advantages, determined by the income level of one's parents. The socio-economic status of one's family is the greatest single determinant of one's own life chances. Those coming from the upper strata have a far better opportunity to maintain their health and develop their performance, attend superior schools, and achieve the advanced professional training, contacts, and influence needed to land the higher paying positions.

More significantly, neither the Rand nor Brookings study actually includes the rich, the people in group A, the top one or two percent who control the lion's share of the nation's wealth largely through inheritance. Both studies instead concentrate on upper-middle-class professionals and managers, who are labeled as "rich" —which indicates that the researchers have no idea how rich the rich really are. The investigators explain that there is a shortage of data on the wealthiest Americans. Being such a tiny percentage, "they're an extremely difficult part of the population to survey," admits James P. Smith, a Rand economist. That they're difficult to survey should not cause him or us to overlook the fact that their existence refutes the findings of these studies. Smith seems to admit as much when he says, "This [study] shouldn't be taken as a statement that the Rockefellers didn't give to their kids and the Kennedys didn't give to their kids." (*New York Times*, 7/25/95) Indeed, most of the really big money is inherited—and by a portion of the population that is so minuscule as to be judged statistically insignificant by some economists.

The Growing Gap

While asserting that the poor create their own poverty, ruling elites pursue policies that take from the needy and give to the greedy. So we have lower wages and salaries for the people in group B, with greater earnings for top corporate executives, shareholders, bondholders, and others in group A; a growing and more regressive tax burden for group B, with multibillion dollar tax cuts for group A; draconian reductions in human services for groups B and C; but ever-increasing government services, protections, and contracts for big business in group A.

In the United States most of the people living below the poverty level, including many homeless people, actually work. If they are poor, it is not because they are lazy but because they are being paid poverty wages while facing exorbitant rents, regressive taxes, and other high costs. In our society the line between the poor and the working class is becoming increasingly blurred. High-paying blue-collar employment has all but disappeared. In its place are millions of new low-paying jobs. Often the wife in the family now brings in a second low income to make up for the male breadwinner's drop in earnings.

In addition, numerous white-collar occupations have been eliminated or downgraded, including medical personnel, middle managers, technicians, and other professionals. When employees are deskilled, they are also disempowered, being more replaceable and thus less able to negotiate conditions of employment.

From 1990 to 1995, as profits achieved record levels and stock prices surged, the great mass of working people saw their wages stagnate or fall, while many of their benefits were reduced or eliminated. In the last twenty years the real income of a U.S. male worker with a high school diploma plunged by 30 percent. Many have lost their health insurance, homes, and savings. About one fourth of the workforce is now doing contract labor, hired on a daily basis, paid hourly with few or no benefits, no job security or collective bargaining.

The ten largest corporations alone have terminated more than 500,000 jobs from 1991 to 1994. Nearly one-third of the work-force is now employed part time. More than 4.5 million part-time employees want full-time jobs. About 75 percent of the workforce has experienced wage stagnation or decline since 1989. Hundreds of thousands of occupations have been downgraded so that fewer than one in five jobs pays enough to support a family of four (*U.S. News & World Report*, 4/3/95).

Meanwhile the gap between haves and have-nots grows still greater. In the United States, between 1973 and 1994, corporate profits jumped 389 percent while real wages fell 21 percent. From 1977 to 1993, the top one percent enjoyed over a 100 percent growth in income. Corporate CEO salaries and benefits jumped from 35 times what the average worker earns to almost 150 times. Today the richest one percent earn as much after-tax income as the bottom 40 percent.

The higher one goes up the income scale, the greater the rate of capital accumulation. Economist Paul Krugman notes that not only have the top 20 percent grown more affluent compared with everyone below, the top 5 percent have grown richer compared with the next 15 percent. The top one percent have become richer compared with the next 4 percent. And the top 0.25 percent have grown richer than the next 0.75 percent.

More than ever, wealth is being funneled upward. The causal relationship between accumulation at the top and decline among the lower strata is clearly demonstrated when various top corpo-rate executives lay off thousands of workers, impose speedups and wage cuts on those remaining, and then—with this increase in productivity and profit to show—vote themselves record salaries, bonuses, and stock options. The leap in CEO and shareholder wealth comes directly at the expense of the workforce.

Keeping the Poor in Their Place

When the poor try to fight for a larger slice of the pie, they are met with the full force of the capitalist state. All over this country, for decades on end, those African Americans, Latinos, and others who have exercised any kind of protest leadership in their communities have been railroaded into jail on trumped-up charges or murdered by the police or subjected to legal lynchings.

Along with the surveillance and suppression by local, state, and federal agencies, social control is exercised by the mass trafficking in drugs, in which the police and other law-enforcement agencies play an active role. The Knapp Commission investigation found that at least half of New York City's police were accepting payoffs, many of them drug-related. It is common knowledge on the inner-city streets that the cops are among the biggest distributors of narcotics. The Reagan and Bush administrations talked a tough line on drugs but drastically cut the Drug Enforcement Agency's investigative staff and halted law-enforcement efforts to keep narcotics out of the United States. Nor did things change much under the Clinton administration.

In addition, as several congressional investigations have discovered, the CIA has been involved in the heroin trafficking from Southeast Asia and the cocaine smuggling from Latin America. Legislation to stop U.S. companies from selling precursor chemicals needed in cocaine production remains unenforced, as do the laws designed to stop the laundering of drug money through established financial institutions. In 1993, Richard Held resigned as head of the FBI's San Francisco office, commenting: "There's never been any war on drugs," just so much manipulation of appearances "to give the public the impression something is being done" (*San Francisco Examiner*, 5/24/93).

The war on drugs is principally a war on drug victims and even more vigorously a war against those in the inner-city communities who attempt to resist the traffickers. African American leaders like Martin Sostre, Frank Shuford, Hurricane Carter, and members of Black Men against Crack were all railroaded into jail on trumped-up charges for trying to resist, among other things, the drug inflow into their communities.

Presiding over all this suppression and drug trafficking are the federal, state, and local agencies whose task is to destroy the militant protest organizations that arise in poor communities. With low wages, lay-offs, high prices, inflated rents, and other "impersonal" forces of the market, the poor are kept poor, no matter how hard they toil. Government imposes the additional burdens of deficient services and regressive taxes that fall unfairly upon lower-income people. Private-sector corporations tend to shun poor neighborhoods. The exception is the waste disposal business, which does much of its toxic dumping near poor communities, taking advantage of their vulnerability and lack of organization resources. And should low-income people try to mobilize their forces, they often are treated to direct applications of force and violence from agencies of the state. The individuals who most persistently denounce the poor for failing to improve their lot are the first to act against them when they attempt to do so.

Poverty deepens when labor is in retreat to capital. When the power of capital is increasingly untrammeled, all of us are put at risk: the environment, the sacred forests, the beautiful and mysterious creatures of the sea, the ordinary people who with their strength and brains and inventiveness create community and give to life so much that is worthy of our respect.

The goal of ruling interests is to keep this society and the entire world open for maximum profitability regardless of the human and environmental costs. The real burden to society is not the poor but the corporate rich. We simply no longer can afford them.

FASCISM IN A PINSTRIPED SUIT

If fascism came to America, some say, it would be an unbearable nightmare drastically disrupting the everyday pattern of our lives. And since our lives seem to retain their normal pattern, it follows that fascism has not taken over. In actuality, however, the fascist state, like all states, has no need to make nightmarish intrusions into the trivia of every citizen's life.

The Orwellian image of Big Brother commanding an obscure citizen to do his morning exercises via two-way television leaves us with a grossly exaggerated caricature of the authoritarian state. Rather than alerting us to more realistic dangers, novels like *1984* cloud our vision with fanciful horrors of the future, thereby making the present look not all that bad in comparison and leaving us the more convinced that there is no cause for alarm.

The dirty truth is that many people find fascism to be not particularly horrible. I once asked some Iranian businesspeople to describe what life had been like under the Shah's police state. "It was perfect," they responded. Workers and servants could be cheaply procured, profits were high, and they lived very well. To be sure, fascism is not perfect for everyone. Mussolini's Italy and Hitler's Germany inflicted a great deal of intentional hardship upon working people, including the destruction of labor unions, the loss of job benefits, and a shift in national income from the lower and middle classes to the upper class. Many among the petty bourgeoisie in Germany, who generally supported the Nazi party, suffered the loss of their small businesses and the dread slippage into working-class ranks — with jobs in the armaments factories when they were lucky enough to find employment. The number of Germans who lived in poverty and want increased substantially as wages were cut by as much as 40 percent.

Those who equate fascism with the horrors of Auschwitz are correct in their moral condemnation but mistaken in their sense of sequence. The worst of Auschwitz did not come until the war years. As late as 1939, the Nazi state was still pursuing a policy of encouraging, and more often forcing, the emigration of Jews to other lands. Mass liquidation as a "final solution" was not seriously considered and was in fact opposed until Hitler's order came (sometime after March 1941, most historians believe).

The concentration camp was never the normal condition for the average gentile German. Unless one was Jewish, or poor and unemployed, or actively leftist or otherwise openly anti-Nazi, Germany from 1933 until well into the war was not a nightmarish place. All the "good Germans" had to do was obey the law, pay their taxes, give their sons to the army, avoid any sign of political heterodoxy, and look the other way when unions were busted and troublesome people disappeared.

Since many "middle Americans" already obey the law, pay their taxes, give their sons to the army, are themselves distrustful of political heterodoxy, and applaud when unions are broken and troublesome people are disposed of, they probably could live without too much personal torment in a fascist state—some of them certainly seem eager to do so. Orwell's imaginings to the contrary, what is so terrifying about fascism is its "normality," its compatibility with the collective sentiments of substantial numbers of "normal" persons—though probably never a majority in any society.

We might do well to stop thinking of fascism as being a simple either-or condition. The political system of any one country encompasses a variety of uneven and seemingly incongruous institutional practices. To insist that fascism does not obtain until every abomination of the Nazi state is replicated and every vestige of constitutional government is obliterated is to overlook, at our peril, the disturbingly antidemocratic, authoritarian manifestations inherent in many states that call themselves democracies.[1]

Selective Repression

It is sometimes argued by those who deny the imminence of American fascism that we are more free today than ever before. One's ability to accept such reassurance partly depends on the class conditions and life chances that one confronts. The affluent individual whose views fit into that portion of the American political spectrum known as the "mainstream" (from rightist Republican to centrist Democrat) and whose political actions are limited to the standardized forms of participation—informal discussion, television viewing, newspaper reading, and voting—

---

[1] In 1971 Bertram Gross and I got into a debate on this point. Gross argued that fascism was a possible but future thing in the United States; it could happen here. I argued that fascistic features already inhered in the state structure of most capitalist democracies including this one. We each wrote an article outlining our positions, he in *Social Policy*, I in *Transactions*. Years later he wrote *Friendly Fascism*, a book in which he adopted my argument. In a subsequent panel he said my article convinced him—though I looked in vain in his book for a citation.

is apt to dismiss the contention that America is fascistic. But those who oppose the existing political orthodoxy and who find themselves under surveillance and subjected to the intimidations, harassments, and sanctions of the U.S. national security state have a less sanguine view.

Over the last several decades just about every African American protest leader who achieved any local or national prominence eventually ended up either under indictment, in jail, on appeal, in hiding, in exile, or murdered by the forces of "law and order." Most of the killings went unreported in the national press. Few if any of the law officers involved were ever convicted of murder by the predominantly white, middle-American juries that pass judgment on these matters.

The leniency displayed by authorities toward those on the right side of the political spectrum stands in marked contrast to the relentless, punitive justice meted out to people of color, the poor, and radicals of all stripes. While the guardians go unguarded, political activists are arrested on trumped-up charges and end up serving astronomical sentences for crimes they never committed or for relatively minor offenses.[2]

The last decade or so has seen a growth in reactionary and racist groups. Yet the government does little about them. In the first half of 1995 alone, a county employee in California who refused a demand by rightist anti-tax activists to remove an IRS lien imposed on one of them, was beaten by two men and slashed with a knife. A judge in Montana was terrorized, threatened with kidnapping, and had a murder contract put out on her by a militia group that claimed she had no jurisdiction over them. A federal wildlife worker received a threat that his wife and children would be bound

---

[2] For a detailed discussion and documentation of this point, see my *Democracy for the Few,* 6th ed. (New York: St. Martin's Press, 1995), chap. 9.

in barbed wire and stuffed down a well. During a forum on Capitol Hill, government workers, environmentalists, and abortion rights activists described incidents of harassment, intimidation, and violence perpetrated by paramilitary groups (*Washington Post*, 7/13/1995). A number of these groups are financed by shady individuals of affluent means. In 1995, the Republican-controlled Congress refused to hold hearings on these paramilitary groups. Meanwhile, the Justice Department has done next to nothing about the menacing arms caches, threats, and openly violent actions these organizations have delivered upon others.

At the same time however, the government's repressive mechanism is geared up against leftist dissenters. The FBI and local police Red squads are once again spying, burglarizing, disrupting, and otherwise targeting various organizations that work for social justice, peace and disarmament, or environmentalism. During the 1980s almost two hundred organizations were labeled, not communist fronts as during the repressive McCarthy era of the 1950s, but "terrorist fronts," including Martin Luther King Jr.'s own Southern Leadership Conference and various church and student organizations. President Clinton lifted not a finger to undo this new round-up list and in 1995 supported a repressive counterterrorist act that gives the president the power to arrest and detain without benefit of evidence or trial or even formal charges individuals deemed to be aiding any group designated as "terrorist" by the president. (The bill passed the Senate by a large majority but was voted down by the House.)

Political Law

In the last two decades one of the fastest growing markets has been in guns, clubs, helmets, bulletproof vests, and other items of domestic warfare sold to law enforcers, and the fastest growing area of public employment has been police and prison guards. The prison populations in most states have grown exponentionally, mostly with small-time drug users. By 1995-96, California was spending more on prisons than on education.

This is not to assume that the police are busy fighting crime. For all their new equipment and personnel, they do little if anything to stop the big drug traffickers, slumlords, sweatshop operators, mobsters, corrupt politicians, spouse beaters, child abusers, rapists, muggers, hate mongers, and others who prey off the most vulnerable among us.

The real function of the police is social control. Their job is to keep in line those elements that might prove potentially troublesome to the powers that be. Take a look at the TV documentary cop shows that are in such abundant supply. What repeatedly comes across is how the police deal not with the victimizers but the victims: the down-and-outs and panhandlers, the homeless, the poor and unemployed, the prostitutes, illegal immigrants, alcoholics and drug addicts, victims who are represented as criminals to the viewing audience.

The social control function of law enforcement operates on three levels within inner-city communities and among potentially "troublesome" populations. First, there is the street-level repression provoked and perpetrated by too many police officers, who use their badges and guns as a cover for venting their racist animosities and personal distortions. All this is a matter of public record, with case after case of police brutality and case after case of settlements. And for every brutality victim who wins damages there are many who never make it into court.

Second, there is the mass trafficking in narcotics, in which the police play an active role as distributors along with federal agen-

cies, such as the CIA, that are linked directly to overseas traffickers. This too is a matter of public record, with findings by three
different congressional committees and sworn testimony by pilots
who have flown narcotics and weapons shipments for the CIA.

On the third level are the coordinated systematic efforts by federal, state, and local authorities to undermine community protest
organizations, because the powers that be prefer demoralized,
divided, disorganized, and drug-ridden populations to people
who are politicized and who mobilize for collective action and
radical change.

Members of various African American and Latino groups, such
as the Young Lords, the Black Panthers, Brown Berets, Black Men
Against Crack, and the Cripps and Bloods (after these gangs
became politicized), can testify that when they were involved in
crime they had less trouble from the police than when they became
politically mobilized against drugs, police brutality, and exploitative social relations within the inner-city communities. In attacks
conducted jointly by local authorities and federal agents, Black
Panther offices across the country were raided and destroyed, their
funds stolen, and their occupants arrested or shot. At least thirty-
four Panthers perished in the repression of the 1970s. Hundreds of
others were incarcerated, many on trumped-up charges. Some, like
Geronimo Pratt, are still in prison over twenty years later.

These three levels of political repression operate symbiotically
with each other. The racist cops and the drug traffickers get an
implicit green light from higher up, and the officials are served in
their larger agenda by the racist cops and the drug pushers. In
addition, the police themselves are often politicized, identifying
with a right-wing application of the law, taking their encouragement from the pronouncements of elected officials who pander to
popular fears about crime.

Familiarity and the "Moderate" Center

It seems that the ability of most middle-class whites to perceive the fascist features of American society is seriously blunted not only by their class experiences but by the aura of familiarity and legitimacy that enshrouds the established political culture. In making comparisons between their society and others, they tend to employ a double standard. Thus the organized forms of police violence in America are seen as isolated, aberrant happenings— on the infrequent occasions they are publicized—rather than as inherent manifestations of our social order. But the same practices in certain other lands are treated as predictable components of totalitarian systems.

The Nazi invasion of Poland is fascism in action; the American invasion of Vietnam is a "blunder" or at worst an "immoral application" of power. The indoctrination of children in Nazi Germany into the myths and rituals of the nation-state is seen as characteristic of fascism; but our own grade-school indoctrination replete with flag salutes, national anthems, and history books espousing the myths of American superiority is "education for citizenship." Many social arrangements and happenings that would evoke strongly negative sentiments if defined as products of a totalitarian state become, by their proximity and cultural familiarity, no cause for alarm when practiced at home.

The political mainstream is frequently characterized, by those who occupy it, as a democratic force fighting a war on two fronts against the extremes of Right and Left. However, a closer reading of history tells us that the Center has been more inclined to make common cause with the Right against the Left rather than oppose both with equal fervor. Far from being a blameless victim when fascism emerges triumphant, the Center is an accomplice. In

Germany, as early as 1918, the Social Democratic leader Ebert
entered an alliance with Field Marshal von Hindenburg "in order
to fight Bolshevism." Throughout the Weimar Republic, as Franz
Neumann records in his book, *Behemoth,* "every law aimed supposedly against both Communists and National Socialists [Nazis]
was invariably enforced against the Socialist party and the entire
left, but rarely against the right." Those leftists who were critical
of the illegal rearmament of Germany found themselves charged
and tried for treason, while rightist assassins and putschists "were
either not prosecuted at all or were dealt with lightly."

The collusion between Center and Right is understandable.
Despite their differences in emphasis and methods (differences
that are not always to be dismissed as insignificant) the Center
and Right share a common commitment to the ongoing corporate class structure, and conservative institutional authority.

While capable of extensive repressive actions at home and
abroad, centrists continue to think of themselves as incapable of
the extremism ascribed to the Right and Left. Indeed, the very linear model they apply to politics (extreme-Left/ Left/ Center/
Right/ extreme-Right), like any line or spectrum, can extend itself
at both ends to allow for limitless extremes but makes no spatial
provision for an extreme Center. The extreme, according to
Webster's, is "the utmost part, the utmost limit, an extremity."
Therefore, the very notion of an extreme Center is a contradiction
in terms. The extremes of the Center on a linear political spectrum, to the extent they can be imagined, are nothing more than
the beginnings of a moderate Left and moderate Right.

But extreme has another meaning, to quote *Webster's,* "an
excessive or immoderate degree, condition or measure." Implicit
in the second definition is the image of the intransigent, dogmatic, and violent extremist, and in common political parlance

this second meaning is often conflated with the first so that the linear relationship, the spectrum, takes on a moral quality of its own. By virtue of a pun, then, the Center becomes incapable of political extremism.

Yet, in truth, it does not follow that those who occupy the extremes of a linear model (a placement made in accordance with beliefs about changing the established social order) must perforce be extremists in the pejorative sense. Those of us designated as "extreme leftists" actually want rather moderate and civil things: a clean environment, a fair tax structure, use of social production for social needs, expansion of public sector production, serious cuts in a bloated military budget, affordable housing, decently paying jobs, equal justice for all, and the like. There is nothing morally extreme about such things. They are "extreme" only in the sense of being extremely at odds with the dominant interests of the status quo. In the face of such gross injustice and class privilege, considerations of social justice and betterment take on the appearance of "extreme" measures.

Nor does it follow that those who occupy the center of any political spectrum are thereby incapable of the kind of brutal, repressive, destructive, intransigent actions usually associated with fascist extremists. It was not the John Birch Society that tried to bomb Indochina into the Stone Age, nor was it the American Nazi Party that perfected napalm and put thalidomide in the defoliants used throughout Indochina. And today it is not the skinheads and Klan that maintain the death squads and other homicidal operations throughout so much of the Third World. It is the best and the brightest of the political Center (with plenty of help from rightists).

Searching for Scapegoats

The way the mainstream shades off into the fascist Right can be seen quite clearly in the Republican party. The GOP socio-economic agenda is not much different from the kind pushed by Mussolini and Hitler: break the labor unions, depress wages, impose a rightist ideological monopoly over the media, abolish taxes for the big corporations and the rich, eliminate government regulations designed for worker and consumer safety and environmental protection, plunder public lands, privatize public enterprises, wipe out most human services, and liberal-bait and race-bait all those opposed to such measures.

Regarding that last point, one of the main tactics of fascism is to direct the legitimate grievances of the populace toward irrelevant foes: Jews, communists, gypsies, labor unions. So today, in the United States, we witness middle Americans beset by real economic difficulties and social frustrations as taxpayers, wage earners, and citizens but too well indoctrinated and too committed to the conventional social order to make any realistic indictment of the multinational corporate system. They are told that the military and the big corporations are the mainstays of Americanism. And they are invited to turn their anger toward irrelevant and often imaginary foes, such as African Americans, Latinos, Jews, the poor, "welfare chiselers," immigrants, feminists, gays, advocates of legal abortions, atheists, the supposedly "liberal" media and other "cultural elites" (whoever they are), the hidden United Nations army that is secretly occupying the USA, and various real and imagined violators of law and order.

While U.S. rulers and the corporate-owned major media regularly ignore the legitimate and pressing grievances of socially deprived groups, there seems no limit to the sympathetic attention they give to angry Klan members, troubled Nazis, and anguished militiamen—almost all of whom are rightist, racist, and armed to the teeth. And rarely if ever do they invite the public to consider whether it actually is the welfare mothers or illegal immigrants who bring us record deficits, war, swollen military budgets, high taxes, poverty, urban blight, inflation, crime, unemployment, and environmental devastation.

As when fascism first emerged in Italy and Germany, the Center shows a tender tolerance for the ultra-Right while seeking to exercise an intimidating and repressive control over the Left. Not surprisingly, many of the same people who support these autocratic, statist measures against democratic dissenters are the first to deny that fascism is a threat in the United States. But growing numbers of us have lost our skepticism. What we fear is not the cataclysm but the drift. In fact, it is less a drift toward fascism than a concerted push by the purveyors of state power. Not only do the higher circles attack the standard of living of the populace, they attack the democratic rights that enable us to launch any kind of counterattack to defend ourselves from being plunged into Third Worldom. In the final analysis, the danger of fascism comes not from the handful of skinheads or militia but from the various enforcement agencies of the national security state, those who would divest us of whatever remains of our livelihoods and democratic rights under the guise of "doing what is best for America."

ROLLBACK

For years U.S. political and economic leaders saw themselves in mortal combat with communist nations for the allegiance of peoples at home and abroad. Time and again, the argument was made that U.S. workers enjoyed a higher standard of living than their opposite numbers who lived under communism. Statistics were rolled out to show that Soviet workers had to toil many more hours than our workers to buy various consumer goods. (No comparisons were offered in regard to medical care, rent, housing, education, transportation, and other services that are heavily subsidized by communist governments). The pressure of being in competition with an alternative economic system set limits on how thoroughly Western politico-economic leaders dared to mistreat their working populations.

To maintain an appearance of "capitalism with a human face," corporate leaders occasionally were compelled to make substantive concessions. All sorts of important victories were won in the better organized sectors of the workforce: the eight-hour day, seniority rights, a minimum wage, social security, unemployment and disability insurance, vacation and health benefits, a guaranteed annual wage, maternity leave, and the like.

The concern about communism also helped the civil rights struggle. Since we supposedly were competing with Moscow for the hearts and minds of nonwhites in Asia, Africa, and Latin America, it was considered imperative that we rid ourselves of Jim Crow here at home and grant equality to our own people of color. Many of the arguments made against segregation were couched in just that amoral opportunistic rhetoric: not racial equality for its own sake but because it would improve America's image in the cold war.

The Third World Comes Home

The overthrow of communism in the Soviet Union and other Eastern European nations caused much rejoicing among the higher circles in this country. Except for a few minor holdouts like Cuba and North Korea, multinational corporate capitalism now seemed to have its grip on the entire globe. Yet, an impatient plaint soon could be detected in conservative publications. It went something like this: "If everywhere socialism is being rolled back by the free market, why is there no rollback here in the United States? Why do we have to continue tolerating all sorts of collectivist regulations and liberal services?"

By 1992, it became clear to many conservatives that now was the time to cast off all restraint and sock it to the employee class. The competition for their hearts and minds was over. There was no alternative system, no place else for them to think of going. Big Capital had scored a total victory and now would be able to write its own ticket at home and abroad. Tolerance toward opposing interests does not increase with a sense of one's own growing power. There would be no more accommodation, not with blue-collar workers, nor even with white-collar professionals or middle management.

Throughout history there has been only one thing that ruling interests have ever wanted—and that is *everything:* all the choice lands, forests, game, herds, harvests, mineral deposits, and precious metals of the earth; all the wealth, riches, and profitable returns; all the productive facilities, gainful inventiveness, and technologies; all the control positions of the state and other major institutions; all public supports and subsidies, privileges and immunities; all the protections of the law with none of its constraints; all the services, comforts, luxuries, and advantages of civil society with none of the taxes and costs. Every ruling class has wanted only this: all the rewards and none of the burdens. The operational code is: we have a lot; we can get more; we want it all.

With the rollback of communism, the politico-economic circles that preside over this country no longer feel they need to tolerate any modus vivendi with those who work for a living. Instead of worrying about lowering unemployment, as during the cold war, corporate elites now seek to sustain a relatively high level of joblessness in order to weaken unions, curb workers, and attain growth without inflation.

Growth without inflation sounds pretty good. But meanwhile we are witnessing the Third Worldization of the United States, the economic downgrading of a relatively prosperous population. Corporate circles see no reason why millions of working people should be able to enjoy a middle-class living standard, with home ownership, surplus income, and secure long-term employment. They also see no reason why the middle class itself should be as large as it is.

As the haves would have it, people must lower their expectations, work harder, and be satisfied with less. The more they get, the more they will expect and be able to demand, until we will end up with a social democracy—or worse. Better to keep them down and hungry with their noses to the grindstone. For the ruling interests, it is time to return to nineteenth-century standards, the kind that currently obtain throughout the Third World—specifically, an unorganized working populace that toils for a bare subsistence; a mass of unemployed, desperate poor who help to depress wages and serve as a target for the misplaced resentment of those just above them; a small, shrinking middle class that hangs on by its bleeding fingers; and a tiny, obscenely rich owning class that has it all.

The haves are pulling out the stops. For them, it's time to cutback drastically on such luxuries as education, medical care, libraries, mass transportation, and other publicly funded human services, so that people will have the opportunity to learn how to take care of themselves. Time to do away with unions, business regulations, minimum-wage laws, occupational safety, consumer safety, environmental protections, and taxes on investment income. All these things cut into profits. Every dollar that goes into the public sector is one less for the private sector. And the haves want it all.

The reactionary offensive in the United States is being replicated throughout most of Western Europe, Canada, Australia, and New Zealand, where we witness repeated moves toward deregulation and privatization and an upward redistribution of income. While the overthrow of communism in Eastern Europe and the decline of social-democratic and communist parties in Western industrial countries has been hailed by some commentators as "the end of class struggle" and even "the end of history,"

the global corporate elites are in fact waging class war more determinedly than ever.

The Fourth World Comes to the Third World

Along with the decline in working and living conditions in the
United States and other Western nations, there has come an economic collapse in many Third World nations. This development
too has been accelerated by the collapse of communism.

During the cold war era, U.S. policymakers sought to contain
communism by ensuring the economic growth and stability of
anticommunist regimes. But Third World development began to
threaten U.S. corporate profitability. By the late 1970s, governments in Brazil, Mexico, Taiwan, South Korea, and other nations
were closing off key sectors of their economies to U.S. investment.
In addition, exports from these countries were competing for
overseas markets with U.S. firms, including within the United
States itself. At the same time, growing numbers of Third World
leaders were calling for more coordinated effort to control their
own communication and media systems, their own resources,
markets, air space, and seabeds.

By the 1980s, U.S. policymakers were rejecting the view that a
more prosperous, economically independent Third World would
work to the interests of U.S. capitalism. Instead, they sought to
subordinate the economies of Third Word nations by rolling back
development programs and weakening the political efficacy of
their governments. The goal has been to create a world free for
maximizing profits irrespective of the human and environmental
costs. And there no longer is a competing communist world to
which Third World leaders might threaten to turn.

One rollback weapon is the debt. Third World governments are burdened with huge debts and desperately strapped for funds. In order to meet payments and receive new credits from the U.S.-dominated World Bank and International Monetary Fund (IMF), these governments have had to agree to heartless "structural adjustments;" including reductions in social programs, cuts in wages, the elimination of import controls, the removal of restrictions on foreign investments, and the privatization of state enterprises.

Such measures are ostensibly designed to curb inflation, boost exports, and strengthen the fiscal condition of the debtor nation. By consuming less and producing more, debtors supposedly will be better able to pay off their debts. In fact, these structural adjustments work wonderfully for the transnational corporations by increasing the level of exploitation and boosting profit rates. They also leave the economies and peoples of these various countries measurably worse off. Domestic industries lose out to foreign investors. There is a general deindustrialization as state enterprises fall by the wayside or are handed over to private owners to be milked for profits. Many small farmers lose their import protections and subsidies and are driven off the land. Unemployment and poverty increase along with hunger, malnutrition, and various attendant epidemics and diseases.

In time, Third World countries like the Philippines, Brazil, and Mexico slip deeper into the desperately absolute poverty of what has been called the "Fourth World," already inhabited by countries like Haiti and Zaire. Thus, in the first ten months of 1995, malnutrition in Mexico City increased sixfold. As many as one-fifth of Mexico's ninety million people are now considered "severely undernourished," while the incidence of cholera, dengue, and other diseases related to malnutrition is nearly ten times higher in 1995 than in the previous year. The Mexican public health system that began to improve markedly in recent years is now at the point

of complete collapse, with overcrowded, underfinanced, and
understaffed hospitals no longer able to provide basic medicines.
Much of this thanks to financial "restructuring."

As a further blow, the richer industrial nations, following the
United States' lead, have been making substantial cuts in nonmil-
itary foreign aid to poor countries. These include sharp reductions in funds for education, environmental protection, family
planning, and health programs. As noted in the *Los Angeles Times*
(6/13/95), "With the decline of the Soviet threat, aid levels fell
off. . . ." Measured as a percentage of gross national product, the
United States gives the least assistance of all industrialized
nations, less than .02 percent.

Reformist governments that try to protect their resources,
develop their economies, and raise their minimum wages are
finding these efforts undermined by the General Agreement on
Tariffs and Trade (GATT), whose latest round of agreements
refashioned the international trade structure to give a free hand to
the transnational corporations and bypass the sovereignty of
individual nations on many essential matters. Not only are Third
World economies now more successfully penetrated but the governments themselves are being undermined and marginalized by
GATT and the whole process of economic globalization. Thus
attempts by Third World governments to institute import protections, public health and insurance services, consumer protections, and environmental regulations are being overruled by
GATT's executive arm, the World Trade Organization, as
"restraints of trade" and "unfair competition."

Reformist governments are attacked not only economically
but, if need be, militarily, as in the case of Libya, Panama, Iraq,
and a dozen revolutionary nations like Grenada, Mozambique,
and Nicaragua. In some cases, they are subjected to dismember-

ment as with Yugoslavia or obliteration as with South Yemen. Yugoslavia's advancing industrial base could no longer be allowed to compete with Germany or France. Secession and war accomplished the goal of breaking up that nation-state into small rightwing client states that are falling under the economic suzerainty of the Western corporations.

The road to development is the road of economic nationalism, and economic nationalism will no longer be tolerated in the New World Order. The nations of the world face a comprehensive, cohesive strategy pursued by U.S. politico-economic elites, whose goal has been to create a world free for maximizing profits irrespective of the human and environmental costs.

Who's Left to Buy It All?

The question is often asked, if the workforces of the world are being downsized and wages are stagnating, where will purchasing power come from? Who will buy all the goods and services produced by overworked and underpaid employees? The elites are cutting their own throats, the argument goes, and will sooner or later have to reverse their policies as consumption diminishes. But there are several mitigating factors.

First, though people may be working for less money in the USA, more of them are working. Despite all the downsizing, millions of new but poorer-paying jobs are being created every year. In many households, the male breadwinner has been joined in the job market by his wife and even oldest child, adding to the nation's aggregate wage.

Second, people are working longer hours. Economists say that the average work week is close to record levels. We not only have the two- and three-job family but the two- and three-job person.

Workers are still buying commodities and services but they have
to work harder and longer to do so.

Third, for the big ticket items like cars, refrigerators, and
homes, there's installment buying. The consumer debt is climbing
precipitously. Those with lots of extra money need to do something with it, so they lend it to those in need—at a price. Among
those in need is the government itself. Deficit spending converts
savings into consumption and consumption into investment
profits. And on it goes.

Fourth, demand is increasing among the rich and the very rich.
Even during recent recession years, the sales of jewelry, antiques,
art work, executive apartments, mansions, vacation homes,
yachts, luxury cars, and fabulous excursions abroad boomed
among upper-class clientele.

Fifth, there will always be some sort of middle class that buys
an ample share of goods and services. In the United States there
are some ten million professionals, upper and middle corporate
managers, government bureaucrats, small investors, and small
but successful entrepreneurs who do well enough. Even in an
impoverished country like India, with a population of about 900
million, there are some 80 million who might be designated as
middle class, constituting a consumer market numerically larger
than in most other countries.

Sixth, it should be noted that the present forced economic
decline in the United States started from an exceptionally high
level of prosperity. With downsizing, the pie may expand at a
slower rate or even get a little smaller, but if the people at the top
get a larger and larger slice, they are not much troubled about
sluggish demand.

Guidance From Above

While they plunder the planet and impoverish the world's population, those at the top proffer a good deal of stern advice for those who fight back. To give only one example: in April 1995, one of the world's leading ruling-class mouthpieces, Pope John Paul II, resplendent in embroidered white robes and a gold-encrusted miter, used his Easter Sunday address to denounce "selfishness and the desire for power" and "all who are tempted to place their hope in weapons" (*New York Times*, 4/17/95). Was he referring to the brutal right-wing plutocrats and militarists who rule and ruin so many nations? Or the CIA-supported bloodletting forces that have slaughtered hundreds of thousands in Mozambique, Angola, Nicaragua, Afghanistan, Guatemala, and scores of other countries? Or the corporate elites who regularly plunder and pollute the planet?

No, not an unkind word for any of them. Instead, the Pope pointed the accusing finger at the Kurds, Palestinians, and indigenous populations of Latin America—those who number among the poorest and most cruelly dispossessed people in the world. If we are to believe John Paul, it is they who should relinquish the use of force, rid themselves of "selfishness," and turn to "dialogue as the only way to promote . . . reciprocal acceptance." Suffering no material miseries of his own, the Pope is able to counsel an admirable forbearance to those who do. In this respect, he differs little from other prominent members of his advantaged class, a class that is not much troubled by the many at home and abroad who are increasingly racked by hardship and want.

Those who pretend to be our leaders are running the cruelest scam in history. There will be hope for the world only when people begin to see that the conditions they face are not the out-

growth of happenstance or "hard times" but the result of concerted and intentional rapacity, the creation of poverty by wealth,
the creation of powerlessness by the powerful.

MAKING THE WORLD
SAFE FOR HYPOCRISY

Why has the United States government supported counterinsurgency in Colombia, Guatemala, El Salvador, and many other places around the world, at such a loss of human life to the populations of those nations? Why did it invade tiny Grenada and then Panama? Why did it support mercenary wars against progressive governments in Nicaragua, Mozambique, Angola, Ethiopia, Afghanistan, Indonesia, East Timor, Western Sahara, South Yemen, and elsewhere? Is it because our leaders want to save democracy? Are they concerned about the well-being of these defenseless peoples? Is our national security threatened? I shall try to show that the arguments given to justify U.S. policies are false ones. But this does not mean the policies themselves are senseless. American intervention may seem "wrongheaded" but, in fact, it is fairly consistent and horribly successful.

The history of the United States has been one of territorial and economic expansionism, with the benefits going mostly to the

U.S. business class in the form of growing investments and markets, access to rich natural resources and cheap labor, and the accumulation of enormous profits. The American people have had to pay the costs of empire, supporting a huge military establishment with their taxes, while suffering the loss of jobs, the neglect of domestic services, and the loss of tens of thousands of American lives in overseas military ventures.

The greatest costs, of course, have been borne by the peoples of the Third World who have endured poverty, pillage, disease, dispossession, exploitation, illiteracy, and the widespread destruction of their lands, cultures, and lives.

As a relative latecomer to the practice of colonialism, the United States could not match the older European powers in the acquisition of overseas territories. But the United States was the earliest and most consummate practitioner of neoimperialism or neocolonialism, the process of dominating the politico-economic life of a nation without benefit of direct possession. Almost half a century before the British thought to give a colonized land its nominal independence, as in India—while continuing to exploit its labor and resources, and dominate its markets and trade—the United States had perfected this practice in Cuba and elsewhere.

In places like the Philippines, Haiti, and Nicaragua, and when dealing with Native American nations, U.S. imperialism proved itself as brutal as the French in Indochina, the Belgians in the Congo, the Spaniards in South America, the Portuguese in Angola, the Italians in Libya, the Germans in Southwest Africa, and the British almost everywhere else. Not long ago, U.S. military forces delivered a destruction upon Vietnam, Laos, and Cambodia that surpassed anything perpetuated by the older colonizers. And today, the U.S. counterinsurgency apparatus and surrogate security forces in Latin America and elsewhere sustain a system of political assassination, torture, and repression unequaled in technological sophistication and ruthlessness.

All this is common knowledge to progressive critics of U.S policy, but most Americans would be astonished to hear of it. They have been taught that, unlike other nations, their country has escaped the sins of empire and has been a champion of peace and justice among nations. This enormous gap between what the United States does in the world and what Americans think their nation is doing is one of the great propaganda accomplishments of the dominant political mythology. It should be noted, though, that despite the endless propaganda barrage emanating from official sources and the corporate-owned major media, large sectors of the public have throughout U.S. history displayed an anti-interventionist sentiment, an unwillingness to commit U.S. troops to overseas actions—a sentiment facilely labeled "isolationism" by the interventionists.

The Rational Function of Policy Myths

Within U.S. ruling circles there are differences of opinion regarding interventionist policy. There are conservatives who complain that U.S. policy is plagued by weakness and lacks toughness and guts and all the other John Wayne virtues. And there are liberals who say U.S. policy is foolish and relies too heavily on military solutions and should be more flexible and co-optive when protecting and advancing the interests of the United States (with such interests usually left unspecified).

A closer look reveals that U.S. foreign policy is neither weak nor foolish, but on the contrary is rational and remarkably successful in reproducing the conditions for the continued international expropriation of wealth, and that while it has suffered occasional setbacks, the people who run the foreign policy establishment in Washington know what they are doing and why they are doing it.

If the mythology they offer as justification for their policies seems irrational, this does not mean that the policies themselves are irrational from the standpoint of the class interests of those who pursue such policies. This is true of domestic myths and policies as well as those pertaining to foreign policy. Once we grasp this, we can see how notions and arrangements that are harmful, wasteful, indeed, destructive of human and social values—and irrational from a human and social viewpoint—are not irrational for global finance capital because the latter has no dedication to human and social values. Capitalism has no loyalty to anything but itself, to the accumulation of wealth. Once we understand that, we can see the cruel rationality of the seemingly irrational myths that Washington policy makers peddle. Sometimes what we see as irrational is really the discrepancy between what the myth wants us to believe and what is true. But again this does not mean the interests served are stupid or irrational, as the liberals like to complain. There is a difference between confusion and deception, a difference between stupidity and subterfuge. Once we understand the underlying class interests of the ruling circles, we will be less mystified by their myths.

A myth is not an idle tale or a fanciful story but a powerful cultural force used to legitimate existing social relations. The interventionist mythology does just that, by emphasizing a community of interests between interventionists in Washington and the American people when in fact there is none, and by blurring over the question of who pays and who profits from U.S. global interventionism.

The mythology has been with us for so long and much of it sufficiently internalized by the public as to be considered part of the political culture. The interventionist mythology, like all other cultural beliefs, does not just float about in space. It must be mediated through a social structure. The national media play a crucial role in making sure that no fundamentally critical views of the rationales underlying and justifying U.S. policy gain national exposure. A similar role is played by the various institutes and policy centers linked to academia and, of course, by political leaders themselves.

Saving Democracy with Tyranny

Our leaders would have us believe we intervened in Nicaragua, for instance, because the Sandinista government was opposed to democracy. The U.S.-supported invasion by right-wing Nicaraguan mercenaries was an "effort to bring them to elections." Putting aside the fact that the Sandinistas had already conducted fair and open elections in 1984, we might wonder why U.S. leaders voiced no such urgent demand for free elections and Western-style parliamentarism during the fifty years that the Somoza dictatorship—installed and supported by the United States—plundered and brutalized the Nicaraguan nation. Nor today does Washington show any great concern for democracy in any of the U.S.-backed dictatorships around the world (unless one believes that the electoral charade in a country like El Salvador qualifies as "democracy").

If anything, successive U.S. administrations have worked hard to subvert constitutional and popularly accepted governments that pursued policies of social reform favorable to the downtrodden and working poor. Thus the U.S. national security state was instrumental in the overthrow of popular reformist leaders such as Arbenz in Guatemala, Jagan in Guyana, Mossadegh in Iran, Bosch in the Dominican Republic, Sukarno in Indonesia, Goulart in Brazil, and Allende in Chile. And let us not forget how the United States assisted the militarists in overthrowing democratic governments in Greece, Uruguay, Bolivia, Pakistan, Thailand, and Turkey. Given this record, it is hard to believe that the CIA trained, armed, and financed an expeditionary force of *Somocista* thugs and mercenaries out of a newly acquired concern for Western-style electoral politics in Nicaragua.

In defense of the undemocratic way U.S. leaders go about "saving democracy," our policy makers offer this kind of sophistry: "We cannot always pick and choose our allies. Sometimes we must support unsavory right-wing authoritarian regimes in order to prevent the spread of far more repressive totalitarian communist ones." But surely, the degree of repression cannot be the criterion guiding White House policy, for the United States has supported some of the worst butchers in the world: Batista in Cuba, Somoza in Nicaragua, the Shah in Iran, Salazar in Portugal, Marcos in the Philippines, Pinochet in Chile, Zia in Pakistan, Evren in Turkey, and even Pol Pot in Cambodia. In the 1965 Indonesian coup, the military slaughtered 500,000 people, according to the Indonesian chief of security (*New York Times*, 12/21/77; some estimates run twice as high), but this did not deter U.S. leaders from assisting in that takeover or from maintaining cozy relations with the same Jakarta regime that subsequently perpetuated a campaign of repression and mass extermination in East Timor.[1]

U.S. leaders and the business-owned mainstream press describe "Marxist rebels" in countries like El Salvador as motivated by a

---

[1] For a more detailed account of Indonesia and East Timor, see "The Invisible Bloodbaths," p. 126.

lust for conquest. Our leaders would have us believe that revolutionaries do not seek power in order to eliminate hunger; they simply hunger for power. But even if this were true, why would that be cause for opposing them? Washington policy makers have never been bothered by the power appetites of the "moderate" right-wing authoritarian executionists, torturers, and militarists.

In any case, it is not true that leftist governments are more repressive than fascist ones. The political repression under the Sandinistas in Nicaragua was far less than what went on under Somoza. The political repression in Castro's Cuba is mild compared to the butchery perpetrated by the free-market Batista regime. And the revolutionary government in Angola treats its people much more gently than did the Portuguese colonizers.

Furthermore, in a number of countries successful social revolutionary movements have brought a net increase in individual freedom and well-being by advancing the conditions for health and human life, by providing jobs and education for the unemployed and illiterate, by using economic resources for social development rather than for corporate profit, and by overthrowing brutal reactionary regimes, ending foreign exploitation, and involving large sectors of the populace in the task of rebuilding their countries. Revolutions can extend a number of real freedoms without destroying those freedoms that never existed under prior reactionary regimes.

Who Threatens Whom?

Our policy makers also argue that right-wing governments, for all their deficiencies, are friendly toward the United States, while communist ones are belligerent and therefore a threat to U.S. security. But, in truth, every Marxist or left-leaning country, from a great power like the Soviet Union to a small power like Vietnam or Nicaragua to a minipower like Grenada under the New Jewel Movement, sought friendly diplomatic and economic relations with the United States. These governments did so not necessarily out of love and affection for the United States, but because of something firmer—their own self-interest. As they themselves admitted, their economic development and political security would have been much better served if they could have enjoyed good relations with Washington.

If U.S. leaders justify their hostility toward leftist governments on the grounds that such nations are hostile toward us, what becomes the justification when these countries try to be friendly? When a newly established revolutionary or otherwise dissident regime threatens U.S. hegemonic globalists with friendly relations, this does pose a problem. The solution is to (1) launch a well-orchestrated campaign of disinformation that heaps criticism on the new government for imprisoning the butchers, assassins, and torturers of the old regime and for failing to institute Western electoral party politics; (2) denounce the new government as a threat to our peace and security; (3) harass and destabilize it and impose economic sanctions; and (4) attack it with counterrevolutionary surrogate forces or, if necessary, U.S. troops. Long before the invasion, the targeted country responds with angry denunciations of U.S. policy. It moves closer to other "outlawed" nations and attempts to build up its military defenses in anticipation of a U.S.-sponsored attack. These moves are eagerly seized upon by U.S. officials and media as evidence of the other country's antagonism toward the United States, and as justification for the policies that evoked such responses.

Yet it is difficult to demonstrate that small countries like Grenada and Nicaragua are a threat to U.S. security. We remember the cry of the hawk during the Vietnam war: "If we don't fight the Vietcong in the jungles of Indochina, we will have to fight them on the beaches of California." The image of the Vietnamese getting into their PT boats and crossing the Pacific to invade California was, as Walter Lippmann noted at the time, a grievous insult to the U.S. Navy. The image of a tiny ill-equipped Nicaraguan army driving up through Mexico and across the Rio Grande in order to lay waste to our land is equally ludicrous. The truth is, the Vietnamese, Cubans, Grenadians, and Nicaraguans have never invaded the United States; it is the United States that has invaded Vietnam, Cuba, Grenada, and Nicaragua, and it is our government that continues to try to isolate, destabilize, and in other ways threaten any country that tries to drop out of the global capitalist system or even assert an economic nationalism within it.

Remember the Red Menace

For many decades of cold war, when all other arguments failed, there was always the Russian bear. According to our cold warriors, small leftist countries and insurgencies threatened our security because they were extensions of Soviet power. Behind the little Reds there supposedly stood the Giant Red Menace. Evidence to support this global menace thesis was sometimes farfetched. President Carter and National Security Advisor Brezinski suddenly discovered a "Soviet combat brigade" in Cuba in 1979—which turned out to be a noncombat unit that had been there since 1962. This did not stop President Reagan from announcing to a joint session of Congress several years later: "Cuba is host to a Soviet combat brigade. . . ."

In 1983, in a nationally televised speech, Reagan pointed to satellite photos that revealed the menace of three Soviet helicopters in Nicaragua. Sandinista officials subsequently noted that the helicopters could be seen by anyone arriving at Managua airport and, in any case, posed no military threat to the United States. Equally ingenious was the way Reagan transformed a Grenadian airport, built to accommodate direct tourist flights, into a killer-attack Soviet forward base, and a twenty-foot-deep Grenadian inlet into a potential Soviet submarine base.

In 1967 Secretary of State Dean Rusk argued that U.S. national security was at stake in Vietnam because the Vietnamese were puppets of "Red China" and if China won in Vietnam, it would overrun all of Asia and this supposedly would be the beginning of the end for all of us. Later we were told that the Salvadoran rebels were puppets of the Sandinistas in Nicaragua who were puppets of the Cubans who were puppets of the Russians. In truth, there was no evidence that Third World peoples took up arms and embarked upon costly revolutionary struggles because some sinister ringmaster in Moscow or Peking cracked the whip. Revolutions are not push-button affairs; rather, they evolve only if there exits a reservoir of hope and grievance that can be galvanized into popular action. Revolutions are made when large segments of the population take courage from each other and stand up to an insufferable social order. People are inclined to endure great abuses before risking their lives in confrontations with vastly superior armed forces. There is no such thing as a frivolous revolution, or a revolution initiated and orchestrated by a manipulative cabal residing in a foreign capital.

Nor is there evidence that once the revolution succeeded, the new leaders placed the interests of their country at the disposal of Peking or Moscow. Instead of becoming the willing puppets of "Red China," as our policy makers predicted, Vietnam found itself locked in combat with its neighbor to the north. And, as noted earlier, almost every Third World revolutionary country has tried to keep its options open and has sought friendly diplomatic and economic relations with the United States.

Why then do U.S. leaders intervene in every region and almost every nation in the world, either overtly with U.S. military force or covertly with surrogate mercenary forces, death squads, aid, bribes, manipulated media, and rigged elections? Is all this intervention just an outgrowth of a deeply conditioned anticommunist ideology? Are U.S. leaders responding to the public's longstanding phobia about the Red Menace? Certainly many Americans are anticommunist, but this sentiment does not translate into a demand for overseas interventionism. Quite the contrary. Opinion polls over the last half-century have shown repeatedly that the U.S. public is not usually supportive of committing U.S. forces in overseas engagements and prefers friendly relations with other nations, including communist ones. Far from galvanizing our leaders into interventionist actions, popular opinion has been one of the few restraining influences.

There is no denying, however, that opinion can sometimes be successfully manipulated by jingoist ventures. The invasion of Grenada and the slaughter perpetrated against Iraq are cases in point. The quick, easy, low-cost wins reaffirmed for some Americans the feeling that we were not weak and indecisive, not sitting ducks to some foreign prey. But even in these cases, it took an intensive and sustained propaganda barrage of half-truths and lies by the national security state and its faithful lackeys in the national media to muster some public support for military actions against Grenada and Iraq.

In sum, various leftist states do not pose a military threat to U.S. security; instead, they want to trade and live in peace with us, and are much less abusive and more helpful toward their people than the reactionary regimes they replaced. In addition, U.S. leaders have shown little concern for freedom in the Third World and have helped subvert democracy in a number of nations. And popular opinion generally opposes interventionism by lopsided majorities. What then motivates U.S. policy and how can we think it is not confused and contradictory?

The answer is that Marxist and other leftist or revolutionary states *do* pose a real threat, not to the United States as a national entity and not to the American people as such, but to the corporate and financial interests of our country, to Exxon and Mobil, Chase Manhattan and First National, Ford and General Motors, Anaconda and U.S. Steel, and to capitalism as a world system.

The problem is not that revolutionaries accumulate power but that they use power to pursue substantive policies that are unacceptable to U.S. ruling circles. What bothers our political leaders (and generals, investment bankers, and corporate heads) is not the supposed lack of *political* democracy in these countries but their attempts to construct *economic* democracy, to depart from the impoverishing rigors of the international free market, to use capital and labor in a way that is inimical to the interests of multinational corporatism.

A *New York Times* editorial (3/30/83) referred to "the undesirable and offensive Managua regime" and the danger of seeing "Marxist power ensconced in Managua." But what specifically is so dangerous about "Marxist power ?" What was undesirable and offensive about the Sandinista government in Managua? What did it do to us? What did it do to its own people? Was it the literacy campaign? The health care and housing programs? The land reform and development of farm cooperatives? The attempt at rebuilding Managua, at increasing production or achieving a more equitable distribution of taxes, services, and food? In large part, yes. Such reforms, even if not openly denounced by our government, do make a country suspect because they are symptomatic of an effort to erect a new and competing economic order in which the prerogatives of wealth and corporate investment are no longer secure, and the land, labor, and resources are no longer used primarily for the accumulation of corporate profits.

U.S. leaders and the corporate-owned press would have us believe they opposed revolutionary governments because the latter do not have an opposition press or have not thrown their country open to Western style (and Western-financed) elections. U.S. leaders come closer to their true complaint when they condemn such governments for interfering with the prerogatives of the "free market." Similarly, Henry Kissinger came close to the truth when he defended the fascist overthrow of the democratic government in Chile by noting that when obliged to choose between saving the economy or saving democracy, we must save the economy. Had Kissinger said, we must save the *capitalist* economy, it would have been the whole truth. For under Allende, the danger was not that the economy was collapsing (although the U.S. was doing its utmost to destabilize it); the real threat was that the economy was moving away from free-market capitalism and toward a more equitable social democracy, albeit in limited ways.

U. S. officials say they *are* for change just as long as it is peaceful and not violently imposed. Indeed, economic elites may sometimes tolerate very limited reforms, learning to give a little in order to keep a lot. But judging from Chile, Guatemala, Indonesia, and a number of other places, they have a low tolerance for changes, even peaceful ones, that tamper with the existing class structure and threaten the prerogatives of corporate and landed wealth.

To the rich and powerful it makes little difference if their interests are undone by a peaceful transformation rather than a violent upheaval. The means concern them much less than the end results. It is not the "violent" in violent revolution they hate; it is the "revolution." (Third World elites seldom perish in revolutions. The worst of them usually manage to make it to Miami, Madrid, Paris, or New York.) They dread socialism the way the rest of us might dread poverty and hunger. So, when push comes to shove, the wealthy classes of Third World countries, with a great deal of help from the corporate-military-political elites in our country, will use fascism to preserve capitalism while claiming they are saving democracy from communism.

A socialist Cuba or a socialist North Korea, as such, are not a threat to the survival of world capitalism. The danger is not socialism in any one country but a socialism that might spread to many countries. Multinational corporations, as their name implies, need the entire world, or a very large part of it, to exploit and to invest and expand in. There can be no such thing as "capitalism in one country." The domino theory—the view that if one country falls to the revolutionaries, others will follow in quick succession—may not work as automatically as its more fearful proponents claim, but there usually is a contagion, a power of example and inspiration, and sometimes even direct encouragement and assistance from one revolution to another.

Support the Good Guys?

If revolutions arise from the sincere aspirations of the populace, then it is time the United States identify itself with these aspirations, so liberal critics keep urging. They ask: "Why do we always find ourselves on the wrong side in the Third World? Why are we always on the side of the oppressor?" Too bad the question is treated as a rhetorical one, for it is deserving of a response. The answer is that right-wing oppressors, however heinous they be, do not tamper with, and give full support to, private investment and profit, while the leftists pose a challenge to that system.

There are those who used to say that we had to learn from the communists, copy their techniques, and thus win the battle for the hearts and minds of the people. Can we imagine the ruling interests of the United States abiding by this? The goal is not to copy communist reforms but to prevent them. How would U.S. interventionists try to learn from and outdo the revolutionaries? Drive out the latifundio owners and sweatshop bosses? Kick out the plundering corporations and nationalize their holdings? Imprison the militarists and torturers? Redistribute the land, use capital investment for home consumption or hard currency exchange instead of cash crop exports that profit a rich few? Install a national health insurance program and construct hospitals and clinics at public expense? Mobilize the population for literacy campaigns and for work in publicly owned enterprises? If U.S. rulers did all this, they would have done more than defeat the communists and other revolutionaries, they would have carried out the communists' programs. They would have prevented revolution only by bringing about its effects — thereby defeating their own goals.

U.S. policy makers say they cannot afford to pick and choose the governments they support, but that is exactly what they do. And the pattern of choice is consistent through each successive administration regardless of the party or personality in office. U.S. leaders support those governments, be they autocratic or democratic in form, that are friendly toward capitalism and oppose those governments, be they autocratic or democratic, that seek to develop a noncapitalist social order.

Occasionally friendly relations are cultivated with noncapitalist nations like China if these countries show themselves in useful opposition to other socialist nations and are sufficiently open to private capital exploitation. In the case of China, the economic opportunity is so huge as to be hard to resist, the labor supply is plentiful and cheap, and the profit opportunities are great.

In any one instance, interventionist policies may be less concerned with specific investments than with protecting the global investment system. The United States had relatively little direct investment in Cuba, Vietnam, and Grenada—to mention three countries that Washington has invaded in recent years. What was at stake in Grenada, as Reagan said, was something more than nutmeg. It was whether we would let a country develop a competing economic order, a different way of utilizing its land, labor, capital, and natural resources. A social revolution in any part of the world may or may not hurt specific U.S. corporations, but it nevertheless becomes part of a cumulative threat to private finance capital in general.

The United States will support governments that seek to suppress guerrilla movements, as in El Salvador, and will support guerrilla movements that seek to overthrow governments, as in Nicaragua. But there is no confusion or stupidity about it. It is incorrect to say, "We have no foreign policy" or "We have a stupid and confused foreign policy." Again, it is necessary not to confuse subterfuge with stupidity. The policy is remarkably rational. Its central organizing principle is to make the world safe for the multinational corporations and the free-market capital-accumulation system. However, our rulers cannot ask the U.S. public to sacrifice their tax dollars and the lives of their sons for Exxon and Chase Manhattan, for the profit system as such, so they tell us that the interventions are for freedom and national security and the protection of unspecified "U.S. interests."

Whether policy makers believe their own arguments is not the key question. Sometimes they do, sometimes they don't.

Sometimes presidents Richard Nixon, Ronald Reagan, George Bush, and Bill Clinton were doing their hypocritical best when their voices quavered with staged compassion for this or that oppressed people who had to be rescued from the communists or terrorists with U.S. missiles and troops, and sometimes they were sincere, as when they spoke of their fear and loathing of communism and revolution and their desire to protect U.S. investments abroad. We need not ponder the question of whether our leaders are motivated by their class interests or by a commitment to anti-communist ideology, as if these two things were in competition with each other instead of mutually reinforcing. The arguments our leaders proffer may be self-serving and fabricated, yet also sincerely embraced. It is a creed's congruity with one's material self-interest that often makes it so compelling.

In any case, so much of politics is the rational use of irrational symbols. The arguments in support of interventionism may sound and may actually be irrational and nonsensical, but they serve a rational purpose. Once we grasp the central consistency of U.S. foreign policy, we can move from a liberal complaint to a radical analysis, from criticizing the "foolishness" of our government's behavior to understanding why the "foolishness" is not random but persists over time against all contrary arguments and evidence, always moving in the same elitist, repressive direction.

With the collapse of the Soviet Union and other Eastern European communist governments, U.S. leaders now have a freer hand in their interventions. A number of left reformist governments that had relied on the Soviets for economic assistance and political protection against U.S. interference now have nowhere to turn.[2] The willingness of U.S. leaders to tolerate economic deviations does not grow with their sense of their growing power.

---

[2] For a discussion of this point, see "Rollback," p. 44.

Quite the contrary. Now even the palest economic nationalism, as displayed in Iraq by Saddam Hussein over oil prices, invites the destructive might of the U.S. military. The goal now, as always, is to obliterate every trace of an alternative system, to make it clear that there is no road to take except that of the free market, in a world in which the many at home and abroad will work still harder for less so that the favored few will accumulate more and more wealth.

That is the vision of the future to which most U.S. leaders are implicitly dedicated. It is a vision taken from the past and never forgotten by them, a matter of putting the masses of people at home and abroad back in their place, divested of any aspirations for a better world because they are struggling too hard to survive in this one.

THE TERRORISM HYPE

The U.S. national security state and its faithful lackeys in the news media designate as "terrorist" those dissident political or nationalist groups that operate against Western governments or against the established interests of global corporations. While applied to the lone gunman or the small circle of conspirators who plant a bomb, "terrorism" is never used to describe the acts of massive repression and destruction perpetrated against whole populations by U.S. forces or by the armies of CIA-supported client states. A bomb planted in a pub by a member of the Irish Republican Army (IRA) is a terrorist act, but not the U.S. aerial bombing of whole working-class neighborhoods in Panama City, or the U.S. bombing of civilian populations in Bagdhad, or the burning of 660 villages in Guatemala by U.S.-supported forces, or the roundups and mass executions of democratic supporters in Chile, Indonesia, Afghanistan, South Yemen, and other countries.

State-supported, right-wing terrorism, as practiced by U.S. client states, is never defined as terrorism, though it is conducted on a far greater scale than the isolated bombings carried out by any Basque, Arab, or IRA group. Also left uncounted is the massive terrorism perpetrated by U.S.-supported "guerrilla" mercenaries, as in Angola, Mozambique, Nicaragua, and several other countries, in which entire countrysides are devastated and massive numbers of people slaughtered.

The Larger Terrorism

As critics of U.S. interventionism have pointed out, what is reported as "terrorism" in the press is "retail terrorism." What goes unnoted is "wholesale terrorism," the massive U.S.-backed, state-supported kind. By any measure other than the peculiar one used by Washington policy makers and propagandists, the U.S. national security state is the greatest purveyor of terrorism in the world today and has been for some time.

Tallying only the death toll inflicted by U.S. armed forces or U.S.-backed surrogate forces around the world, the estimates are as follows: 3,000,000 in Vietnam, 1,000,000 in Cambodia, 1,000,000 in Mozambique, 500,000 to 1,000,000 in Indonesia, 600,000 in Angola, 300,000 in Laos, 250,000 in East Timor, 200,000 in Iraq, 200,000 in Afghanistan, 150,000 in Guatemala, 100,000 in Nicaragua, 90,000 in El Salvador, and tens of thousands in Chile, Argentina, Zaire, Iran (under the Shah), Colombia, Bolivia, Brazil, Panama, Somalia, South Yemen, Western Sahara, and other countries.[1]

Against the blowing up of a building or an airliner, how do we measure this U.S.-sponsored terrorism? To be sure, we must not dismiss or make light of individual acts of terror. Yet we might

---

[1] For details and documentation on the U.S.-imposed postwar holocaust in the Third World, see my *The Sword and the Dollar* (New York: St. Martin's Press, 1989); Edward Herman, *The Real Terror Network* (Boston: South End Press, 1982); William Blum, *Killing Hope: U.S. Military and CIA Interventions Since World War II* (Monroe, Maine: Common Courage Press, 1995).

wonder why they are the only ones that warrant publicity and condemnation. The wholesale terrorism of aerial massacres, death squads, mass executions, torture, and intimidation orchestrated by the U.S. national security state either goes unreported altogether or is represented as the legitimate activity of governments defending themselves from insurgencies and terrorists.

Even on those rare occasions when atrocities *are* reported, the corporate-owned media never make the link between such horrific events and the policies of intervention and repression directed from Washington. The question is never asked: "Why do successive U.S. governments support the kind of elements that are capable of commiting such acts? What interests are bolstered and what interests retarded when whole villages of men, women, and children are slaughtered by a military that is supplied and trained by the U.S. government?

Those isolated acts of violence the press defines as terrorist are subjected to a highly slanted mode of reportage. Consider that the White House charged Libya with orchestrating the destruction of Pan Am flight 103 in 1988 over Lockerbie, Scotland, an incident resulting in the loss of 270 lives. In fact, there were strong signs pointing to terrorist groups in Syria and Iran. No matter, Washington wanted to target Libya. Two Libyan "intelligence agents" were named in the U.S. media as having committed the act of terrorism. In fact, all we really knew about them was that they were Libyan airline employees, yet they were repeatedly identified as "secret agents." The *New York Times* ran an editorial demanding that they be brought to justice and that the Libyan government, particularly its leader Muammar el-Qaddafi, be held accountable. The Libyans understandably refused to hand over the two men because no evidence was ever presented linking any Libyan to the Pan Am bombing.

Everybody, Here Come the Assassins!

Libya has been targeted on other occasions. In 1981, U.S. planes attacked that country and shot down two Libyan training jets. In 1985, U.S. planes bombed two cities, killing a number of people, including Qaddafi's young daughter. (They were aiming for Qaddafi.) Neither of these terrorist attacks was condemned in the U.S. press.

An incident of terrorism hype that had the U.S. press hot and bothered for the better part of two months, occurred in late 1981, when the U.S. government announced that a Libyan team of assassins, assisted by "East German terror experts," under orders from Colonel Qaddafi, had entered the United States. Supposedly armed with surface-to-air missiles, they were intending to kill President Reagan and ten or so top officials including the secretary of state and the secretary of defense.

The media's response to this fantastic tale was to treat it as solid fact. On ABC-TV evening news (11/26/1981) Frank Reynolds stated that it was "known" that Libyan agents were "in this country for the purpose of assassinating the highest officials in the U.S. government." CBS anchor Dan Rather announced on December 4, "A squad of terrorists infiltrated the United States on a mission to kill the president and his top aides. It sounds like the stuff of a suspense novel . . . but American security officials tonight are taking the word of an informant seriously."

That same evening, NBC began its report by asking, "Is it true?" and then promptly treated it as if it were. An NBC correspondent asked President Reagan if he was "worried about the assassination plot." "Yes, of course," said Reagan. The camera cut to Secret Service men leaping out of cars and racing around the president's limousine—an image which itself suggested that the president was under imminent attack.

ABC's "Nightline" (12/4/1981) presented a special on the "Libyan Assassination Plot," featuring Ray Cline, a former deputy director of the CIA, who claimed that Libyan terrorist groups were organized "basically and initially by the Soviet Union," and that our "open society" made our officials "sitting ducks" because "we have been busy handcuffing the CIA and FBI for a number of years, and only President Reagan is trying to turn them loose a bit to deal with these threats."

For the sake of balance, the right-wing Cline was joined by right-wing journalist Arnaud de Borchgrave, introduced as a "terrorism expert." He, too, assured viewers that the Libyans were working for the Soviet Union and that Qaddafi, whom de Borchgrave claimed to have interviewed "five times in my life," was a "pathological liar."

For added political diversity the panel included the right-winger Marvin Zonis, a Likud cheerleader described as a "Mideast expert," who said that "Colonel Qaddafi had a conversation with another leader of a Middle Eastern country in which he discussed very coolly and in a rational way how he intended to go about assassinating President Reagan." No one questioned Zonis about his source or asked how it was possible that a leader of one nation would openly discuss his plans to assassinate the U.S. president with the leader of another nation who might impart this information to others. No one appeared on the show to inject a cautionary note or question the remarkable statements made by these three cold warriors.

The networks did their share to keep the White House's conspiracy fantasy alive, running no less than twenty-four evening news reports about the hit teams in one month. Viewers were told there were three, five, ten, twelve, or thirteen hit men, depending on what network and what evening you watched. The assassins had entered the U.S. from Canada (ABC, CBS), from Mexico (CBS), and not from Mexico (ABC). The hit squad was composed of three Libyans (ABC, NBC), three Iranians (CBS, NBC), two Iranians (ABC), and three Syrians (NBC). All three networks agreed that there was one Palestinian, one Lebanese, and one East German. By the third week there was said to be *two* hit squads. Never before had assassins received such advanced billing. It should have been enough to deter all but the wildest publicity hounds among them.

The national media were filled with accounts of FBI agents fanning out across the country to hunt the assassins and heavily armed security teams roosting on the White House roof. In addition, there was film footage of Libyan soldiers firing "Soviet missile launchers" to shoot down helicopters "such as the one the president used." Police composite sketches of six would-be assassins, looking like sinister, comic-book Third World characters, were carried by newspapers across the country, including the *Washington Post* and the *New York Times,* and flashed repeatedly across the TV screen.

The sketches were allegedly composed from descriptions provided by an unidentified informant, who somehow was privy to the whole plot and endowed with an exceptional memory for facial detail. They were distributed to the media by columnist Jack Anderson who later regretted doing it and wrote that he had been set up by an unnamed "intelligence agency."

Needless to say, the nonexistent hit team(s) never materialized. It remained for *TV Guide* (6/12/1986) to admit, in a cover story entitled: "Why American TV Is so Vulnerable to Foreign Propaganda," that the "assassination plot" consisted of nothing but wild conjectures. *TV Guide* then disinformed its millions of readers by asserting that the whole incident was probable evidence of a KGB campaign to use alarmist rumors "to destabilize public opinion in the West." Or perhaps the story was planted by Qaddafi himself, who "is no madman" but "a shrewd Bedouin" "who is sitting back and laughing over this." Thus *TV Guide* accused Qaddafi of deliberately planting stories that implicated him in assassination plots against the president of the United States, presumably so that he might give U.S. leaders an excuse to deliver another murderous military retaliation upon him and his country.

In our "open society," continued *TV Guide,* where "anything can get reported," the press should be more wary of the false stories floated by "Soviet intelligence sources." This assertion was as outlandish as the original story itself. It ignored the fact that the assassination-team fairy tale emanated from the White House rather than from any foreign source. Indeed the press had been once again willingly duped—by Washington, not Moscow.

The White House learned some things after it floated the "assassination plot" story of 1981. In regard to the Pan Am bombing, it came up with the names of two specific Libyan "agents," Abdel Basset Ali al-Megrahi and Lamen Khalifa Fhimah, so that no embarrassment need be suffered when imaginary assassins fail to materialize. The White House also learned that it can inflict more durable pain and punishment with economic sanctions than with a few air strikes. So Libya has been repeatedly hit with trade sanctions.

Qaddafi's Real Sins

Still, we might ask what motivates all this hostility against Libya? Why has a country of three million inhabitants with a ragtag army of 55,000 been singled out by U.S. leaders and media as a major threat to U.S. national security? And why is Libya still targeted today with oil and trade embargoes? Is it because U.S. policy is just stupid or mean? More likely, the attacks have been motivated by Washington's concern that Libya is one of those renegade countries that refuses client-state status, not unlike Nicaragua (under the Sandinistas), Islamic Iran, nationalist Iraq, and communist Cuba and North Korea.

There are countries that do not want to be an integrated part of the global free-market system. They do not want to open their land, labor, markets, and natural resources to U.S. investors, saying in effect, "Come on in, it's all yours. There are no occupational safety laws, no corporate taxes, no environmental standards, no limit to what you can carve out of our land at outrageously low prices, no minimum wage, no real labor unions. And if the workers or peasants get out of line, our police and military, who are trained and equipped by your military, will take care of them, for there are no constitutional protections either. You give us oligarchs a generous cut and the rest is all yours. You make this society safe for us and we will open it completely to you." The nations that refuse this contract with America run the risk of being targeted as "terrorist states."

After Qaddafi took power in the 1969 colonels' rebellion, he nationalized Libya's oil industry and set about transforming a country that resembled Saudi Arabia into a more egalitarian society, using a larger portion of its capital and labor for popular needs rather than corporate profits, building health clinics, schools, and public housing, and implementing massive reforestation programs.

Independent, reform-minded Third World leaders like Qaddafi have a chancy future in the New World Order. They do not have the right politics. They do not represent the right class interests. For that reason we, the American people, ought to get to know more about what they are doing and find out how we too can produce leaders who do not worship at the altar of global free-market corporate capitalism, "dangerous" leaders who put public need before private greed.

Meanwhile we are not likely to see a swift end to the terrorism hype. Indeed, in 1995, President Clinton sponsored the "Omnibus Counter-terrrorism Act," which the U.S. Senate passed by a vote of ninety-one to eight. Among other things, the bill authorized the president to unilaterally designate as "terrorist" any group anywhere in the world—without offering a shred of evidence. Any challenge to the president's declaration would have been a criminal offense. Any donation of money or aid or other kind of support to the "terrorist group" would have been punishable with ten years in prison and a $50,000 fine. The bill would also have allowed the FBI to infiltrate, wiretap, and investigate groups and individuals with no previous proof of criminal activity.[2]

With the overthrow of most communist states, U.S. leaders face a shortage of adversaries needed to justify U.S. global interventionism. "Fighting terrorism" now takes the place of "fighting communism" as the rationale for a huge military state and a repressive national security apparatus at home and abroad, the true function of which is to keep the world safe for those who own it. The real danger we face is not from terrorism but from what is being done under the pretext of fighting it.

---

[2] The bill was voted down in the House of Representatives in December 1995 by a coalition of civil-liberties minded Democrats and conservative Republicans, the latter concerned that the bill would infringe on the rights of ultra-rightist groups and the gun lobby.

FREE SPEECH—AT A PRICE

What does it mean to say we have freedom of speech? Many of us think free speech is a right enjoyed by everyone in our society. In fact, it does not exist as an abstract right. There is no such thing as a freedom detached from the socio-economic reality in which it might find a place.

Speech is a form of interpersonal behavior. This means it occurs in a social context, in homes, workplaces, schools, and before live audiences or vast publics via the print and electronic media. Speech is intended to reach the minds of others. This is certainly true of political speech. But some kinds of political speech are actively propagated before mass audiences and other kinds are systematically excluded.

Ideologically Distributed

In the political realm, the further left one goes on the opinion spectrum the more difficult it is to gain exposure and access to larger audiences. Strenuously excluded from the increasingly concentrated corporate-owned media are people on the Left who go beyond the conservative-liberal orthodoxy and speak openly about the negative aspects of big capital and what it does to people at home and abroad. Progressive people, designated as "the Left," believe that the poor are victims of the rich and the prerogatives of wealthy and powerful interests should be done away with. They believe labor unions should be strengthened and the rights of working people expanded; the environment should be rigorously protected; racism, sexism, and homophobia should be strenuously fought; and human services should be properly funded.

Progressives also argue that revolutionary governments that bring social reforms to their people should be supported rather than overthrown by the U.S. national security state, that U.S.-sponsored wars of attrition against reformist governments in Vietnam, Nicaragua, Angola, and a dozen other countries are not "mistakes" but crimes perpetrated by those who would go to any length to maintain their global privileges.

To hold such opinions is to be deprived of any regular access to the major media. In a word, some people have more freedom of speech than others. People who take positions opposing the ones outlined above are known as conservatives or right-wingers. Conservative pundits have a remarkable amount of free speech. They favor corporations and big profits over environmental and human needs, see nothing wrong with amassing great wealth while many live in poverty, blame the poor for the poverty that has been imposed upon them, see regulations against business as a bureaucratic sin, and worship at the altar of the free market. They support repressive U.S. interventions abroad and pursue policies opposed to class, gender, and racial equality.

Such rightists as Rush Limbaugh, William F. Buckley Jr., John McLaughlin, George Will, and Robert Novak enjoy much more

exposure to mass audiences than left liberals and populists like
Jim Hightower, Jerry Brown, or Ralph Nader. And all of them,
conservatives and liberals, enjoy more exposure than anyone on
the more "radical" or Marxist Left.

It is the economic power of the rich corporate media owners
and advertisers that provides right-wingers with so many mass
outlets, not the latter's wit and wisdom. It is not public demand
that brings them on the air; it is private corporate owners and
sponsors. They are listened to by many not because they are so
appealing but because they are so available. Availability is the first
and necessary condition of consumption. In this instance, supply
does not merely satisfy demand; supply *creates* demand. Hence,
those who align themselves with the interests of corporate
America will have more freedom of expression than those who
remain steadfastly critical.[1]

People on the Left are free to talk to each other, though sometimes they are concerned their telephones are tapped or their
meetings are infiltrated by government agents and provoca-
teurs—as has so often been the case over the years. Leftists are
sometimes allowed to teach in universities but they usually run
into difficulties regarding what they say and write and they risk
being purged from faculty positions.[2] Leftists are free to work for
labor unions but they generally have to keep their politics care-
fully under wraps, especially communists. People on the Left can
even speak publicly, but usually to audiences that seldom number
more than a few hundred. And they are free to write for progressive publications, which lack the promotional funds to reach mass
readerships, publications that are perennially teetering on the

---

[1] For further discussion of this, see "The 'Liberal Media' Myth," p. 97.
[2] For an account of my own experiences with repression in academia, see
"Struggles in Academe," p. 235.

edge of insolvency for want of rich patrons and corporate advertisers.

In sum, free speech belongs mostly to those who can afford it. It is a commodity that needs to be marketed like any other commodity. And massive amounts of money are needed to reach mass audiences. So when it comes to freedom of speech, some people have their voices amplified tens of millions of times, while others must cup their hands and shout at the passing crowd.

The Freedom of Power

We are taught to think of freedom as something antithetical to power. And there is something to this. The people's hard-won democratic rights do sometimes act as a restraint on the arbitrary power of rulers. But to secure our freedom we have to mobilize enough popular power to check state power. In other words, freedom and power are not always antithetical; they are frequently symbiotic. If one has no power, one has very little freedom to protect one's interests against those who do have power. Our freedoms are realities only so far as we have the democratic power to make them so.

People on the Left have freedom only to the extent they have rallied their forces, have agitated, educated, and organized strikes, boycotts, and demonstrations, and have fought back against the higher circles. They have no freedom to reach mass audiences because popular power and iconoclastic opinion have not penetrated the corporate citadels that control the mass communication universe.

We were never "given" what freedoms we do have, certainly not by the framers of the Constitution. Recall that the Bill of Rights was not part of the original Constitution. It was added after ratification, as ten amendments. When Colonel Mason of Virginia proposed a Bill of Rights at the Constitutional Convention in Philadelphia in 1787, it was voted down almost unanimously (Massachusetts abstained). Popular protests, land seizures by the poor, food riots, and other disturbances made the men of property who gathered in Philadelphia uncomfortably aware of the need for an effective central authority that could be sufficiently protective of the propertied classes. But such popular ferment also set a limit on what the framers dared to do. Belatedly and reluctantly they agreed during the ratification struggle to include a Bill of Rights, a concession made under threat of democratic agitation and in the hope that the amendments would ensure ratification of the new Constitution.

So the Bill of Rights was not a gift from that illustrious gaggle of rich merchants, land and currency speculators, and slaveholders known as our "Founding Fathers." It was a product of class struggle. The same was true of the universal franchise. It took mass agitation from the 1820s to the 1840s by workers and poor farmers to abolish property qualifications and win universal white male suffrage. Almost a century of agitation and struggle was necessary to win the franchise for women. And a bloody civil war and subsequent generations of struggle were needed to win basic political rights for African Americans, a struggle still far from complete.

During the early part of the twentieth century a nationwide union movement in this country called the Industrial Workers of the World (the "Wobblies") struggled for the betterment of working people in all occupations. To win gains, the Wobblies had to organize, that is, they had to be able to speak out and reach people. To speak out, they had to confront the repressive tactics of local police who would beat, arrest, and jail their organizers. The

Wobblies discovered that if they went into a town with five hundred people instead of five, then the sheriff and his deputies could do little to stop them from holding public meetings.

The right to free speech was established de facto during the course of class struggle. The Wobblie free speech fights were simultaneously a struggle for procedural democracy impelled by a struggle for substantive economic democracy. This fight continued into the Great Depression, as mass organization and agitation brought freedom of speech to hundreds of local communities, where police had previously made a practice of physically assaulting and incarcerating union organizers, syndicalists, anarchists, socialists, and communists.

So it went with other freedoms and democratic gains like the eight-hour day, Social Security, unemployment and disability insurance, and the right to collective bargaining. All such democratic economic rights, even though they may be seriously limited and insufficiently developed, exist to some degree because of popular struggle against class privilege and class power.

Freedom for Criminal Intelligence Agencies?

Like other freedoms, free speech is situational. It exists in a social and class context, which is true of democracy itself. Once we understand that, we can avoid the mistaken logic of a news columnist like Nat Hentoff who repeatedly attacks left activists who commit civil disobedience protesting CIA campus recruiters and military recruiters. Hentoff says they interfere with the freedom of speech of those students who want to talk to the recruiters (as if students had no other opportunity to do so). Hentoff also is worried that the CIA was having its rights abridged.

Such a view of freedom of speech has no link to the realities of human suffering and social justice, no connection to the realities of class power and state power, no link to the *democratic* struggle against the murderous force of the CIA, no acknowledgment that the CIA routinely suppresses the basic rights of people all over the world in the most brutal fashion. With a $25 billion yearly budget, with its tens of thousands of operatives unleashing death squads and wars of attrition against democratic forces and impoverished peoples around the world, with its control of hundreds of publications, publishing houses, and wire services, with thousands of agents pouring out disinformation, the CIA has more "free speech" than all those who protest its crimes—because it is backed by more money and more power.

With his tendency to treat rights as something apart from socio-economic realities, Hentoff would have us think that the CIA is just another participant in a democratic campus dialogue. In fact, the CIA is itself one of the greatest violators of free speech both at home and abroad. Those who take the one-dimensional Hentoff approach say nothing about the freedom of speech that millions might gain by shutting down the CIA and all such agencies of violence and repression, nothing about the lives that would be saved and the freedom salvaged in Third World countries that feel the brunt of the CIA onslaught.

By coercively limiting CIA recruitment, the campus demonstrators made a statement that goes beyond discourse and becomes part of the democratic struggle. By dramatically—through direct confrontation—questioning the CIA's legitimacy on college campuses and thereby challenging (even in a small way) its ability to promote oppressive political orders around the world, the demonstrators were expanding the realm of freedom, not diminishing it.

Of course, this has to be measured against the violations these same protestors commit, specifically the inconveniencing of some upper- and upper-middle-class students who don't want to have to travel off campus in order to ask CIA recruiters about pursuing a career of political crime. This latter right seems to weigh more heavily in Hentoff's mind than all the attendant misdeeds perpetrated by the CIA.

If we take Hentoff's position, there can be no direct actions, no civil disobedience by the powerless against the established powerful because these would constitute infringements on the recruitment efforts of the CIA. Hentoff's failure to deal with the context of power and wealth in free speech issues leaves him in the ridiculous position of defending the CIA's freedom of speech—and worse, its freedom of action. It is the same position that led to the overthrow of the Fairness Doctrine: the corporate media bosses were being limited in their free speech because they had to grant it to others.

Struggle for More Democracy

If the Reagan-Bush-Clinton years have taught us anything, it is that our freedoms are neither guaranteed nor secure—unless we agitate and show our strength. If democratic struggle has taught us anything, it is that our rights are not things that must be "preserved." Rather, they must be vigorously used and expanded. As with the physical body, so with the body politic: our capacities are more likely to grow if exercised and developed. Freedom of speech needs less abstract admiration and more militant exercise and application. Use it or lose it.

Democracy is not a "precarious fragile gift" handed down to us like some Grecian urn. Rather, it is a dynamically developing process that emerges from the struggle between popular interests and the inherently undemocratic nature of wealthy interests.

Rather than fear an "excess of democracy"[3] as do some of our media pundits and mandarin academics, we must struggle for more popular power, more victories for labor and human services, more victories against racism, sexism, and militarism, and against capitalism's apparent willingness to destroy the environment. And we need to muster more opposition to U.S. interventions around the world.[4]

We must push for more not-for-profit economic development, more democratic ownership of productive forces and services, more ideological variety and dissidence in the mainstream media, more listener-controlled access to radio and television stations. In every field of endeavor we must learn to see the dimensions of the struggle that advances the interests of the many and opposes the interests of the outrageously privileged, overweening few; in other words, a struggle for more *democracy*, of the kind that brings an advance in social conditions for everyone, a socially conscious allocation of community resources for the sake of the community rather than for the greed of private investors, and an equalization and improvement of life standards that in effect brings less freedom for the CIA and the interests it serves but more freedom for the rest of us. Essential to such an agenda is a freedom of speech that is not limited to media moguls and their acolytes but is available to persons of all ideological persuasions.

---

[3] A term used by, among others, Harvard political scientist and cold war apologist Samuel P. Huntington.

[4] On U.S. interventionism, see "Making the World Safe for Hypocrisy," p. 55.

TERM LIMITS:
TRICK OR TREAT?

There is much urgent talk about the need to limit incumbency in the U.S. Congress, most of it coming from the Right. In California and a number of other states, things went further than talk. The liberal leadership of the state legislature was forced out of office after voters passed a proposition limiting Assembly tenure to six years and Senate tenure to eight years. During the 1990 campaign, President Bush and Vice President Quayle made a point of journeying to California to support term limits.

Unfortunately, a number of people of progressive persuasion are standing shoulder to shoulder with the right-wingers on this issue. The appeal is understandable. Term limits supposedly would rid the Congress of entrenched oligarchs who long ago sold their souls to the moneyed interests. Competition would improve the quality of candidates and limit the influence of PACs. Infusions of fresh blood would also bring fresh and creatively progressive ideas and a more democratic performance.

A Conservative Scheme

If all that were true, why would right-wingers like George Bush, Dan Quayle, and George Will favor term limits and a swifter turnover of congressional occupants? Is it because they are desirous of seeing the entrenched moneyed interests routed and a more democratic and progressive Congress emerging? I suspect they have a different agenda.

Conservatives have nothing against incumbency when it is their people who are filling the slots. Some conservatives, most notably President Nixon and, more vehemently, President Reagan during his last days in office, have wanted to abolish the 22nd Amendment, which places a two-term limit on presidential incumbents. Conservatives feel they have the inside track on the presidency for several reasons. First, the defection of the South into the GOP column has given the Republicans a built-in head start in the electoral college, the very same head start once enjoyed by the Democratic Party when the South was solidly Democratic. Second, the electoral college gives two extra votes to each state regardless of population, thereby padding the number of electors claimed by numerous smaller and more conservative states.

Third, and most important of all, it takes hundreds of millions of dollars to win a presidential nomination and election. The presidency has been priced out of the reach of any progressives. The decline of grassroots party organizations and the domination of national campaigns by television has only increased the need for big money and decreased popular input. No wonder the Republicans would like to get rid of term limits in regard to the presidency.

To my knowledge, no conservative has uttered a word favoring a constitutional amendment that would limit the terms of Supreme Court justices or federal judges. Judges must be "independent" from politically partisan pressures, they argue, so that they may remain judiciously objective in their judgments. The dirty truth is that the judiciary was thoroughly packed during the Reagan and Bush administrations with hundreds of relatively young, conservative ideologues, who will be handing down decisions into the third decade of the next century. The Clinton appointees to the federal courts are mostly people of conventional or unpronounced political orientation, who are more or less at home with the conservatives on most issues.

Why do many conservatives, who see nothing wrong with limitless terms for presidents and lifelong appointments for judges, want limited terms for Congress?[1] Ronald Reagan gave us the answer. Just before leaving office he commented that the executive and judiciary "are fine" but the legislature still remains "a problem." He meant that a substantial liberal political formation still survived in Congress. These liberals occasionally favor the democratic interest over moneyed interests. They call, albeit weakly, for taxing the rich. They have passed (watered-down) laws for occupational safety, public housing, public transportation, clean air, clean water, and bigger cuts in military spending. They support at least minimum levels of human services for the indigent and stricter regulations of the banking industry, the timber industry, and other plunderers. And many of them keep getting reelected. Though pitifully inadequate in terms of what is really needed, all this is enough to annoy any right-winger.

For decades political scientists pointed out that the congres-

---

[1] As far as I know, only one prominent conservative, Pat Buchanan, has come out for term limits for federal judges, as of October 1995. And he does not push the issue very strongly.

sional seniority system allowed for the entrenchment of conservatives of both parties. They presided like petty tyrants over their
committee satrapies and accumulated power over the legislative
process by virtue of being repeatedly elected. For decades such
criticisms were ignored. Today the seniority system isn't what it
used to be but it is still operative. And for the first time, when liberals and even some left progressives like Ron Dellums and John
Conyers moved into committee chairs, suddenly the issue of
incumbency was targeted by conservatives and publicized in the
national media. It became an issue for the corporate mainstream
media because it had become a conservative crusade.

An Amateur Congress

With term limitations we will be faced with a rotating amateur
Congress, one perpetually populated by freshmen and sopho-
mores, who must leave office after their second or third stint, facing off against a well-entrenched national security state, a large
professional bureaucracy, and corporate lobbyists who are elected
by no one but who will be far more experienced and long-lived
than the term-limited legislators.

The legislative amateurs will still need large sums of money to
get elected and will be even more vulnerable than before to powerful professional lobbyists. They will also be increasingly dependent on congressional staffers, who are elected by no one. And
when one recalls that it takes many years and sometimes decades
of struggle to pass major legislation that could offer some protection of public interests, we might wonder who in Congress will be
able to stick around long enough to see things through.

I suspect that is why conservatives suddenly became so enthusiastic about rotation of *legislative* office. A more rapid turnover

would wipe out any potential seniority of the Democratic liberals in Congress and would pit short-term transient legislators against an entrenched and increasingly conservative state power. Unlike some liberals, people like Reagan and Bush do not treat process and performance as if existing in a social vacuum. They are keenly aware of how ongoing institutional arrangements advance or retard their political interests. They understand power because they have so much of it and have so much to protect with it.

In 1994, for the first time in decades, the Republicans won a majority in both houses of Congress. Most of the conservative ideologues among them still remained committed to term limits. A bill proposing term limits was defeated after a close vote. In the years since, feeling they have a good chance to retain control of Congress, conservatives seem to have quieted down about the issue.

In any case, before progressive people jump on any bandwagon to "throw the rascals out," they better check on who else is going along for the ride.

THE "LIBERAL MEDIA" MYTH

It is a widely accepted belief in this country that the press suffers from a liberal bias. Television pundits, radio talk-show hosts, and political leaders, including presidents of both parties, help propagate this belief. And their views are widely disseminated in the media. In contrast, dissident critics, who maintain that the corporate-owned press exercises a conservative grip on news and commentary, are afforded almost no exposure in the supposedly liberal media.

Consider the case of David Horowitz. When Horowitz was a radical author and editor of *Ramparts,* the mainstream press ignored his existence. But after he and former *Ramparts* colleague Peter Colliers surfaced as new-born conservatives, the *Washington Post Magazine* gave prominent play to their "Lefties for Reagan" pronunciamento. Horowitz and Colliers soon linked up with the National Forum Foundation, which dipped into deep conservative pockets and came up with hundreds of thousands of dollars to enable the two ex-radicals to do ideological battle with the Left. Today Horowitz is a rightist media critic, who has his own radio show and who appears with dismaying frequency on radio and television to whine about how radio and television shut out the conservative viewpoint.

Then there is the multitude of talk-show hosts, of whom Rush Limbaugh is only the best-known, who rail against the "pinko press" on hundreds of local television stations and thousands of radio stations owned by wealthy conservatives and underwritten by big business firms. To complain about how the media are dominated by liberals, Limbaugh has an hour a day on network television, an hour on cable, and a radio show syndicated by over 600 stations.

There are well-financed, right-wing, media-watch organizations, such as Reed Irvine's Accuracy in Media (AIM). In a syndicated column appearing in over one hundred newspapers and a radio show aired on some two hundred stations, Irvine and his associates complain that conservative viewpoints are frozen out of the media. Many left critics would like to be frozen out the way AIM, Limbaugh, and Horowitz are.

Not to be overlooked is National Empowerment Television (NET), a new cable network available in all fifty states, offering round-the-clock conservative political commentary. In the words of its founder Paul Weyrich, NET is dedicated to countering media news that "is riddled with a far-left political bias" and "unacceptable" notions about "gender norming, racial quotas, global warming, and gays in the military."

Political leaders do their share to reinforce the image of a liberal press. During the Iran-contra affair, President Reagan likened the "liberal" media to "a pack of sharks." More recently President Clinton complained that he had "not gotten one damn bit of credit from the knee-jerk liberal press." Clinton is confused. Almost all the criticism hurled his way by the so-called liberal press is coming from conservatives.

He Who Pays the Piper

There is no free and independent press in the United States. The notion of a "free market of ideas" is as mythical as the notion of a free market of goods. Both conjure up an image of a bazaar in which many small producers sell their wares on a more or less equal footing. In fact—be it commodities or commentary—to reach a mass market you need huge sums of money to buy exposure and distribution. Those without big bucks end up with a decidedly smaller clientele, assuming they are able to survive at all.

Who owns the big media? The press lords who come to mind are Hearst, Luce, Murdoch, Sulzberger, Annenberg, and the like, personages of markedly conservative hue who regularly leave their ideological imprint on both news and editorial content. The boards of directors of print and broadcast news organizations are populated by representatives from Ford, General Motors, General Electric, Alcoa, Coca-Cola, Philip Morris, ITT, IBM, and other corporations in a system of interlocking directorates that resembles the boards of any other corporation. Among the major stockholders of the three largest networks are Chase Manhattan, J.P. Morgan, and Citibank. The prime stockholder of this country's most far-reaching wire service, Associated Press, is the Wall Street brokerage firm, Merrill Lynch. NBC is owned outright by General Electric, a corporation that frequently backs conservative causes and candidates. In 1995, CBS was bought up by Westinghouse for $5 billion and Time Warner prepared to take over Ted Turner's CNN.

Not surprisingly, this pattern of ownership affects how news and commentary are manufactured. Virtually all chief executives of mainstream news organizations are drawn from a narrow, high-income stratum and tilt decidedly to the right in their political preferences. Media mogul Rupert Murdoch was once asked in an interview: "You're considered to be politically conservative. To what extent do you influence the editorial posture of your newspapers?" He responded with refreshing candor: "Considerably . . . my editors have input, but I make the final decisions." In 1995, Disney bought ABC and all other Capital Cities media holdings for $19 billion, then wasted no time moving the network's editorial policies still further to the right, firing one remaining liberal editor and populist commentator, Jim Hightower, and forcing ABC to recant its exposé of how cigarette manufacturers manipulate nicotine levels to increase addiction.

Corporate advertisers exercise an additional conservative influence on the media. They cancel accounts not only when stories reflect poorly on their product but when they perceive liberal tendencies creeping into news reports and commentary.

As might be expected from business-dominated media, the concerns of labor are regularly downplayed. Jonathan Tasini, head of the National Writers Union, studied all reports dealing with workers' issues carried by ABC, CBS and NBC evening news during 1989, including child care and minimum wage: it came to only 2.3 percent of total coverage. No wonder one survey found that only 6 percent of business leaders thought the media treatment accorded them was "poor," while 66 percent said it was "good" or "excellent."

Religious media manifest the same gross imbalance of right over left. The fundamentalist media—featuring homophobic, sexist, reactionary, televangelists like Pat Robertson—comprise a $2-billion-a-year industry, controlling about 10 percent of all radio outlets and 14 percent of the nation's television stations. In contrast, the Christian Left lacks the financial backing needed to gain major media access.

The Petroleum Broadcasting System

A favorite conservative hallucination is that the Public Broadcasting System is a leftist stronghold. In fact, more than 70 percent of PBS's prime-time shows are funded wholly or mostly by four giant oil companies, earning it the sobriquet of "Petroleum Broadcasting System." PBS's public affairs programs are underwritten by General Electric, General Motors, Metropolitan Life, Pepsico, Mobil, Paine Webber, and the like. One media watchdog group found that corporate representatives constitute 44 percent of program sources about the economy; activists account for only 3 percent, while labor representatives are virtually shut out. Guests on National Public Radio (NPR) and PBS generally are as ideologically conservative as any found on commercial networks. Even "Frontline" and Bill Moyer's "Listening to America"—favorite GOP targets—use Republicans far more frequently than Democrats.

Conservatives like Horowitz make much of the occasional muckraking documentary that is aired on public television. But most PBS documentaries are politically nondescript or centrist. Progressive works rarely see the light of day. Documentaries like *Faces of War* (revealing the brutality of the U.S.-backed counterinsurgency in El Salvador), *Building Bombs* (on nuclear weapons proliferation), *Coverup* (on the Iran-contra conspiracy), *Deadly Deception* (an Academy Award-winning critique of General Electric and the nuclear arms industry) and *Panama Deception* (an Academy Award-winning exposé of the U.S. invasion of Panama) were, with a few local exceptions, denied broadcast rights on both commercial and public television.

A rightist perspective dominates commentary shows like NBC's "McLaughlin Group," PBS's "One on One" (with

McLaughlin as host), CNBC's "McLaughlin Show" (with guess who), PBS's "Firing Line" with William F. Buckley, CNN's "Evans and Novak" and "Capital Gang," and ABC's "This Week with David Brinkley." The spectrum of opinion on such programs, as on the pages of most newspapers, ranges from far right to moderate right or center, in a display of false balancing. Facing Pat Buchanan on CNN's "Crossfire," Michael Kinsley correctly summed it up: "Buchanan is much further to the right than I am to the left."

On foreign affairs the press's role as a cheerleader of the national security state and free-market capitalism seems almost without restraint. Virtually no favorable exposure has ever been given to indigenous Third World revolutionary or reformist struggles or to protests at home and abroad against U.S. overseas interventions. The media's view of the world is much the same as the view from the State Department and the Pentagon. The horrendous devastation wreaked upon the presumed beneficiaries of U.S. power generally goes unmentioned and unexplained—as do the massive human rights violations perpetrated by U.S.-supported forces in dozens of free-market client states.

Why Do Conservatives Complain?

If news and commentary are so preponderantly conservative, why do rightists blast the press for its supposedly left bias? For one thing, such attacks help create a climate of opinion favorable to the Right. Railing against the press's "liberalism" is a way of putting the press on the defensive, keeping it leaning rightward for its respectability, so that liberal opinion in this country is forever striving for credibility within a conservatively defined framework.

Ideological control is not formal and overt as with a state censor but informal and usually implicit. Hence it works with imperfect effect. Editors sometimes are unable to see the troublesome implications of one or another story. As far as right-wingers are concerned, too much gets in that should be excluded. Their goal is not partial control but perfect control, not an overbearing advantage (which they already have) but total dominance of the communication universe. Anything short of unanimous support for a rightist agenda is treated as evidence of liberal bias. Expecting the press corps to be a press chorus, the conservative ideologue, like an imperious maestro, reacts sharply to the occasionally discordant note.

The discordant notes can be real. The news media never challenge the free market ideology but they do occasionally report things that might put business and the national security state in a bad light: toxic waste dumping by industrial firms, price gouging by defense contractors, bodies piling up in Haiti, financial thievery on Wall Street, and the like. These exposures are more than rightists care to hear and are perceived by them as a liberal vendetta.

The problem faced by conservatives is that reality itself is radical. The Third World really is poor and oppressed. The U.S. usually does side with Third World oligarchs. Our tax system really is regressive. Millions of Americans do live in poverty. Public services are really being ruthlessly cut. Our children do face a less promising economic future than did we. The corporations do plunder and pollute the environment. Real wages for blue-collar workers have declined. And the rich have dramatically increased their share of the pie. Despite its best efforts, there are limits to how much the press can finesse these realities.

The limits of reality sometimes impose limits on propaganda, as Dr. Goebbels discovered when trying to explain to the German public how invincible Nazi armies could win victory after victory while retreating on both fronts in 1944 and 1945. Although it sees the world through much the same ideological lens as do corporate and government elites, the press must occasionally report some of the unpleasantness of life—if only to maintain its credibility. On such occasions, rightists complain bitterly about a left bias.

Rightist ideologues object not only to what the press says but to what it omits. They castigate the press for failing to tell the American people that federal bureaucrats, "cultural elites," gays, lesbians, feminists, and abortionists are destroying the nation, that the U.S. military and corporate America are our only salvation, that there is no health care problem, that eco-terrorists stalk the land, that the environment is doing just fine—and other such loony tunes.

Self-Censorship

Reporters often operate in a state of self-censorship and anticipatory response. They frequently wonder aloud how their boss is taking things. They recall instances when superiors have warned them not to antagonize big advertisers and other powerful interests. They can name journalists who were banished for turning in the wrong kind of copy. Still, most newspeople treat these incidents as aberrant departures from a basically professional news system and insist they owe their souls to no one. They claim they are free to say what they like, not realizing it is because their superiors like what they say. Since they seldom cross any forbidden lines, they are not reined in and they remain unaware that they are on an ideological leash.

While incarcerated in Mussolini's dungeons from 1928 to 1937, Antonio Gramsci wrote about politics and culture in his prison notebooks. But he had to be careful to disguise his references to capitalism, class power, and class conflict so as not to antagonize the fascist censor. (The fascists knew what class they were working for.) Today most of our journalists and social commentators exercise a similar caution. However, unlike Gramsci, they are not in prison. They don't need a fascist censor breathing down their necks because they have a mainstream one implanted in their heads.

These internalized forms of self-censorship are far more effective in preserving the dominant ideology than any state censor could hope to be. Gramsci knew he was being censored. Many of our newspeople and pundits think they are free as birds—and they are, as long as they fly around in the right circles.

For conservative critics, however, the right circles are neither right enough nor tight enough. Anything to the left of themselves, including moderate rightist and establishment centrist, is defined as "leftist." Their campaign against the media helps to shift the center of political gravity in their direction. By giving such generous publicity to conservative preachments and pronouncements, while amputating everything on the Left, the press limits public debate to a contest between Right and Center, including the debate about bias in the media.

On the American political scene, the Center is occupied by conservative Democrats like Bill Clinton, who are happy to be considered the only alternative to the ultra-Right. This Center is then passed off and attacked as "liberal." Meanwhile real liberalism and everything progressive remain out the picture—which is just what the mainstream pundits, publishers, politicians, and plutocrats want.

FABRICATING A
"CULTURAL DEMOCRACY"

In the United States and most other countries, the movie and television entertainment industry is controlled by transnational corporations. These corporations are highly concentrated capital formations whose primary functions are (a) making a profit for their investors and (b) supporting an opinion climate favorable to corporate economic dominance. Big companies and banks have had a stake in the movie industry since its earliest days. By 1936, all the major studios had come under the suzerainty of either the Morgan or Rockefeller financial empires.

Today, the majors no longer dominate production. Independent producers have proliferated and some have become the source of politically aware quality films like *Missing, Executive Action, Sounder, Silkwood, Reds,* and *The Milagro Beanfield War.* Still, independent production does not guarantee support for independent ideas. Film making remains an enterprise open only to a relatively select few. In 1995, the average cost of producing a movie was over $35 million, not counting promotional expenses—which sometimes equal production costs. Investment support, even for most independent films, still comes from the major studios and from the corporations that own the studios and the banks that finance the corporations. Not all that much has changed since the days of the Hollywood mogul.

The major studios still finance the promotion and distribution of films. An independent usually has no way of gaining access to a national audience without dealing with the majors. Hundreds of films are made that never are released because the majors decide they lack "commercial viability," or because they contain controversial political content. Sometimes it is a combination of both, as industry bigwigs presume to equate political controversy with lack of commercial appeal.

What is true of films is equally true of television. The three networks CBS, ABC, and NBC enjoy a dominant position, selling over 86 percent of all TV advertising intended for a national audience. To the extent that their hegemony is challenged, it is by other highly financed networks like Fox, owned by billionaire reactionary Rupert Murdoch. The dramatic giant mergers of 1995 make it still clearer that our "free and independent" entertainment media are in the grip of ever more concentrated wealthy conservative interests. The mass media are class media.

Nothing Too Critical

Do the big owners and advertisers determine the media's ideological content? Isn't this done by politically liberal directors, scriptwriters, actors—and you, the viewing audience? An investigation of the hundreds of films and television shows offered each year suggests that a truly leftist movie or teleplay, offering a class analysis of power and wealth, is something rarely to be expected from the major media.

While persons of left persuasion often have worked in the film industry, they rarely have been able to insert much, if any, of their politics into the movies they created. Films that deviate from the mainstream political credo usually have to be toned down, rewritten, and larded with stars in order to be funded. Once made, they are accorded limited publicity and distribution, as was true of *Reds, Matewan,* and Bertolucci's *1900.* The dissident *Romero,* the story of the Salvadoran archbishop who was murdered by a death squad, was denied funding by major studios and networks. It saw the light of day only because funds were forthcoming from sympathetic Catholic agencies, and even then it received scant distribution.

Television scripts that offer a critical perspective fare no better. For years, TV's biggerst advertiser, Proctor and Gamble, imposed an editorial policy on its shows that read in part:

> There will be no material that may give offence either directly or by inference to any commercial organization of any sort. There will be no material on any of our programs which could in any way further the concept of business as cold, ruthless and lacking all sentimental or spiritual motivation. . . . Members of the armed forces must not be cast as villains. If there is any attack on American customs, it must be rebutted completely on the same show.

Televison shows are often prescreened by advertisers. Eastman Kodak noted: "In programs we sponsor on a regular basis, we do preview all scripts before the airing of the program. If we find a script is offensive, we will withdraw our commericals from the program."

The TV movie *Shootdown,* which showed that the Korean pas-

senger plane shot down over the Soviet Union had been inten-
tionally sent that way by U.S. authorities to test Soviet defense
responses, was subjected to drastic cuts. According to the show's
producer Leonard Hill, NBC censors "played the role of grand
inquisitor. It was quite a relentless interrogation and it turned
into a war of attrition." And the TV movie *Roe vs. Wade,* dealing
with the struggle for safe, legal abortions, was subjected to seventeen rewrites because network censors did not want the final
product to seem too pro-choice.

Ideological Sanitizers

On one of the rare occasions it has acknowledged the existence
of media censorship, the *New York Times* (11/27/88) noted that
while network "production and standards" departments have
reduced their policing of sexual and other cultural taboos, "the
network censors continue to be vigilant when it comes to over-
seeing the political content of television films."

Censorship is far more widespread than the few publicized incidents suggest. According to a poll conducted by the Writers Guild
of America, 86 percent of the writers who responded found from
personal experience that censorship exists in television. Many
claim that every script they have written, no matter how seemingly
innocuous, has been censored. And 81 percent believe that "television is presenting a distorted picture of what is happening in this
country today—politically, econmomically and racially."

Even more common is precensorship. In the early 1980s the
word was out in Hollywood that politically controversial film and
TV scripts were not welcome. Studio and network bosses and corporate advertisers are almost all politically conservative, as are
their financial backers. By defining beforehand what are the

saleable subjects, media chiefs predetermine the kind of scripts they will get. In short time, writers and producers bury dissident story ideas before they ever get on paper.

There are other censors: the U.S. military censors scripts for the many shows and movies that use its equipment and bases. The FBI has censored scripts and TV series about the FBI. Ultra-conservative censors like the Moral Majority and the Coalition for Better Television have exercised a censorial influence far out of proportion to their numbers because they can win support from conservative advertisers and network bosses.

The dissident views that manage, in one form or another, to survive the maulings perpetrated by investors, studio moguls, insurance underwriters, government officials, right-wing watchdogs, corporate advertisers, and network bosses must then face another group of ideological gatekeepers: the TV and film critics who do the reviews. If they treat progressive story lines too favorably, their employers may charge them with diverging from their roles as objective cultural evaluators. Generally, there is little need to rein them in, since they already have been ideologically preselected and are not likely to take unacceptable positions.

The entertainment industry's definition of a political film is itself political. The dissident political offering is readily identified disparagingly as "agitprop" and "preachy." In contrast, films and teleplays laden with political values and images that are well within acceptable parameters are less likely to be perceived as ideologically inspired. Thus the various films that glorify state-sponsored high-tech terrorism and militarism are seen as pure entertainment.

Creating Mass Audiences

Representatives from the entertainment industry maintain that media offerings are determined democratically through consumer sovereignty. In their quest for profits, corporate broadcasters and film makers strive for the largest possible audiences by giving the public what it wants. If entertainment media are filled with violence, authoritarianism, superpatriotism, materialism, militarism, sexism, and racism, it's because that's what the public prefers. Thus millions flocked to the *Rambo* movies, while only some thousands view a film like *Salvador*, a drama about the U.S.-supported, counterrevolutionary repression in El Salvador. In effect, what we have is a free-market "cultural democracy." So the argument goes.

It should be noted, however, that *Salvador* was turned down by every major Hollywood studio. One of them described it as "a hateful piece of work." Such a vehement rejection had less to do with market considerations than with political convictions. The film was eventually financed by British and Mexican investors and achieved only limited distribution in a handful of theaters around the country. In contrast, each of the *Rambo* flicks opened in over 2,000 movie houses.

Salvador was gripping and action-packed, just the things the public supposedly wants. Is it really the public that is not interested in seeing films like *Salvador*—or *Romero, Burn, 1900, Gaijin,* and other such well-made politically dissident movies? Or is it that, given their conservative ideological biases, studio bosses and financial backers are not interested in producing and distributing them?

The entertainment industry does not merely give the people what they want: it is busy shaping those wants. If a *Rambo* film had a naturally vast audience, it would not be necessary to spend $20 million on a pre-release publicity hype. Conversely, it is misleading to say that dissident films fail to appeal to large audiences when in fact they are kept from the general public by poor distribution, limited publicity, and politically hostile reviewers.

In sum, it is not simply a matter of demand creating supply. Often it is the other way around: supply creates demand. The first condition for all consumption is accessibility to the product. The whole advertising industry is predicated on the notion that the public can be taught or at least influenced to want certain things and that—be it movies, cars, or soft drinks—consumption will depend in large part on how available and well-hyped the product is. Prime-time TV shows, along with movies that open in every shopping mall in America, win large audiences not because there is a spontaneous wave of popular demand carrying them to the top, but because there is a lot of strenuous pulling *from* the top.

"Giving people what they want" is too simple an explanation of what the media do. Shows that are ideologically conservative will sometimes get vigorous publicity and distribution no matter what their box-office draw. The Pentagon/John Wayne production of *The Green Berets,* a movie filled with militaristic and superpatriotic hype, appeared at the height of the protests against the Vietnam War when there was no great public demand for that kind of film. Though it flopped, it was given wide distribution, playing to sparsely attended theaters in just about every mainstream movie chain in America. Likewise, shoot-'em-ups like *Cobra, Rambo 3,* and *The Dead Pool* were box-office disappointments despite multimillion-dollar publicity campaigns. This suggests that even people who have been conditioned to consume junk begin to tire of the same old junk.

What Does the Public Want?

Media production involves a lot more than just satisfying the public. The first audience a producer must please consists of the show's financial backers, its would-be corporate sponsors, and studio and network bosses. Because most movies and television series are completed before they are shown to the public, they cannot be altered to reflect audience feedback. Letters from individual viewers are usually not considered representative of the general public. Market research and rating services also are not that helpful, since they seldom tell anything about reactions to specific content. The only direct feedback is from the people who preside over the productive process, hardly a representative sample of the public.

Those who claim to give us what we like do everything they can to make us like what they give. In the early 1980s, the network brass, having decided that the public was in a conservative mood, produced a number of law-and-order television series like "Walking Tall," "Today's FBI," and "Strike Force," all of which suffered dismal ratings and died early deaths.

Usually producers give us what *they* like. Les Brown notes that, in defiance of the usual market criteria, golf receives more television exposure than other more popular sports. Since golf is a favorite recreation of media executives, agency men, and corporate sponsors, they assume "everyone" wants the game regularly televised.

When media bosses actually do try to ascertain what the public wants, the outcome can be surprising. Various surveys, including one conducted by the National Association of Broadcasters and suppressed for many years, reveal that though people watch a lot of television, they rate it poorly. One Roper poll reported that only 8 percent of viewers felt "very satisfied" with TV entertainment shows, and a majority wanted "more relevant" programs. A survey in Great Britain yielded similar results. Coverage of the royal family—thought to be close to the hearts of most British viewers—held an attraction for only 22 percent. Over 55 percent of the British public wanted serious news and documentaries, while 35 percent preferred game shows.

Shows that win substantial audiences may nevertheless be canceled because of ideological considerations. In 1982 the series "Lou Grant" came under right-wing attack because of its consistently liberal themes and the outspokenly progressive political activities of its star, Ed Asner. Though "Lou Grant" was sixth from the top among some ninety shows and its supporters launched letter-writing campaigns and public rallies, the network replaced it with a show that had a lower rating.

Media bosses tell us that most people desire to escape reality, not confront it. In fact, there exist large interested publics that respond positively to quality real-life dramas. The TV miniseries *Roots* lacked all the usual promotional glamour yet it reached record audiences, including many people who normally do not watch television. Other quality made-for-television movies with socially relevant messages have won impressive viewing audiences, including *The Autobiography of Miss Jane Pittman, A Matter of Sex, The Burning Bed, Shootdown,* and *Roe vs. Wade.* Quality movies containing politically progressive themes have been box-office successes, such as *Julia* (winner of three Oscars), *Reds* (winner of one Oscar), *Norma Rae, Missing, JFK,* and *Malcolm X.* Contrary to what network and studio bosses think, audiences do not eschew controversial themes.

Free-Market Democracy?

Much of what has been said about entertainment is true of the entire political universe. Political consciousness does not evolve in a social vacuum. Often it is shaped by a communication universe that regularly disinforms the public on crucial issues, offering a severely limited range of candidates and policies. Supply so thoroughly preempts demand that people often are unable to articulate the nature of their grievances. Public life devolves into increasingly irrelevant, sensationalist, or downright reactionary levels of discourse.

Be it "cultural democracy" or "political democracy," be it mental production or commodity production, in monopoly capital's "free market" the offerings consist of thoroughly processed and selectively distributed products. What we end up with is an illusion of choice with little of the substance. When exposed to nothing better, people are inclined to seek diversion in whatever is offered. And as already noted, this preconditioned consumption is then treated as evidence that the public is getting what it wants.

What is remarkable is that, despite all their exposure to trash, millions are still interested in quality productions that go beyond apolitical idiocy or mainstream orthodoxies. As the success of issue oriented films suggest, much of the public responds with alacrity to politically iconoclastic themes in ways that the mass-market hucksters never anticipated. In both the entertainment world and the arena of political struggle, there exist large interested publics that want something better than what is being offered. Many of them organize and agitate around vital issues and themselves can be the source of creative ideas and choices. Therein lies some cause for hope.

As of now the dirty truth is that we are being more than enter-

tained. The entertainment media are no less free from conservative political bias and ideological control than the news media. Of
this we must become aware if we are going to fight back in any
kind of organized way. And fight back we must. The struggle for
cultural hegemony is an important part of the struggle for political democracy itself.

GIVING LABOR THE BUSINESS

Why do so many people have a negative view of workers and labor unions? In part, it is because of what is fed to them by the corporate-owned news media. A 1990 City University of New York study found that programs devoted to "elite" personages consumed "nearly ten times more PBS prime-time programming hours than programs devoted to workers." Less than half of one percent of the programming dealt with workers—and it was mostly with British rather than American ones. A *Los Angeles Times* survey found that newspaper editors favored business over labor by 54 to 7 percent. My reading of this nation's newspapers leaves me to wonder who the 7 percent might be.

The media's pro-business bias is pronounced enough for anyone to see. The major newspapers and weeklies have no labor section to go along with their business section. They have whole staffs reporting on business news but not more than one labor reporter, if that. And usually "labor" reporters, judging from the ones I have met, show no special grasp of labor's struggles or sensitivity toward workers' issues. If they did, they would not last at that assignment and would be judged as "getting too close" to their subject.

The media's devotion to corporate America is manifested in the many TV and radio commentary shows that are glutted with conservatives. Public affairs programming is crowded with offerings like "Wall \$treet Week," "American Enterprise," "Adam Smith's Money World," "Nightly Business Report," and "Marketplace."

The network evening news regularly reports the Dow Jones average but offers no weekly tabulations on lay-offs, industrial accidents, and long-term occupational illness. When the stock market has a good day, for some reason this is treated as good news for all of us. The press seldom refers to the politico-economic power of corporations. The economy itself is presented as something government and business attend to, while organized labor tags along at best as a very junior and often troublesome partner.

Selfish Strikers

Labor news is seldom reported except when there is a major strike. Even then coverage is minimal and usually favors management. The press regularly presents labor as unwilling to negotiate in good faith when in fact management—in pursuit of high-profit policies—is usually the side that refuses a contract and forces a strike. Frequently, the workers do not walk out because they don't like management's offers but because management refuses to negotiate an acceptable contract and seeks to destroy the union and the collective bargaining process—a fact seldom noticed by the press. Instead, the union is depicted as making "demands" and management as making "offers."

The news media's anti-labor bias is never more pronounced than during contract disputes. To offer one example among many: In 1989, members of the United Mine Workers took over a coal processing plant owned by Pittston in southwest Virginia. It was the first major plant takeover since the historic Flint, Michigan, sit-down strike by auto workers in 1937. "The event had every element of a good journalistic story: conflict, drama, colorful characters and, for television, tremendous footage," commented Jonathan Tasini. "Yet, as far as the national media were concerned the historic action did not occur."

While the long and bitter strike against Pittston was receiving scant exposure, the networks and newspapers were lavishing sympathetic coverage on a coal miners' strike in the Soviet Union. During a nine-day period, the Soviet miners received a total of over 37 minutes of prime-time news coverage on the major networks. Contrasts were made between the living standards of Soviet bosses and coal miners—something the media never thought of doing in regard to the Pittston owners and miners. The Soviet strikers also were portrayed glowingly as fighters for self-betterment and social justice—a kind of representation never accorded U.S. workers.

Finally, in July of 1989, CBS's weekly television news show "48 Hours" did devote an entire hour to the Pittston strike. Reporters interviewed company executives who said they wanted to resume production but they couldn't get the union to cooperate. Scabs said they wanted to work and didn't need a union to tell them what to do; they spoke at length of threats and mistreatment from strikers. State troopers were portrayed as neutral peacekeepers just doing their job, clearing the roads as they arrested strikers who tried to keep "replacement workers" (scabs and strikebreakers) from entering the mines.

In a show of balanced reportage, CBS also interviewed strikers who said they were struggling for a contract and had to stick together until victory was theirs. Strikers were shown at home, at rallies, and on the picket lines. Never were they shown telling the viewers what the strike was about, what actually was at stake. Missing from the entire program was any reference to the issues, the *content* of the conflict. Why were the miners striking? Not once did CBS mention that Pittston wanted to make deep cuts in wages and benefits. Nor did CBS mention that Pittston was facing serious charges of unfair labor practices.

A few such pertinent facts would have put the whole conflict in a different light. As presented by the network, the strike seemed to be a mindless contest of wills, pitting the stubborn, shrill, and rather foolish miners against patient, softspoken managers who only wanted to resume production, "neutral" police who only wanted to keep the peace, and "replacement workers" (scabs) who only wanted the freedom to work without union interference.

Likewise, national coverage of the 1990 Greyhound bus strike offered little opportunity for the public to ascertain what was on the minds of striking workers. Company officials were afforded ample opportunity to comment, but union leaders and rank-and-file drivers received almost no exposure. Management's offer consisted of a moderate wage increase and drastic cuts in bene-fits—which taken together amounted to a real-wage deduction. Yet the press treated management's proposal, riddled as it was with selective arithmetic, as a generous one. The union's proposals were accorded almost no media attention. Management was depicted as using "replacement workers" to "rebuild its fleet" and maintain services for the public when in fact it was trying to break the strike and destroy the union. Throughout the strike, the images were of a besieged, responsible management versus violent, angry strikers, the latter showing a selfish indifference to the disruptive effects their strike was having on the economy and the public.

The media's anti-labor biases should come as no surprise. Media owners themselves are among the most exploitative, anti-union employers and strikebreakers. Over the years, the *Washington Post,* the *Los Angeles Herald-Examiner,* the *New York Daily News,* CBS, NBC ,and numerous other news organizations have been locked in bitter strikes that ended with unions being seriously weakened or totally crushed. As *Washington Post* owner Katharine Graham is reportedly fond of saying: "Unions interfere with freedom of the press."

When not on strike, unions and workers practically vanish from the national media. Issues that concern them—occupational safety, declining real-wages, seniority, job security, under-employment, health benefits, workplace racism and sexism, consumer safety, affordable housing, tax reform, and human services—are routinely ignored or given paltry exposure.

Taboo Topics

The media treat labor-management disputes as isolated incidents having no linkage to larger economic forces. Strikes are treated as aberrant disruptions of normal life, not as systemic conflicts endemic to industrial capitalism. The mutual support that strikers provide for each other and the aid that unions sometimes extend to other unions is usually ignored by the news media. During past coal strikes there was almost nothing on how farmers were bringing food to the miners. By ignoring instances of worker solidarity and mutual assistance within and between occupations, the press denies the class dimensions of the strike and underplays the support strikers have among other sectors of the public.

While the media will talk about "management," they have little to say about *capital*, little about the enormous wealth accumulated by owners. The billions paid out in stock dividends and interest on bonds represent a hugely inequitable upward distribution of the productive earnings of labor, a transfer of wealth from those who work to those who live mostly off those who work. Such exploitative arrangements go unnoticed or are implicitly accepted as the natural order of things.

Nor is the media much bothered by the damage done to labor and job opportunities in general as big companies export jobs to cheap Third World labor markets, where the margin of profit is several times higher than at home.

Also left untouched are the anti-union biases written into the laws. Under the National Labor Relations Act of 1935, employees won the right to organize and bargain collectively. Union membership grew dramatically. But the passage of the Taft-Hartley Law in 1947 and various right-to-work laws passed by the states imposed drastic restrictions on strikes, boycotts, and labor organizing, resulting in a decline in union membership from 35 percent of the work force in 1950 to 15 percent today. Union busting has become a major industry with more than a thousand consulting firms teaching companies how to prevent workers from organizing and how to get rid of existing unions. Lacking adequate support from the pro-business Clinton administration, a bill that would have protected striking workers from being permanently replaced by scabs failed to win congressional approval. Most of these anti-labor developments go unheralded in the pro-business media.

The National Labor Relations Board (NLRB), a federal agency intended to protect labor's right to organize and deal with grievances against management, was stacked during the Reagan-Bush years with pro-business appointees who refused to act on complaints and move against the many unfair, anti-labor practices and who delayed decisions for years. The NLRB has failed to protect employees from being illegally fired for union activities and has imposed only token fines on management for serious violations. The media has had almost nothing to say about these things.

Instead, the press treats the government as a neutral arbiter acting on behalf of the "national interest" in the struggle between management and labor. It is assumed that the public's interest is best served by avoiding strikes or getting strikers back into production as soon as possible, regardless of the terms of settlement. The police—along with the courts, the president, and the rest of the state apparatus—are presented as guardians of the peace, defenders of the public interest, rather than as protectors of corporate property and bodyguards for strikebreakers.

Invisible Workers

Like the news media, the entertainment media of Hollywood films and TV dramas also underrepresent or misrepresent working people. With few exceptions, such as the movie *Norma Rae,* blue-collar workers of both genders and whatever ethnic background play minor walk-on roles as waiters, service people, gas station attendants, and the like in an affluent, upper-middle-class, media-created world. When they do make a more substantial appearance, they are portrayed as emotional, visceral, simplehearted and simple-minded, incapable of leadership or collective action. Given the hostility that network and studio bosses have manifested toward organized labor in the entertainment industry, it is no wonder that labor unions are almost always portrayed in an unsympathetic light, as doing the workers more harm than good.

Generally speaking, whether it's a movie about factory workers, cops and crime, or the invasion of galactic monsters, it is individual heroics rather than collective action that save the day. Solutions and victories are never won by good ordinary people struggling for mutual betterment but by the hero in combat, defying the odds and sometimes even the authorities to vanquish the menace and let justice triumph.

No wonder the American people (including many otherwise liberal individuals) have a somewhat negative image of organized labor. No wonder some persons who are critical of racist, sexist, and anti-gay attitudes still harbor anti-working-class and anti-union sentiments of the kind propagated by the business-oriented media.

The situation is so bad that even the U.S. Congress felt obliged to take note. House Report 102-363, accompanying the Public Telecommunications Act of 1991, calls on the public broadcasting community to stop ignoring "class differences and the plight of American working people" and to make greater efforts to meet its "obligation to encourage diversity in programming, including programming which addresses the lives and concerns of American workers and their families, in documentaries, dramas, and public affairs programs." The report also noted that "public television station boards typically are dominated by business interests, even though working Americans are key supporters of public television." Unfortunately the report had little to say about the media's treatment of labor unions, an omission that itself may be a reflection of the anti-union bias that permeates the business-dominated political culture.

With its monopoly over mass communication, business has

been able to present a largely unchallenged picture of "Big Labor" as an avaricious and narrowly self-interested force that does itself, the economy, and the public no good, driving up prices with its incessant demands, serving only itself while creating costs that must be passed on to the rest of us. Labor has no direct means of countering this negative image among the general public. If there exists for labor a free market of ideas, it is not to be found in the corporate-owned mass media.

THE INVISIBLE BLOODBATHS

A common method of deception practiced by U.S. leaders and the U.S. news media is omission. Rather than outright lying, rather than twisting and embellishing the truth, leaders and their faithful flacks in the mainstream media frequently just ignore or greatly downplay events that might prove too troublesome for officialdom and too edifying for the U.S. public.

This is especially true when it comes to matters relating to the national security state. Reports can appear now and then in the news regarding an irresponsible business firm, a catastrophic oil spill too large to keep hidden, a corrupt banker or broker, an incident of sexism in the armed services, and so forth. Out of bounds are the fundamental questions about the use of state power in the service of corporate class interests at home and abroad. Critical discussions of global capitalism and what it is doing to the world are not likely to be countenanced by either U.S. leaders or the corporate-owned media.

The various methods of U.S. interventionism in other countries include both the overt forms of military invasion and the covert actions of the CIA and other counterinsurgency agencies; they include everything from bribes and rigged elections to death squads and mass slaughter. The purpose of these actions is to eliminate individual leaders, political parties, social movements, and governments that in any way challenge the existing global politico-economic arrangements that advocate egalitarian social change, be it toward a social democracy or socialism or even a conservative economic nationalism that strives for some kind of independent development.

Acceptable Holocaust

Consider the case of Indonesia. In the period following World War II, after a successful war of independence against the Dutch, Indonesia adopted an anti-imperialist stance on foreign policy and pursued progressive domestic programs. Among President Achmed Sukarno's supporters was the Indonesian Communist Party (PKI). One of the largest communist parties in the world, with a broad political organization right down to the village level, the PKI built schools, libraries, clinics, cooperatives, and day-care centers. It sponsored literacy and health programs, and encouraged democratic participation by villagers and others. When the Indonesian army overthrew Sukarno in 1965, it embarked upon a campaign to eradicate the PKI and the entire left, slaughtering about one-half million people (some estimates are as high as a million) in what was the greatest genocidal action since the Nazi Holocaust.

The massacre went on for weeks, but U.S. leaders murmured not a word of protest, though they were well aware of what was happening and even played a strategic hand in the events, supplying the generals with arms, tactical assistance, and money. It was over two months before the story broke in the U.S. press, in *Time* (12/17/65), which gave a matter-of-fact account of the massacres, complete with a description of rivers clogged with bodies. A month later the *New York Times* carried a relatively brief report. Spotty accounts appeared elsewhere over the ensuing weeks.

As with the overthrow of democracy in Guatemala, Chile, and a score of other countries, aided and abetted by the U.S. national security state, this mass atrocity by the fascist Right against the progressive Left was treated, if at all, in a fatalistic tone, with a striking lack of official indignation in Washington or critical editorial comment in the press. It was as if the victims were just the personae in some messy incident preordained by destiny. Thus the *New York Times* (7/6/66) quoted, without any reference to the moral horror of it all, the late Prime Minister of Australia, Harold Holt, who happily told the River Club of New York City that "with 500,000 to 1,000,000 Communist sympathizers knocked off, I think it is safe to assume a reorientation has taken place." Not a hint that these "Communist sympathizers" were human beings trying to build a more egalitarian democratic life for masses of people.

Some press commentary was blatantly upbeat in tone. James Reston, writing in the *New York Times* (6/19/66), saw the "savage transformation" from a leftist Sukarno government to "a defiantly anti-Communist policy under General Suharto" as one "of the more hopeful political developments . . . in Asia." Reston's column, entitled "A Gleam of Light in Asia" praised the U.S. government for the aid and assistance it gave to the coup. Except for one or two passing references, the press as usual had almost nothing to say about the critical role played by the CIA and the U.S. military in assisting the Indonesian generals before, during, and after the bloody takeover. The admission by State Department official George Aldrich that "roughly 90 percent" of the Indonesian military equipment and supplies were provided by the United States was treated as no cause for official comment or editorial condemnation.

Also deemed too trivial to earn much exposure was the plight of the several hundred thousand political prisoners rounded up in the coup, many of whom committed suicide or sickened and died under unspeakably inhumane conditions of captivity. Subsequent references in the news turned truth on its head and depicted the communists as the instigators of the massacre. Thus the *Los Angeles Times* (11/15/78) reported in retrospect that the Indonesians had broken relations with China in 1965 "when the Mao-inspired Communist Party, now outlawed, attempted to seize power and subjected the country to a bloodbath."

The press had little to say about developments in Indonesia after the military coup: the abolition of Sukarno's land reform program, the massive dispossession of peasants, the widening gap between village rich and poor, and the return of Dutch and Japanese corporations. Not a word about Indonesia's reentry into the International Monetary Fund, the power exercised by the "Tokyo Club" of financiers who rescheduled Indonesia's debts in exchange for more exploitative investment terms, and the U.S. and other Western firms that took hold of Indonesia's mineral resources.

What happened in Indonesia was no different from what has happened in scores of other countries: a populist, reformist government overthrown by a reactionary military armed and abetted by the U.S. national security state, accompanied by massive executions, murders, torture, and imprisonment of those deemed guilty of reformist inclinations, massive corruption by the new military autocrats, privatization of public properties, widespread plunder of natural resources and ecological preserves, the suppression of wages, a surge in unemployment, the reintroduction of foreign finance and loans, and an explosion of the national debt under arrangements worked out by the International Monetary Fund and related institutions.

Repeat Performance

The subsequent slaughter perpetrated by the Indonesian military in East Timor from 1976 on is another terrible story suppressed by official Washington and underplayed by the U.S. press. When East Timor, a Portuguese island colony at the edge of the Indonesian archipelago was granted independence by Lisbon in 1975, a brief struggle ensued between Timorese elites and a left-populist organization called Fretilin, with the latter swiftly gaining a popular base and emerging triumphant. Western observers, including Australian reporters, parliamentarians, and members of an Australian aid mission, reported that the reformist Fretilin government enjoyed strong support from the population.

This was enough reason for the CIA-sponsored Indonesian military to invade East Timor, engaging in a counterinsurgency campaign that included crop destruction, defoliation, and the systematic annihilation of whole villages. Thousands of Timorese starved to death or died of disease in concentration camps.

In 1977 Australian journalist James Dunn testified that when the Indonesian army captured the villages of Remexic and Aileu, all the inhabitants, except children under the age of three, were shot—because they were considered to be "infected with the seeds of Fretilin." After an extensive investigation of the evidence, an Australian political scientist, Pat Flanagan, concluded: "There can be no question that, if the articles of the 1948 United Nations

Geneva Convention defining 'genocide' are applied, what we have in East Timor is precisely that." (*Monthly Review,* May 1980)

The Indonesian intervention destroyed about half of the Timorese people. In 1974 the diocese of Dili, the capital of East Timor, placed the nation's population at 690,000. In 1978, Jakarta's security chief in East Timor reported a surviving populace of 330,000.

How did U.S. leaders and their media flunkies respond to genocide in East Timor? Hardly at all. Reports about the Indonesian military campaign trickling out of that unhappy land, mostly from Australian journalists and Timorese refugees, were ignored or downplayed by the White House and State Department. The index to the *New York Times* gave six full columns of citations to Timor in 1975, when the fate of the Portuguese colony was of great concern to the State Department and the CIA, and the left-oriented Fretilin was emerging victorious. (By left-oriented, I mean Fretilin was dedicated to land reform and public programs directed toward public needs rather than private investment.) But through 1977, when the Indonesian army's war of annihilation had reached awesome proportions, the *Times* index gave Timor only five lines.

Normally tireless in seeking out refugee reports alleging atrocities in countries not under Western capitalist domination, the U.S. press failed to interview any of the many Timorese refugees in Portugal and elsewhere. The *New York Times* (4/19/78) reported that Fretilin consisted only of "scattered groups" that were losing their hold over most of the Timorese people who had been "forced" to live "under their control" and that many Timorese were now fleeing into areas controlled by the Indonesian invaders. The image was a familiar one. As in the press's treatment of Vietnam, the Timorese were not fleeing the

Indonesian invaders' slash-and-burn campaigns, they were not forcibly evacuated by the military. As the *Times* would have us believe, they were choosing to leave their lands and ancestral birthplaces to live in Indonesian-run internment camps because of their dislike of the "totalitarian guerrillas" and their own love of freedom.

The *Times* reported that Fretilin's only outside support was "limited to highly vocal groups of Australian leftwing students." Not true. As the *Times* should have known, the United Nations General Assembly and also the Nonaligned Nations group had for several years in a row adopted resolutions supporting self-determination for East Timor, and anti-imperialist organizations on several continents supported the Timorese independence struggle.

Not surprisingly, the U.S. government, being one of the perpetrators and movers of the suppression, was determined to leave these momentous events unnoticed. Predictably, the U.S. media followed the official line, to wit: East Timor was a matter of no great moment; the Indonesians had "stabilized" the situation; and nothing much—and certainly nothing terrible—was happening there.

Maintaining silence about a dirty truth is another way of lying, a common practice in high places. Meanwhile the horror, torture, slaughter, grief, and misery inflicted upon dedicated people in Indonesia and East Timor over the last thirty years remain one of the great atrocities of history, made no less horrendous in the scales of human suffering for being studiously downplayed by its sponsors, who would have us believe they are defending democracy at home and abroad.

YELTSIN'S COUP AND THE
MEDIA'S ALCHEMY

One seldom hears about capitalism in the capitalist-owned media. For decades we were told that the cold war was a contest between freedom and communism, without any references to the interests of global capitalism. But with the collapse of communism in Eastern Europe and the Soviet Union, U.S. leaders began intimating that there was something more on their agenda than just free elections for the former "captive nations" — namely free markets. Of what use was political democracy, they seemed to be saying, if it allowed the retention of an economy that was socialistic or even social democratic? So they publicly acknowledged that a goal of U.S. policy was to restore *capitalism* in the former communist nations.

The propaganda task was to treat capitalism as inseparable from democracy (while ignoring the many undemocratic capitalist regimes from Guatemala to Indonesia to Zaire). However, "capitalism" still sounded, well, too capitalistic, so the preferred terms were "free market" and "market economy," concepts that appeared to include more of us than just the Fortune 500. So President Clinton announced before the United Nations on September 27, 1993: "Our overriding purpose is to expand and strengthen the world's community of market-based democracies." In a similar vein, the *New York Times* (10/5/93) noted that "[President Boris] Yeltsin remains the best hope for democracy and a market economy in Russia."

Far from being wedded to each other, capitalism and democracy are often on a fatal collision course—as demonstrated by the horrific events in Russia during the autumn of 1993. Multiparty electoral democracy is useful when it can be used to destabilize one-party socialism. But when it becomes a barrier to an untrammeled capitalism, democracy runs into trouble. The first ominous signs came in 1992, when the presidents of Poland, Czechoslovakia, and Russia demanded that their parliaments be suspended and they be allowed to rule by ukase. On cue, the U.S. media started making sympathetic noises about obstructionist legislators, letting us know that parliamentary democracy was getting in the way of "democratic market reforms." Washington threw its full support behind repressive executive leaders like Boris Yeltsin, a champion of the free market.

Orwell Lives

Those of us who have repeatedly challenged the outrageous misrepresentations perpetrated by that gaggle of concubines who compose "our free and independent press" still must marvel at the media's newspeak and doublethink treatment of Yeltsin's bloody coup in Russia in 1993. I had thought that George Orwell's model of propaganda as reality-in-reverse was crudely overdone.

Propaganda is most effective when it relies on emphasis, tones, and overall framing rather than when it blatantly inverts reality. But the U.S. media's treatment of Yeltsin's bloody coup is a real-life replication of Orwell's model: "tyranny is freedom," the blatant reversal of reality, the unblinking propagation of the crassest lies. Here we have an executive leader who tears up his country's constitution, disbands parliament, abolishes the Constitutional Court, launches an armed attack upon the parliamentary building, kills hundreds of resisters and demonstrators, jails opposition leaders without bail, arrests and detains tens of thousands, puts hundreds of elected and appointed officials under investigation, expels thousands of non-Russians from Moscow, bans labor unions from political activities, exercises monopoly control over all broadcast media, suppresses dozens of publications and television shows, and permanently outlaws fifteen political parties— and who is hailed by U.S. leaders as a savior of democracy.

With self-confirming momentum, the news media did not merely excuse the repression as a necessary evil but celebrated it as a step forward. This transformation of a violent putsch into a heroic salvation of democracy was truly one of the marvels of modern propaganda. Here is how it was done.

The Unconstitutional Constitution

It is a rare democracy in which conflicts do not arise between the executive and the legislature. What often happens is that a compromise is worked out. But compromise was just what Yeltsin and his Western allies were not interested in. "I will not agree to any compromise with any bodies. Categorically not." he is quoted as saying (*New York Times*, 9/28/93). Yet from the beginning he was portrayed as the moderate and compromising proponent while his adversaries were described (*Times*, 9/22/93) as "communists and nationalists who have blocked [his] legislation at every turn."

Once Yeltsin tore up the constitution, that document was seen as seriously defective. Appearing on "One on One" (10/3/93), Zbigniew Brzezinski falsely dismissed the Russian Constitution as "the old Brezhnev one." The next day, NPR's "All Things Considered" interviewed a member of Yeltsin's party in parliament who called it "the Stalin Constitution," another false assertion that went unchallenged by the NPR host.

The *New York Times* (9/22/93) approvingly repeated Aleksander Solzhenitsyn's untruthful charge that "this was less a parliament in Western terms than a gang of party hacks, more selected than elected in 1989, when the Soviet Union still existed and the Communist Party held sway." A front-page headline in the *Los Angeles Times* (10/3/93) announced: "Bill of Wrongs: Constitution in Mess in Russia." The accompanying story stated, "The weakest link in the legal structure is the constitution itself, enacted in its most recent incarnation in 1978, under Soviet power."

Truth peeked through only once in the *New York Times*. In an op-ed piece (10/2/93), historian Robert Daniels pointed out that every member of parliament had been freely elected in 1990. The Russian parliament was *not* operating under a Brezhnev or Stalin constitution but under the fully democratic reforms of 1989. It was not to be confused with the earlier Soviet parliament, which did have some nonelective seats but went out of existence two years before.

When not faulting the constitution, the *Times* berated the Russian people themselves: "There was nothing in the upbringing of these people that would equip them to appreciate the notion that above the laws there could be principles, that a constitution itself could be 'unconstitutional' if it served only a small clique"

(9/26/93). Russia's democratic institutions were undermined because "they were created . . . before the fledgling businessmen learned to defend their interests through politics" (10/10/93). Russia is populated by a "people steeped in socialist propaganda" who "are outraged by the vulgar display of the new rich" (10/5/93) — certainly not the right attitude for building capitalism.

Unlawful Lawmakers

Most of the Russian legislators were noncommunists and erstwhile Yeltsin allies. Yet they were repeatedly labeled by the press as "communists and ultranationalists," "communist holdovers," "unrepentant communists," "armed fascist-communist rebels," "the old elites," and "die-hard communists." In contrast, Yeltsin's former Communist Party affiliation was rarely mentioned. To be sure, some of the legislators were communists. That they were freely elected to office was of no matter; they still were considered anti-democratic simply by virtue of being communists.

The lawmakers were depicted as opposed not only to reforms but to *democratic* reforms and therefore to democracy itself. The *Times* (9/22/93) told us "this remains at its heart a battle between those who broke early with the totalitarian, centralized state and those who are trying to maintain its essence." In fact, the repressive centralization was being carried out by Yeltsin and his administration, not his opponents in parliament.

The largest formation in the Russian parliament, the Civic Union, favored slowing down the pace of privatization and retaining public ownership of those plants and collectives that were showing a profit. In this, they were moving contrary to capitalist state policy, which normally nationalizes sick industries at public expense and hands the profitable ones to private corporate interests, also at public expense. Far from being "hardliners," the Russian legislators were charting a mixed-economy course between total collectivization and Yeltsin's hardline free-market policy. Their real sin was that they were neither dismantling the public sector swiftly enough nor putting the interests of capitalist investors above all other considerations.

Minimizing the Slaughter

Yeltsin was given a generous rewrite when he abolished not only parliament but every other elected representative body in the country, including many city councils and the regional councils or soviets. The *New York Times* (10/10/93) dismissed the soviets as "creatures of the early Bolshevik era." Left unmentioned was that the councils had been recently democratically elected and that the president had no authority to abolish or restructure them.

The armed attack launched by President Yeltsin against the parliament earned a complete whitewash from the U.S. press. In what sounded like a replay of the Waco assault on the Branch Davidians, CNN commentators (10/4/93) tirelessly referred to the "very heavy weaponry inside the White House [the Russian parliamentary building]," including perhaps "rocket propelled grenades and anti-tank weaponry" and even "surface-to-air missiles." No evidence of such heavy weaponry ever materialized. The only footage we saw of those who occupied the White House showed only a makeshift collection of light arms.

There supposedly was a "very heavy exchange of fire from both sides." The "exchange" was actually a one-sided slaughter caused by a bombardment of the parliament building by Yeltsin forces, using 125mm and 75mm artillery shells, fragmentation bombs, and heavy-caliber machine-gun fire.

The U.S. press accepted the official count of 144 dead. But the president of the Kalmyk Republic, who spent all of October 4 in the parliament building, reported seeing hundreds of bodies and estimated the final toll at 1,000. His observations were reported by Moscow correspondent Mike Davidow in the *People's Weekly World* (10/30/93) and nowhere else in the U.S. press. Davidow noted that a number of Russian publications, including the pro-Yeltsin *Komsomolskaya Pravda* (10/15/93), reported 1,000 deaths and mass cremations. The *New York Times* (11/11/93) finally acknowledged that "many Russians" believe that 1,052 people were killed but assured its readers that these reports were unconfirmed.

The Violent Renegades versus Boris the Gentle

During CNN's October 4 daylong live coverage of the assault, the anti-coup legislators were described as "very hardline communists" who "have nothing to lose" and "renegade lawmakers." CNN reporter Ailene O'Conner turned instant psychiatrist, noting that many of the rebels were "social misfits" and some were "definitely mentally ill." A *New York Times* report (10/5/93) informed us that "the parliamentary plot jumped right out of the communist textbook on revolution." That same issue admiringly described the attack on the parliament as "a textbook example of the decisive application of military power."

The perpetrator of the coup, Boris Yeltsin, was portrayed as a leader who "seems to rely on popularity not brute force" (*Times*, 9/26/93) and who shows "commendable restraint" (*Times*, 10/5/93). As the parliament building was going up in flames and dead and wounded were being carried out, CNN's Bob Cain concluded with a straight face that we were witnessing "a measured action by Yeltsin forces, not an all-out assault." Cain and other CNN commentators assured us that Yeltsin "really doesn't want to fire on his countrymen." They noted the "relatively restrained response from the government," and claimed falsely that "Yeltsin made an attempt to reach a negotiated settlement but was rebuffed."

Final Solution

The U.S. press failed to point out that "market reforms" have brought disaster to Russia. The lifting of price controls spurred an inflation that dissolved real wages and reduced the majority of the population to virtual penury. By 1993, Russia's health system was crumbling; the education system was deteriorating; cholera, diphtheria, and tuberculosis were spreading, as was poverty, hunger and homelessness; and crime, corruption, and prostitution were flourishing. Whatever economic democracy the communists had managed to put together—including the guaranteed right to a job, medical care, and education, and subsidized food, housing, and utilities—was being scuttled. Russia became a juicy chunk of the Third World, with immense reserves of cheap labor, a vast treasure of natural resources, and industrial assets to be sold off at giveaway prices.

Yeltsin did what other desperate defenders of capitalism-in-crisis have done, he suppressed all opposition. This tyranny was given its fig leaf in the form of a rigged constitution and a showcase electoral system that poses no real challenge to executive state power. The Duma was reduced to a debating society, while Yeltsin went on to rule largely by executive decree. One thing is certain, U.S. leaders and their mouthpieces in the mainstream media will always be there, cheering on the Yeltsins of the world.

NOW FOR THE WEATHER

The media's most common method of distortion is omission. We are misled not only by what is reported but by what is left unmentioned. This is true even with weather reports.

Impending Disaster

There are catastrophic things happening with the weather, one of which is ozone depletion. Damage to the earth's protective ozone layer causes skin cancer, cataracts, crop damage, and climatic aberrations. Some 2.6 billion pounds of ozone-depleting chemicals are emitted into the air every year. Some of the biggest polluters are military-industrial contractors who are also among the biggest TV advertisers. One of the worst, General Electric, owns NBC.

Another potentially calamitous development is global warming. Auto exhaust, industrial air pollution, and other fossil fuel emissions act like a blanket to create and trap heat close to the earth's surface, causing it to warm. Every day the number of vehicles spewing emissions into the atmosphere increases. In 1950, the United States had 75 percent of the world's automobiles. Today it has only 25 percent even though the actual number of vehicles in this country has more than doubled in that period. Now the car is everywhere in Asia, Africa, and Latin America, wreaking its devastation on the land, ground water, and air.

The nine warmest years (average global temperature) ever recorded in the last century were during the last fifteen years. Every year, in various cities and other locales, "record temperatures" are announced. We have discovered that the earth's capacity to absorb heat from energy consumption is limited. We face an ecological crisis whose momentous dimensions we are just beginning to grasp. One effect of global warming is drought: from California to Vermont to England to Russia to New Zealand. Unless reversed, drought leads to starvation, as Africa has been the first to know.

When the evening news tells us "what's happening with the weather," these potentially cataclysmic developments are not mentioned. "Weather" is defined in a limited way: cloudy and clear, cold and warm. The weather is reported the way politics is reported: isolated daily particulars unconnected to the larger structural forces that help create them.

Sunny Disinformation

Worse still, the ill effects of global warming and ozone depletion are actually celebrated by TV weather reporters, who operate by an unwritten code: "sunny" and "warm" are good, "rainy" and "cold" are bad. Weathercasters in various locales get absolutely rhapsodic over the strangely mild winters we have been having in recent years. They exult over the "beautiful spring-fever weather" that now seems to come in December and January. We are told to "get out there today and catch some of these lovely rays." Not a word about watching out for skin damage because of ozone depletion. Not a word about drought—or if drought *is* mentioned, not a word about the global warming that is causing it and not a word about the commercial industrial base and mode of vehicular transportation that are causing the global warming.

Conversely, weathercasters frown when "the weather is bad," when temperatures drop and January begins to resemble January. We are told "the outlook is not good" because rain "threatens." Another winter with very little snow? "That's good news," said one announcer, good for all of us except "you skiing fans." Forget that snow is a major source of our water supply, that it shields the topsoil from the sun, helping it to retain its sponginess. Forget that the scarcity of snow is making it increasingly difficult for forests in northern climes to renew themselves.

In California, where a six-year drought threatened to devastate agribusiness, there was at least some belated awareness among weather reporters that endless sunny days were not good news. But even there, the reportage was misleadingly upbeat. Thus the rain that finally came to Northern California in early 1991 was cheerfully greeted as raising reservoir levels, with no acknowledgment of how dangerously insufficient such levels remained. And even after the rains filled the reservoirs, as happened in 1993-94 and the water emergency was declared over, no mention was made that the state's water-storage facilities, even at full capacity, were insufficient for growing population and business needs. In other words, the emergency was not over.

On rare occasions, the threat of environmental catastrophe is obliquely acknowledged only to be denied. Thus TV weathercasters, who usually never mention global warming, were quick to

assert that the record-breaking high temperatures for May 1991
in our nation's capital were not an indication of global warming,
since other parts of the country had been cooler than usual that
same month and "it all averaged out." What the weather people
do not seem to understand is that temperature increase is only a
part of the global warming problem. Even more ominous is the
carbon dioxide buildup that causes such unusual weather aberrations as record storms, floods, hurricanes, and drought; hot and
sunny winter days in Seattle and San Francisco, snow in Los
Angeles one day and record freezing temperatures in Florida
another.

During an ABC weather report in Washington, D.C. (10/5/91),
an announcer asked if the increasing number of days with temperatures over 90 degrees was indicative of global warming. The
weathercaster replied: "The record is too short. You've got to look
over hundreds of years to get a perspective." In effect, he was
treating the question of global warming as untestable and
unprovable in anyone's lifetime or any one era, leaving us with the
soothing assumption that we have the luxury of "hundreds of
years" to study the problem. The dirty truth is that every leading
scientific body in the world now recognizes global warming to be
a dangerous fact of life on this planet and that human causes are
a major factor.

During the Gulf War, bias in weather coverage showed forth in
a new unabashedly political way, as evening reports began to fea-
ture aerial weather maps of the Gulf region. When the skies were
clear over Iraq, announcers would look pleased. When cloudy,
they looked concerned; as one of them said, "It's gonna interfere
with our air strikes."

Conservatives say that left critics deny "the autonomy of culture." Not true. Most of us recognize that culture does not oper-

ate in perfect harmony with the dominant socio-economic order. We understand that dissident cultural forces can arise and have a self-generating impact. But when it comes to the kind of mass culture manufactured by the media, I want to plead guilty to the charge. There is little autonomy to speak of. Be it entertainment, news, advertising, sports, or weather, it is all subject to various degrees of political bias. And no one is more political than those who instinctively know how to avoid politically troubling realities.

SOME CALL IT CENSORSHIP

Our "free and independent" news media are actually controlled by publishers and network bosses who see to it that their own preferred views prevail. They will refuse to run letters, guest columns, and occasionally even their regularly syndicated features and comic strips if the material does not suit their political proclivities. They punish editors and journalists by passing them over for promotion, transferring them to remote posts, and even firing them if they don't learn soon enough what is and is not ideologically fit to print or broadcast. Such actions should be exposed for what they are: *censorship*. But news organizations are the last to publicize their own transgressions. Instances of censorship are simply not treated as newsworthy.

The hardest kinds of censorship to detect are the preemptive forms. In a profession that is literally awash with right-wing pundits, there are few, if any, progressives who appear regularly as TV commentators or as nationally syndicated columnists in the major dailies. The Left does not have to be censored; it is excluded from the start. It does not have to be reined in; it is never even put into harness.

Here I would like to recount two incidents of media suppression drawn from my own experience. These events hardly exhaust my encounters with political censorship but they illustrate a kind of suppression that is seldom publicized.

Overruled

Some years ago, when I lived in Washington, D.C., an acquaintance urged me to call upon the editor of *City Paper* and suggest to him that I write a weekly column for his publication. It seemed worth a try. *City Paper* is a handout "alternative" weekly that affects a kind of *Village Voice* stylistic and cultural liberalism. It treats various taboo subjects with more candid detail than would be allowed in the mainstream media and it offers—or used to offer in those days—an occasional liberal muckraking article. It claims a readership of 50,000 and is picked up by a lot of people both in local government and on Capitol Hill.

The editor greeted me warmly in his office. Professing to be an admirer of my writing, he responded most positively to my offer to do a column. He was delightedly surprised that someone with my "credentials" would be willing to become a regular contributor for a local publication like *City Paper*. Would I consider doing a media watchdog column, one that could eventually be syndicated in other alternative weeklies? I said yes. He would call me within a week with a final go-ahead.

Three weeks later, having not heard from him, I telephoned his office. He sounded like a different person. Whereas before he had been ebullient and enthusiastic, now he spoke in a flat, dismissive tone, saying only: "Uh, no, we're not going to do it." No explanation, no regrets. The conversation went no further. He abruptly hung up. Later on, I heard from someone who used to write for *City Paper* that he had been overruled by his publishers.

Cokie, Kevin, and Michael?

The second incident involves a national media organization. In February 1990 I received a telephone call from the senior editor of National Public Radio's "Morning Edition." She said words close to these: "We have been thinking of broadening our range of commentary on 'Morning Edition,' and your name keeps coming up. Would you be interested in becoming one of our regular commentators along with Cokie Roberts and Kevin Philips?" She went on to tell me that along with the commentaries I might expect to participate in an occasional weekend retreat with Kevin and Cokie and a few of the senior staff to exchange ideas and impressions. A whole weekend listening to Cokie Roberts do her spin analyses was my idea of purgatory. Still I said okay. The editor said she would get back to me soon.

Friends asked me why I wasn't more enthusiastic about the pending offer from NPR; I replied, "Because it will never happen." Our "free and independent" media can harbor all sorts of conservative and reactionary pundits but would never have a progressive like myself as a regular commentator. Indeed, the "Morning Editon" senior editor never got back to me. I later learned she was no longer at that post.

Seven months later I received another call from another senior editor of "Morning Edition." "We haven't forgotten about you," she said. She asked if I had something they could use as a commentary. (There was no further mention of weekend retreats or becoming a regular third member of the Cokie-Kevin team.) I suggested a short commentary drawn from an article I had just written on the U.S. armed assault against Iraq, entitled "Bush's Splendid Little War." I sent the script—maximum allowed length of 400 words—to her. After a few changes by her, we taped it at the NPR studio.

Canceled

My commentary was hardly a class analysis of imperialism but it did make some pointed criticisms of Bush's intervention in the Gulf region—of a kind I had not heard on NPR or any other mainstream outlet. I noted that the president had a taste for splendid little wars, that the invasion of Panama had brought dire results for the Panamanians, and that an attack against Iraq (the fighting had not yet begun) would be disastrous for the Iraqi people. I said: "One wonders what this military venture is all about. Saddam Hussein is not a Sandinista, a Castro, a Qaddaffi, nor even a Noriega. By that I mean, he doesn't have leftist or populist leanings. He doesn't advocate the kind of economic equality that rich conservatives like Bush find so loathsome. Hussein is a right-wing dictator, who like other such autocrats, has received U.S. aid . . . . So why is Bush now coming down so hard on him?" I stated that the intervention had a self-serving purpose for the president. It distracted the public from the sagging economy and the savings-and-loans scandal. It secured oil profits for the big corporations. It bolstered the case for military spending and boosted Bush's opinion poll ratings.

The editor was pleased with the taping and told me it would run the next morning. As I left, she asked if I had anything else I would like to do. I mentioned an idea I had about the Supreme Court, and she indicated a desire to start on it in the next few days.

The following morning I listened to NPR's "Morning Edition" but did not hear my commentary. Later I called the senior editor. She told me that the executive producer Bob Ferrante had listened to my tape and had canceled it because, as he put it, "I'm not hearing anything new." Nothing new? What previous "Morning Edition" commentary had touched on Bush's hidden agenda in the Gulf war, especially his dedication as a wealthy conservative to economic inequality and oil profits? "No," I said to her, "your boss vetoed that tape because there *was* something new in it." She responded: "I only work here."

She added that she wouldn't mind having me try another commentary but she feared it might again be canceled—and that would be a waste of my time. So ended my career with National Public Radio.

There were questions I could have asked that editor, such as: Is it a regular practice to have the executive producer exert prior censorship over the commentaries? Had he killed any other contributions? If so, how many? whose? and for what reasons? Did he ever cancel one that seemed too conservative? Did he really hear something new in every Kevin and Cokie commentary? Hadn't he run numerous commentaries that offered the same old predictable notions, the same perspective and familiar information?

If the above incidents tell us anything, it is that editors and reporters are not as free and independent to invite a variety of opinions as they might think. They are free to say what they like only as long as their bosses like what they say. They are free to produce what they want if their product remains within acceptable political boundaries. You will have no sensation of a leash around your neck if you sit by the peg. It is only when you stray that you feel the restraining tug.

I can draw one consolation from the above incidents: they support the Left's critical analysis of the press as being neither free nor independent but highly controlled by its corporate owners and their faithful lieutenants. In the stories and commentary they run or refuse to run, and the people they hire or refuse to hire, the mass media demonstrate the accuracy of what we progressive critics say about them.

THE JFK ASSASSINATION I: DEFENDING THE GANGSTER STATE

Much of history is a chronicle of immense atrocities. Whenever surplus wealth accumulates in any society, whenever people emerge from a cooperative subsistence economy, some portion of the population will do everything it can to exploit the labor of the rest of the people in as pitiless a manner as possible. This is true whether it be the slaveholders of ancient Egypt, Greece, Rome, and the antebellum American South; or the feudal aristocracy of medieval Europe; or the financial moguls of modern capitalist society. Today, throughout much of the capitalist Third World and increasingly in the United States and other industrialized nations, people are being driven into desperation and want, made to work harder for less, when able to find work.

The Gangster State

The state is the instrument used in all these societies by the wealthy few to impoverish and maintain control over the many.

Aside from performing collective functions necessary for all societies, the state has the particular task of protecting the process of
accumulating wealth for the few. Throughout our country's history, people have fought back and sometimes gained a limited
degree of self-protective rights: universal suffrage, civil liberties,
the right to collective bargaining, the eight-hour day, public education, social security, and some human services. While these
democratic gains are frequently violated and prove insufficient
as a restraint against state power, their importance should not
be denied.

Today in the much-vaunted western democracies there exists a
great deal of unaccountable state power whose primary function
is to maintain the existing politico-economic structure, using
surveillance, infiltration, sabotage, judicial harassment, disinformation, trumped-up charges and false arrests, tax harassment,
blackmail, and even violence and assassination to make the world
safe for those who own it.

There exists a state within the state, known as the national
security state, a component of misgovernment centering around
top officers in the various intelligence agencies, the Pentagon,
and policy makers in the Executive Office of the White House.
These elements have proven themselves capable of perpetrating
terrible crimes against dissidents at home and abroad. National
security state agencies like the CIA, in the service of dominant
economic interests, have enlisted the efforts of mobsters, drug
traffickers, assassins, and torturers, systematically targeting peasant leaders, intellectuals, journalists, student leaders, clergy, labor
union leaders, workers, and community activists in numerous
countries. Hundreds of thousands of people have been murdered
to prevent social change, to destroy any government or social
movement that manifests an unwillingness to reduce its people to

economic fodder for the giant corporations that rule the world's economy.[1]

JFK, the Media Mugging

Occasionally an incident occurs that reveals in an unusually vivid manner the gangster nature of the state. The assassination of President John Kennedy in November 1963 is such an occasion. The dirty truth is that Kennedy was heartily hated by right-wing forces in this country, including many powerful people in the intelligence organizations. He had betrayed the national interest as they defined it, by refusing to go all out against Cuba, making overtures of rapproachment with Castro, and refusing to escalate the ground war in Vietnam. They also saw him as an anti-business liberal who was taking the country down the wrong path. Whether Kennedy really was all that liberal is another matter. What the national security rightists saw him to be was what counted.

To know the truth about the assassination of John Kennedy is to call into question the state security system and the entire politico-economic order it protects. This is why for over thirty years the corporate-owned press and numerous political leaders have suppressed or attacked the many revelations about the murder unearthed by independent investigators like Mark Lane, Peter Dale Scott, Carl Oglesby, Harold Weisberg, Anthony Summers,

---

[1] Colonel L. Fletcher Prouty, a military intelligence chief closely connected with the CIA, tells of his visit to "a special 'village' in the Mediterranean where a highly select group of stateless 'mechanics' in the CIA are hit-men, assassins, and other related specialists. They are absolutely anonymous"; see his introduction to Mark Lane's *Plausible Denial* (New York: Thunder's Mouth Press, 1991). For a further discussion on U.S. repression abroad, see "Making the World Safe for Hypocrisy," p. 55; also my two books *Against Empire* (San Francisco: City Lights Books, 1995); and *The Sword and the Dollar* (New York: St. Martin's Press, 1989).

Philip Melanson, Jim Garrison, Cyril Wecht, Jim Marrs, Gaeton Fonzi, Sylvia Meagher, Michael Canfield, James DiEugenio, and many others.

These investigators have been described as "assassination buffs." The term "buff" is a diminishing characterization, describing someone who pursues odd hobbies. For the same reason that we would not refer to "Holocaust buffs," so should we not refer to these serious investigators as "assassination buffs." Their efforts reveal a conspiracy to assassinate the president and an even more extensive conspiracy to hide the crime.

While ignoring their revelations, the media have given fulsome publicity to the likes of Gerald Posner, author of a grotesque whitewash of the assassination. Posner's book was not a sloppy, confused work but a deliberate contrivance that used outright untruths to conclude that Lee Harvey Oswald was a disgruntled lone leftist who killed Kennedy. Posner could get away with his misrepresentations because those who have written systematic exposures of his book were either ignored by the corporate-owned media or roughed up by unsympathetic reviewers and editors.[2]

An end run around the media blackout was achieved by Oliver Stone's movie *JFK*, a film that directly reached millions of viewers with an accurate account of the specifics of the assassination. The movie could not be ignored because it was reaching a mass audi-

---

[2] For telling critiques of Posner's *Case Closed,* see Peter Dale Scott, "Gerald Posner and the False Quotation Syndrome," *Prevailing Winds,* premiere issue, 1995 (published by Prevailing Winds Research, Santa Barbara, Calif.), 58-63; also Scott's review of Posner's book in that same issue; George Costello's critique in *Federal Bar News and Journal,* May 1994; Gary Aguilar, "Gerald Posner and the Evidence," *Open Secrets,* November 1995; Dan Beckman and Wallace Milam, *Loss of Faith: A Critique of the Warren Report,* Case Closed *and the Single Assassin-Theory* (forthcoming); Stewart Galanor, *Coverup* (forthcoming); Harold Weisberg, *Case Open: The Omissions, Distortions and Falsifications of* Case Closed (New York: Carroll & Graff Publishers, 1994)

ence. So the press savaged it. As far as I know, *JFK* is the only movie in film history that was attacked, six months *before* it was released, in just about every major broadcast and print outlet. The *Washington Post*, for instance, gave George Lardner Jr. the whole front page of its Sunday "Outlook" section (5/19/91) to slam Stone for "chasing fiction." Lardner was an interesting choice to review this particular movie, being the *Post* reporter who covered the CIA and who never wrote a harsh word about that agency.

The media's ideological gatekeepers threw restraint to the wind when dealing with Stone's film. Conservative news columnist George Will, not known for writing movie reviews, penned a rant against *JFK*, calling it "a cartoon history" and "a three-hour lie." Will describes Stone as "an intellectual sociopath, combining moral arrogance with historical ignorance . . . a specimen of the sixties' arrested development. . . . Intellectually, Stone is on all fours . . . part of a long fringe tradition . . . banally venal, reckless, cruel" (*Washington Post*, 12/27/91). By relying on invective, Will avoided the more difficult task of rebutting the points made in Stone's film.

Shoulder to shoulder with conservatives like Will stood liberal centrists like Daniel Schorr, the NPR radio commentator who attacked Stone three times on the air, always in sarcastic and general terms, without ever coming to grips with the information proffered by the movie.

Then there was Tom Wicker, a syndicated columnist who also had never done a movie review, but when *JFK* came out, he wrote one that covered a whole page, complete with photos (*New York Times*, 12/15/91). In it, Wicker said something revealing:

> If the wild assertions in Oliver Stone's movie are taken at
> face value, Americans will have to accept the idea that most of

the nation's major institutions conspired together and carried
out Kennedy's murder. In an era when mistrust of government
and loss of confidence in institutions—the press not the
least—are widespread and virulent, such a suggestion seems a
dubious public service.

In so many words Wicker was disclosing the basic reason why
such a merciless attack had been launched against Stone's movie.
A full exposure of the assassination conspiracy would invite serious discredit upon the legitimacy of the dominant institutions of
state and class. Playing before mass audiences, *JFK* did not accuse
a cabal of malevolent perpetrators, but pointed to the national
security state itself, inviting millions of viewers to question the
kind of state system under which they lived.

JFK is the only movie I know that continues to be attacked four
years after its run. Reviewers and commentators persist in making gratuitous references, describing Oliver Stone as "the man
who reinvented history with movies such as *JFK*" (*Oakland
Tribune*, 10/13/95), referring to "Oliver Stone's near-pathological
monkeying with history" (*East Bay Express*, 12/14/95), and
describing him as "a man who makes his living being a ranting
maniac" and a "dangerous fellow" (*San Francisco Examiner*
1/9/96). If anyone is ranting, it's the press.

Sociologist David Simone compiled a study of the books published on the Kennedy assassination, some 600 titles, and found
that 20 percent of them blamed either a lone assassin or the mafia
or the Cubans or Russians. The other 80 percent ascribed the
assassination to a conspiracy linked to U.S. intelligence agencies;
some of these also said that mobsters were involved at the operational level. Ignoring this 80 percent of the literature, publications
like the *New York Times* and *Washington Post* have listed the vari-

ous theories about the JFK assassination as follows: (a) lone assassin, (b) mafia, (c) Cubans/Soviets, and (d) the "Oliver Stone movie theory." In other words, they ignore the existence of a vast literature from which the movie is derived and ascribe the critical theme presented within the film solely to the imagination of a film maker. The press would have us believe that the notion of a state-sponsored assassination conspiracy and cover-up came out of a movie—when actually the movie was based on a rich and revealing investigative literature.

Like the Warren Commission, the press assumed a priori that Oswald was the killer. The only question it asked was: Did Oswald act alone? The answer was a loudly orchestrated *yes*. Meanwhile, almost every in-depth investigator had a different conclusion: Oswald did not act at all. He was not one of the people who shot Kennedy, although he was involved in another way, as a fall guy, in his own words "just a patsy."

The media have been tireless in their efforts to suppress the truth about the gangster state. In 1978, when a House Select Committee concluded that there was more than one assassin involved in the Kennedy shooting, the *Washington Post* (1/6/79) editorialized:

> Could it have been some other malcontent who Mr. Oswald met casually? Could not as much as three or four societal outcasts with no ties to any one organization have developed in some spontaneous way a common determination to express their alienation in the killing of President Kennedy? It is possible that two persons acting independently attempted to shoot the President at the very same time?

It is "possible," but also most unlikely and barely imaginable. Instead of a conspiracy theory the *Post* creates a one-in-a-billion "coincidence theory" that is the most fanciful of all explanations.

Ignored Evidence, Unanswered Questions

David Garrow, author of a biography of Martin Luther King, condescendingly says: "A large majority of the American people do believe in assassination conspiracies. That allows events to have large mysterious causes instead of small idiosyncratic ones." Contrary to Garrow, the question of whether a conspiracy exists in any particular situation has to be decided by an investigation of evidence, not by patronizing presumptions about the public mind. Investigators who concluded there were conspiracies in the Kennedy and King murders did not fashion "large mysterious causes" but came to their conclusions through painstaking probes of troubling discrepancies, obvious lies, and blatant cover-ups. They have been impelled not by the need to fashion elaborate theories but by the search for particular explanations about some simple and compelling truths.

Many people talk about finding the "smoking gun" behind this or that mystery, the one evidentiary item that dramatically resolves the case and puts to rest all further questions. Unlike fictional mysteries, in real life there usually is no smoking gun. Historians work by a process of accretion, putting piece by piece together until a picture emerges. In the Kennedy murder, the pieces make an imposing picture indeed, leaving one with the feeling that while there may not be a smoking gun there is a whole fusillade of impossibilities regarding the flight of bullets, the nature of the wounds, the ignored testimony of eye witnesses, the sudden and mysterious deaths of witnesses, the disappearance and deliberate destruction of evidence, and the repeated acts of official cover-up that continue to this day regarding the release of documents.

Let us focus on just a small part of the immense brief that has been assembled by investigators. Consider the background of Lee

Harvey Oswald. During the week of the thirtieth anniversary of the JFK assassination, one repeatedly heard on television that Oswald was an incompetent "loner" and not very bright. Gerald Posner, transforming himself into an instant psychiatric expert, announced that Oswald "had a very disturbed childhood, and he was a passive-aggressive." A passive-aggressive assassin? He was also repeatedly labeled a "loner" and a "leftist." The truth is something else.

Lee Harvey Oswald spent most of his adult life not as a lone drifter but directly linked to the U.S. intelligence community. All of his IQ tests show that he was above average in intelligence and a quick learner. At the age of eighteen in the U.S. Marines he had secret security clearance and was working at Marine Air Control in Atsugi Air Force base in Japan, a top-secret location from which the CIA launched U2 flights and performed other kinds of covert operations in China. The next year he was assigned to El Toro air station in California with security clearance to work radar.

Strange things began to happen. While at El Toro, Oswald emerged as a babbling Russophile and a "communist." He started playing Russian-language records at blast level in his barracks and addressing his fellow Marines in Russian, calling them "comrade." He read Russian books and hailed Soviet Communism as "the best system in the world." If Oswald was a Soviet or a Cuban spy, as some people now claim, he certainly had a novel way of building a cover.

Philip Melanson, author of *Spy Saga*, a book about Oswald's links to intelligence, reminds us that the U.S. Marine Corps in 1958 was not exactly a bastion of liberal tolerance and freethinking. But in this instance, for some strange reason, Oswald's Marine commanders did not seem to mind having a ranting commie sympathizer in their midst. He kept his security clearance and retained access to a wealth of sensitive radar information and classified data from secret facilities.

Other odd things happened. In February 1959, he failed the Marine Corps proficiency test in Russian. Six months later he had developed some fluency in that language. In 1974, a document classified by the Warren Commission—and dislodged mostly by Harold Weisberg's legal efforts—revealed that Oswald had attended the U.S. Army's School of Languages at Monterey. Monterey is not open to just anyone who happens to have a language hobby. One is sent by the government, for training in a specific language pertaining to a specific assignment. Oswald learned Russian at Monterey.

Another curious thing: Oswald applied for an early dependency discharge from the Marines because his mother had injured her foot—the accident had occurred a year earlier. He was released one week after putting in his request, a decision so swift as to astonish his fellow Marines.

Oswald then "defected" to the USSR, but how? Melanson notes that such a trip would have cost at least $1,500 in those days, but Oswald's bank account showed a balance of $203. And how did he get from London to Helsinki on October 11, 1959, when no available commercial flight could have made it in one day? He must have had some kind of private transportation to Helsinki.

Once in Russia, he went to the U.S. embassy and openly renounced his U.S. citizenship, declaring that he was going to give military secrets to the Soviets. Embassy officials made no effort to detain him. As the KGB files opened in 1991 show, the Soviets kept him under constant surveillance. KGB defector Yuri Nosenko, who had been responsible for investigating every contact Oswald made in the USSR, reported that the young American had never been associated with Soviet intelligence and that the KGB suspected he was connected with U.S. intelligence.

While in Russia Oswald belonged to a gun club at the factory in which he worked, though he showed no interest in guns. He reportedly used to join in rabbit shoots but could never score a hit. Someone would have to stand behind him and shoot the rabbit while he was firing. His performance became something of a joke among his co-workers. His marksmanship in the U.S. Marines had been no better.

U.S. intelligence mysteriously departed from normal procedure and made no damage assessment of Oswald's "defection," or so they claimed. Another odd thing: after two-and-a-half years, Oswald's sudden request to return to the United States was immediately granted by U.S. officials—all this after he had threatened to give away state secrets to the Soviets. Instead of being arrested for treason, Oswald was accepted with open arms by U.S. authorities.

The CIA claimed it had no record of debriefing him and was never near him. Their explanation before the Warren Commission was that there were so many tourists coming in and out and there was nothing particularly unusual about Oswald that would have caught their attention. One might wonder what was needed to catch the CIA's attention.

Yet, CIA officials claimed they had suspected all along that he was a Soviet spy—which makes it even more curious that they did not debrief him. In fact, they did debrief him in Holland. But being so eager to cover up any association with Oswald, they could not recognize how in this instance the truth would have been a less suspicious cover than the improbable lie they told about not noticing his return.

State Department officials also behaved strangely. They paid all travel and moving expenses back to the United States for Oswald and his wife. Without a moment's delay they gave him back his passport with full rights to travel anywhere in the world. Another curious thing: his wife was exempted from the usual immigration quotas and granted immediate entry. Years earlier she had belonged to the Soviet Komsomol, the Communist youth organization, which automatically would have barred her from the United States. Yet in violation of U.S. immigration laws, she was allowed into the country.

In Dallas, Lee Harvey Oswald settled under the wing of White Russian émigré and former cavalry officer George de Mohrenschildt, an associate of oil millionaires H. L. Hunt and Clint Murchinson and other Dallas economic elites. In de Mohrenschildt's telephone book was found the name of George "Pappy" Bush. A correspondence existed between Bush and de Mohrenschildt indicating that they were personal acquaintances.

De Mohrenschildt and his wife Jeanne were identified by the Warren Commission as the people closest to Oswald just before the assassination. An investigator for the House Select Committee, Gaeton Fonzi, noted, "Given his background, it seemed strange that de Mohrenschildt would have spontaneously befriended someone with the look of a working-class drifter like Lee Harvey Oswald." That was not the only strange thing about de Mohrenschildt. He also was part of a network of ex-Nazis contracted by the CIA.

A CIA memorandum written not long after Oswald returned from Russia advised de Mohrenschildt on how to handle the young "defector." De Mohrenschildt also had a close friendship with J. Walter Moore, who was an agent of the CIA's Domestic Contacts Division. As de Mohrenschildt told one investigator just before his sudden death, it was Moore who encouraged him to see Oswald. Investigator Jim Marrs observes in his book *Crossfire:*

"The CIA memos, Moore's closeness, and de Mohrenschildt's own testimony all confirm that a certain relationship existed between the CIA and the man closest to Oswald in early 1963. While this does not necessarily involve the Agency in a plot to kill Kennedy, it raises questions about what Agency officials might have known regarding such a plot."

Oswald embarked on a series of short-lived public forays as a "leftist." He started a one-person Fair Play for Cuba chapter in New Orleans, without ever bothering to recruit another member. He never met with a single member of the Communist Party or any other left organization, although he wrote friendly letters to the Communist Party and to the Socialist Workers Party—two groups that were not even talking to each other—supposedly asking for instructions. Again, all this was a novel way for a Soviet agent and would-be assassin to act.

He blazed a highly visible trail as a "leftist" agitator: managing to get exposure on local TV in New Orleans after getting involved in some fistfights while leafleting. One of the leaflets he distributed showed that his organization was on Camp Street in the very same building that a former FBI bureau chief, Guy Banister, had his office. Banister retained close working relations with émigré Cuban right-wing groups and with Lee Harvey Oswald.

When he wasn't playing the communist agitator, Oswald spent most of his time with rabid anticommunists, including émigré Cubans and CIA operatives. Besides Banister and de Mohrenschildt, there was David Ferrie. (In his book *First Hand Knowledge,* Robert Morrow, a conservative businessman and CIA operative, tells how he served as a pilot on CIA missions with Ferrie.) Oswald also knew businessman Clay Shaw who was CIA, as later confirmed by the agency's director Richard Helms. These were hardly the sort of friends we would expect for a loudmouthed "Marxist revolutionary" just returned from giving away classified secrets in the USSR.

The attorney general of Texas, Waggoner Carr, told the Warren Commission that Oswald was an FBI informant or contract agent, with assigned number S-172 or S-179. For his services, Oswald was paid two hundred dollars a month by the FBI.[3] Orest Pena, a Cuban émigré and FBI informant, told Mark Lane that Oswald worked for the FBI and met with FBI personnel from time to time.

If not paid by security agencies, how did Oswald support himself during his forays into New Orleans and Dallas? He was employed for a brief time in 1962 by a printing company in Dallas that specialized in highly classified government work, including the making of secret maps of the Soviet Union for U.S. Army Intelligence—again hardly the sort of job to assign an openly Russophilic communist agitator. Oswald's overall employment record and income sources remain something of a mystery. To this day, the government refuses to release his tax returns, with no explanation as to what issue of national security is at stake.

We are asked to believe that Oswald just happened to get a job at the Texas School Book Depository five weeks before the assassination, when it had not yet been publicized that Kennedy's limousine was going to pass in front of that building. In fact, George de Morenschildt got him the job.

We are asked to believe that Oswald, who could not hit the side of a barn, chose a Mannlicher-Carcano to kill the president, a

---

[3] The Warren Commission reacted with extreme alarm toward Carr's testimony. Its general counsel, J. Lee Rankin said that evidence linking Oswald to the FBI "is very damaging to the agencies that are involved in it, and it must be wiped out insofar as it is possible to do so by this commission." The "wipe out" consisted of a statement from Hoover reassuring the commission that Oswald never worked for the FBI. In the *New York Times* edition of the Warren Commission report, Waggoner Carr's testimony is nowhere to be found.

cheap, poor-performance Italian rifle that the Italians said never killed anyone on purpose and caused them to lose World War II. Dallas District Attorney Henry Wade initially announced that the murder weapon was a German Mauser. Later informed that Oswald owned a Manlincher-Carcano, Wade declared that the murder weapon was an "Italian carbine."

We are asked to believe that Oswald would forgo shooting President Kennedy when he had a perfect target of him as he rode right down Houston Street directly toward the Texas School Book Depository. Instead he supposedly waited until the car had turned down Elm Street and was a half-block away. With the President's head and shoulders barely visible through a tree, Oswald supposedly fired rapidly, getting off three shots in record time, one missing the limousine by twenty-five feet and the other two hitting their target with devastating accuracy and record rapid succession, a feat the best marksmen in the country found impossible to emulate even after much practice and after the sights on the Mannlicher-Carcano were properly reset in a laboratory.[4]

We are asked to believe that Oswald then left his rifle at the window, complete with a perfect palm print and, they now say, his fingerprints (but no fingerprints on the clip or handloaded cartridges), along with three spent shells placed on the floor neatly in a row, in a manner no spent shells would fall.

We are asked to believe that a bullet would go through John Kennedy, pause in mid-air, change direction, and wound

---

[4] In his political memoirs, Speaker of the House Tip O'Neil writes that Kenneth O'Donnell, a top JFK aide, said he was sure he had heard two shots that came from behind the fence on the grassy knoll. "I told the FBI what I had heard, but they said it couldn't have happened that way and that I must have been imagining things. So I testified the way they wanted me to." O'Neil reports that another top Kennedy aide, Dave Powers, who was present when O'Donnell made this statement, said he had the same recollection of the shots.

Governor Connally in several places—something Connally never believed—and reappear perfectly intact wedged into the flap of a stretcher in Parkland Hospital, supposedly having fallen out of Connally's body but obviously pushed into the flap by hand.

We are asked to believe that only three shots were fired when in fact six bullets were noted: one that entered the president's throat and remained in his body; the second extracted from Governor Connally's thigh; a third discovered on the stretcher; a fourth found in fragments in the limousine; a fifth that missed the president's car by a wide margin, hitting the curb according to several witnesses, and wounding onlooker James Thomas Tague on his face; a sixth found in the grass by Dallas police directly across from where the president's vehicle had passed.

The Secret Service took possession of the presidential limousine, ignored reports in the *St. Louis Post-Dispatch* (12/1/63) that there was a bullet hole in the windshield, and rejected all requests to inspect the vehicle. We are asked to believe that the inside of limousine, a trove of physical evidence, was then quickly torn out and rebuilt, with no thought of covering up anything.

We are asked to believe that Kennedy's autopsy was innocently botched and his brain just accidentally disappeared. The X-ray purporting to be Kennedy's head now shows a rear entry wound, different from the rear exit wound all the pathologists saw. Someone cropped the jaw out of the picture, so there is no opportunity to determine by dental identification if the X-ray really is the president's.

We are asked by people like Max Holland, writing in the *Nation*, to believe that the "infamous picture of Oswald posing with rifle in hand" is not a forgery. Actually there are two pictures, both proven composites, with bodies of different sizes but with the identical head that matches neither body, and with shadows going in incongruous directions. Who fabricated these photos?

"The lone leftist assassin" Oswald was a friend of Jack Ruby, a gangster with links to Cuban exiles and the FBI. Ruby once worked for Congressman Richard Nixon and the House Un-American Activities Committee in Chicago when his name was still Jack Rubenstein. He also worked for the FBI in Dallas during the years before the JFK assassination. Ruby claimed he was just an ordinary private citizen, moved to kill Oswald in order to avenge the suffering Oswald had inflicted upon the Kennedy family.[5]

While in prison Ruby pleaded with the Warren Commission to be taken to Washington where he could tell the whole story. He feared for his life and claimed "they are killing me here." Indeed, he died in jail, supposedly of natural causes.

We are asked to believe that when twenty-four persons who had information related to the case met violent deaths, this was a colossal coincidence.[6] In 1978, after the House Select Committee investigation got underway, Anthony Summers records that another sixteen connected to the case died violently. This, too, supposedly was just a coincidence. This latter group included George de Mohrenschildt, killed by a gun blast to the head three hours after a House Assassinations Committee Investigator had tried to contact him. De Mohrenschildt had been worried that he would be murdered. His daughter Kressy Keardon believes it "impossible" that he shot himself. The sheriff's office in Palm

---

[5] At a Washington, D.C. conference in October 1995, assassination investigator John M. Williams reported on an interview he had with Robert Morrow, March 10, 1994. Morrow said that on the day after JFK's assassination, Marshall Diggs, the man who recruited Morrow as a CIA operative, confided to him a warning of Oswald's impending assassination: "He won't be around to testify for his trial."

[6] See Penn Jones, Jr., *Pardon My Grief* vols. 1 and 2 for details about the death of these twenty-four.

County, Florida, found the shooting "very strange." But it was ruled a suicide. Generally, people who voice fears that they might be killed do not then kill themselves.

William Sullivan, number-three man in the FBI, was secretly on the CIA payroll, according to CIA operative Robert Morrow. He was scheduled to appear before the House Select Committee but before he could do so, he was shot outside his home by a man who claimed to have mistaken him for a deer. The killer was charged with a misdemeanor and released in custody of his father, a state policeman.

While under government protection, mobster Sam Giancana was shot dead one day before he was to testify before the House Select Committee about mob and CIA connections. One of the things that emerges from this whole story is the widespread linkages between the CIA and organized crime, between the gangster state and the gangsters.

When the House committee was putting its staff together, it was heavily pressured to employ only persons acceptable to the CIA, the very agency it was supposed to investigate. In his book *Plausible Denial*, Mark Lane reports that when Bernard Fensterwald, an independent-minded Washington lawyer, was offered the job of general counsel, a CIA representative called on him and said that the Agency would hand him "his head on a platter" if he took the assignment. Fensterwald turned it down.

Is the Kennedy assassination conspiracy just a lot of hoopla kicked up by "conspiracy buffs?" Most of the independent investigators I have met seem to be serious politically literate people. Their struggle to arrive at the truth is not impelled by a love of conspiracies but by a concern for the political and historic importance of the case. They seek the truth no matter how dirty it might be. That process of confronting the machinations of the national security state is not a conspiracy hobby. It is an essential part of the struggle for democracy.

THE JFK ASSASSINATION II:
CONSPIRACY PHOBIA
ON THE LEFT

Almost as an article of faith, some individuals believe that conspiracies are either kooky fantasies or unimportant aberrations. To be sure, wacko conspiracy theories do exist. There are people who believe that the United States has been invaded by a secret United Nations army equipped with black helicopters, or that the country is secretly controlled by Jews or gays or feminists or black nationalists or communists or extraterrestial aliens. But it does not logically follow that all conspiracies are imaginary.

Conspiracy is a legitimate concept in law: the collusion of two or more people pursuing illegal means to effect some illegal or immoral end. People go to jail for committing conspiratorial acts. Conspiracies are a matter of public record, and some are of real political significance. The Watergate break-in was a conspiracy, as was the Watergate cover-up, which led to Nixon's downfall. Iran-contra was a conspiracy of immense scope, much of it still uncovered. The savings and loan scandal was described by the Justice Department as "a thousand conspiracies of fraud, theft, and bribery," the greatest financial crime in history.

Conspiracy or Coincidence?

Often the term "conspiracy" is applied dismissively whenever one suggests that people who occupy positions of political and economic power are consciously dedicated to advancing their elite interests. Even when they openly profess their designs, there are those who deny that intent is involved. In 1994, the officers of the Federal Reserve announced they would pursue monetary policies designed to maintain a high level of unemployment in order to safeguard against "overheating" the economy. Like any creditor class, they preferred a deflationary course. When an acquaintance of mine mentioned this to friends, he was greeted skeptically, "Do you think the Fed bankers are deliberately trying to keep people unemployed?" In fact, not only did he *think* it, it was *announced* on the financial pages of the press. Still, his friends assumed he was imagining a conspiracy because he ascribed self-interested collusion to powerful people.

At a World Affairs Council meeting in San Francisco, I remarked to a participant that U.S. leaders were pushing hard for the reinstatement of capitalism in the former communist countries. He said, "Do you really think they carry it to that level of conscious intent?" I pointed out it was not a conjecture on my part. They have repeatedly announced their commitment to seeing that "free-market reforms" are introduced in Eastern Europe. Their economic aid is channeled almost exclusively into the private sector. The same policy holds for the monies intended for other countries. Thus, as of the end of 1995, "more than $4.5 million U.S. aid to Haiti has been put on hold because the Aristide government has failed to make progress on a program to privatize state-owned companies" (*New York Times* 11/25/95).

Those who suffer from conspiracy phobia are fond of saying: "Do you actually think there's a group of people sitting around in a room plotting things?" For some reason that image is assumed to be so patently absurd as to invite only disclaimers. But where else would people of power get together—on park benches or carousels? Indeed, they meet in rooms: corporate boardrooms, Pentagon command rooms, at the Bohemian Grove, in the choice dining rooms at the best restaurants, resorts, hotels, and estates, in the many conference rooms at the White House, the NSA, the CIA, or wherever. And, yes, they consciously plot—though they call it "planning" and "strategizing" —and they do so in great secrecy, often resisting all efforts at public disclosure. No one confabulates and plans more than political and corporate elites and their hired specialists. To make the world safe for those who own it, politically active elements of the owning class have created a national security state that expends billions of dollars and enlists the efforts of vast numbers of people.

Yet there are individuals who ask with patronizing, incredulous smiles, do you really think that the people at the top have secret agendas, are aware of their larger interests, and talk to each other about them? To which I respond, why would they not? This is not to say that every corporate and political elite is actively dedicated to working for the higher circles of power and property. Nor are they infallible or always correct in their assessments and tactics or always immediately aware of how their interests are being affected by new situations. But they are more attuned and more capable of advancing their vast interests than most other social groups.

The alternative is to believe that the powerful and the privileged are somnambulists, who move about oblivious to questions of power and privilege; that they always tell us the truth and have nothing to hide even when they hide so much; that although most of us ordinary people might consciously try to pursue our own interests, wealthy elites do not; that when those at the top employ force and violence around the world it is only for the laudable reasons they profess; that when they arm, train, and finance covert actions in numerous countries, and then fail to acknowledge their role in such deeds, it is because of oversight or forgetfulness or perhaps modesty; and that it is merely a coincidence how the policies of the national security state so consistently serve the interests of the transnational corporations and the capital-accumulation system throughout the world.

Kennedy and the Left Critics

In the winter of 1991-92 Oliver Stone's film *JFK* revived popular interest in the question of President John Kennedy's assassination. As noted in part I of this article, the mainstream media launched a protracted barrage of invective against the movie. Conservatives and liberals closed ranks to tell the public there was no conspiracy to murder the president for such things do not happen in the United States.

Unfortunately, some writers normally identified as on the Left have rejected any suggestion that a conspiracy occurred. While the rightists and centrists were concerned about preserving the legitimacy of existing institutions and keeping people from seeing the gangster nature of the state, the leftists had different concerns, though it was not always clear what these were.

Noam Chomsky, Alexander Cockburn, and others challenge the notion that Kennedy was assassinated for intending to withdraw from Vietnam or for threatening to undo the CIA or end the cold war. Such things could not have led to his downfall, they argue, because Kennedy was a cold warrior, pro-CIA, and wanted a military withdrawal from Vietnam only with victory. Chomsky claims that the change of administration that came with JFK's assassination had no appreciable effect on policy. In fact, the massive ground war ordered by Johnson and the saturation bombings of Vietnam, Cambodia, and Laos ordered by Nixon represented a dramatic departure from Kennedy's policy. On some occasions, Chomsky says he refuses to speculate: "As for what JFK might have done [had he lived], I have nothing to say." Other times he goes on to speculate that Kennedy would not have "reacted differently to changing situations than his close advisers" and "would have persisted in his commitment to strengthen and enhance the status of the CIA" (*Z Magazine,* 10/92 and 1/93).

The evidence we have indicates that Kennedy observed Cambodian neutrality and negotiated a cease-fire and a coalition government in Laos, which the CIA refused to honor. We also know that the surviving Kennedy, Robert, broke with the Johnson administration over Vietnam and publicly stated that his brother's administration had committed serious mistakes. Robert moved with the tide of opinion, evolving into a Senate dove and then a peace candidate for the presidency, before he too was murdered. The two brothers worked closely together and were usually of like mind. While this does not provide reason enough to conclude that John Kennedy would have undergone a transition comparable to Robert's, it still might give us pause before asserting that JFK was destined to follow in the direction taken by the Johnson and Nixon adminstrations.

In the midst of this controversy, Chomsky wrote a whole book arguing that JFK had no intention of withdrawing from Vietnam without victory. Actually, Kennedy said different things at different times, sometimes maintaining that we could not simply abandon Vietnam, other times that it ultimately would be up to the Vietnamese to fight their own war.[1]

One of Kennedy's closest aides, Kenneth O'Donnell, wrote that the president planned to withdraw from Vietnam after the 1964 elections. According to Colonel L. Fletcher Prouty, who headed military support for the clandestine operations of the CIA, Kennedy dictated "the rich parts" of NSAM 263, calling for the withdrawal not only of all U.S. troops but all Americans, meaning CIA officers and agents too. Prouty reflects that the president thereby signed "his own death warrant." The Army newspaper *Stars and Stripes* ran a headline: "President Says — All Americans Out by 1965." According to Prouty: "The Pentagon was outraged. JFK was a curse word in the corridors."

Concentrating on the question of withdrawal, Chomsky says nothing about the president's unwillingness to *escalate* into a ground war. On that crucial point all Chomsky offers is a speculation ascribed to Roger Hilsman that Kennedy might well have introduced U.S. ground troops in South Vietnam. In fact, the same Hilsman, who served as Kennedy's Assistant Secretary of State for Far Eastern Affairs, the officer responsible for Vietnam, noted in a long letter to the *New York Times* (1/20/92) that in 1963 "President Kennedy was determined not to let Vietnam become an American war — that is, he was determined not to send U.S.

---

[1] Kennedy's intent to withdraw is documented in the Gravel edition of the *Pentagon Papers* ("Phased Withdrawal of U.S. Forces, 1962-1964," vol. 2, pp. 160-200). It refers to "the Accelerated Model Plan . . . for a rapid phase out of the bulk of U.S. military personnel" and notes that the administation was "serious about limiting the U.S. commitment and throwing the burden onto the South Vietnamese themselves." But "all the planning for phase-out . . . was either ignored or caught up in the new thinking of January to March 1964" (p. 163) — the new thinking that came after JKF was killed and Johnson became president.

combat troops (as opposed to advisers) to fight in Vietnam nor to bomb North Vietnam." Other Kennedy aides such as Arthur Schlesinger Jr. and General Maxwell Taylor made the same point. Taylor said, "The last thing he [Kennedy] wanted was to put in our ground forces. . . . I don't recall anyone who was strongly against [the recommendation], except one man and that was the President." Kennedy opposed the kind of escalation embarked upon soon after his death by Lyndon Johnson, who increased U.S. troops in Vietnam from 17,000 to approximately 250,000 and committed them to an all-out ground war.

Kennedy and the CIA

Chomsky argues that the CIA would have had no grounds for wanting to kill JFK, because he was a dedicated counterinsurgent cold warrior. Chomsky arrives at this conclusion by assuming that the CIA had the same reading of events in 1963 that he has today. But entrenched power elites are notorious for not seeing the world the way left analysts do. To accept Chomsky's assumptions we would need a different body of data from that which he and others offer, data that focuses not on the Kennedy administration's interventionist pronouncements and policies but on the more private sentiments that festered in intelligence circles and related places in 1963.

To offer a parallel: We might be of the opinion that the New Deal did relatively little for working people and that Franklin Roosevelt actually was a tool of the very interests he publicly denounced as "economic royalists." From this we might conclude that the plutocrats had much reason to support FDR's attempts to save big business from itself. But most plutocrats damned "that man in the White House" as a class traitor. To determine why, you would have to look at how *they* perceived the New Deal in those days, not at how we think it should be evaluated today.

In fact, President Kennedy was not someone the CIA could tolerate, and the feeling was mutual. JFK told one of his top officials that he wanted "to splinter the CIA in a thousand pieces and scatter it to the winds" (*New York Times*, 4/25/66). He closed the armed CIA camps that were readying for a second Bay of Pigs invasion and took a number of other steps designed to bring the Agency under control. He fired its most powerful and insubordinate leaders, Director Allen Dulles, Deputy Director Charles Cabell, and Deputy Director for Plans Richard Bissell. He tried to reduce its powers and jurisdiction and set strict limits as to its furture actions, and he appointed a high-level committee to investigate the CIA's past misdeeds.

In 1963, CIA officials, Pentagon brass, anti-Castro Cuban émigrés, and assorted other right-wingers, including FBI chief J. Edgar Hoover, hated JFK and did not believe he could be trusted with the nation's future. They referred to him as "that delinquent in the White House." Roger Craig records the comments of numerous Dallas police officers who wanted to see Kennedy done away with. Several years ago, on a San Francisco talk show on station KGO, I heard a listener call in as follows: "This is the first time I'm saying this. I worked for Army intelligence. In 1963 I was in Japan, and the accepted word around then was that Kennedy would be killed because he was messing with the intelligence community. When word came of his death, all I could hear was delighted comments like 'We got the bastard.'"

In his book *First Hand Knowledge,* CIA operative Robert Morrow noted the hatred felt by CIA officers regarding Kennedy's "betrayal" in not sending the U.S. military into the Bay of Pigs fiasco. One high-level CIA Cuban émigré, Eladio del Valle, told

Morrow less than two weeks before the assassination: "I found out about it last night. Kennedy's going to get it in Dallas."[2] Morrow also notes that CIA director Richard Helms, "knew that someone in the Agency was involved" in the Kennedy assassination, "either directly or indirectly, in the act itself—someone who would be in a high and sensitive position. . . . Helms did cover up any CIA involvment in the presidential assassination."

Several years after JFK's murder, President Johnson told White House aide Marvin Watson that he "was convinced that there was a plot in connection with the assassination" and that the CIA had something to do with it (*Washington Post,* 12/13/77). And Robert Kennedy repeatedly made known his suspicions that the CIA had a hand in the murder of his brother.

JFK's enemies in the CIA, the Pentagon, and elsewhere fixed on his refusal to provide air coverage for the Bay of Pigs, his unwillingness to go into Indochina with massive ground forces, his no-invasion guarantee to Khrushchev on Cuba, his overtures for a rapproachment with Castro and professed willingness to tolerate countries with different economic systems in the Western hemisphere, his atmospheric-test-ban treaty with Moscow, his American University speech calling for reexamination of U.S. cold war attitudes toward the Soviet Union, his antitrust suit against General Electric, his curtailing of the oil-depletion allowance, his fight with U.S. Steel over price increases, his chal-

---

[2] Del Valle's name came up the day after JFK's assassination when Dallas District Attorney Henry Wade announced at a press conference that Oswald was a member of del Valle's anti-communist "Free Cuba Committee." Wade was quickly contradicted from the audience by Jack Ruby, who claimed that Oswald was a member of the leftish Fair Play for Cuba Committee. Del Valle, who was one of several people that New Orleans District Attorney Jim Garrison sought out in connection with the JFK assassination, was killed the same day that Dave Ferrie, another suspect met a suspicious death. When found in Miami, del Valle's body showed evidence of having been tortured, bludgeoned, and shot.

lenge to the Federal Reserve Board's multibillion-dollar monopoly control of the nation's currency,[3] his warm reception at labor conventions, and his call for racial equality. These things may not have been enough for some on the Left but they were far too much for many on the Right.

Left Confusions and the Warren Commission

Erwin Knoll, erstwhile editor of the *Progressive,* was another left critic who expressed hostility toward the conspiracy thesis and Oliver Stone's movie in particular. Knoll admitted he had no idea who killed Kennedy, but this did not keep him from asserting that Stone's *JFK* was "manipulative" and provided false answers. If Knoll had no idea who killed Kennedy, how could he conclude that the film was false?

Knoll said Stone's movie was "a melange of fact and fiction" (*Progressive,* 3/92). To be sure, some of the dramatization was fictionalized—but regarding the core events relating to Clay Shaw's perjury, eyewitness reports at Dealey Plaza, the behavior of U.S. law officers, and other suspicious happenings, the movie remained faithful to the facts unearthed by serious investigators.

In a show of flexibility, Knoll allows that "the Warren Commission did a hasty, slipshod job" of investigation. Here too he only reveals his ignorance. In fact, the Commission sat for fifty-one long sessions over a period of several months, much longer than most major investigations. It compiled twenty-six volumes of testimony and evidence. It had the investigative

---

[0] The bankers of the Federal Reserve System print paper money, then lend it to the government at an interest. Kennedy signed an executive order issuing over $4 billion in currency notes through the U.S. Treasury, thus bypassing the Fed's bankers and the hundreds of millions of dollars in interest that would normally be paid out to them. These "United States Notes" were quickly withdrawn after JFK's assassination.

resources of the FBI and CIA at its disposal, along with its own professional team. Far from being hasty and slipshod, it painstakingly crafted theories that moved toward a foreordained conclusion. From the beginning, it asked only a limited set of questions that seemed to assume Oswald's guilt as the lone assassin.

The Warren Commission set up six investigative panels to look into such things as Oswald's background, his activities in past years and on the day of the assassination, Jack Ruby's background, and his activities on the day he killed Oswald. As Mark Lane notes, there was a crying need for a seventh panel, one that would try to discover who killed President Kennedy. The commission never saw the need for that undertaking, having already made up its mind.

While supposedly dedicated to bringing the truth to light, the Warren Commission operated in secrecy. The minutes of its meetings were classified top secret, and hundreds of thousands of documents and other evidence were sealed for seventy-five years. The Commission failed to call witnesses who heard and *saw* people shooting from behind the fence on the grassy knoll. It falsely recorded the testimony of certain witnesses, as they were to complain later on, and reinterpreted the testimony of others. All this took careful effort. A "hasty and slipshod" investigation would show some randomness in its errors. But the Commission's distortions consistently moved in the same direction in pursuit of a prefigured hypothesis.

Erwin Knoll talks disparagingly of the gullible U.S. public and says he "despises" Oliver Stone for playing on that gullibility. In fact, the U.S. public has been anything but gullible. It has not swallowed the official explanation the way some of the left critics have. Surveys show that 78 percent of the public say they believe there was a conspiracy. Both Cockburn in the *Nation* and

Chomsky in *Z Magazine* dismiss this finding by noting that over 70 percent of the people also believe in miracles. But the fact that people might be wrong about one thing does not mean they are wrong about everything. Chomsky and Cockburn are themselves evidence of that.

In any case, the comparison is between two opposite things. Chomsky and Cockburn are comparing the public's gullibility about miracles with its *unwillingness* to be gullible about the official line that has been fed to them for thirty years. If anyone is gullible it is Alexander Cockburn who devoted extra column space in the *Nation* to support the Warren Commission's tattered theory about a magic bullet that could hit both Kennedy and Connolley while changing direction in mid-air and remaining in pristine condition.

Chomsky says that it is a "curious fact that no trace of the wide-ranging conspiracy appears in the internal record, and nothing has leaked" and "credible direct evidence is lacking" (*Z Magazine*, 1/93, and letter to me, 12/15/92). But why would participants in a conspiracy of this magnitude risk everything by maintaining an "internal record" (whatever that is) about the actual murder? Why would they risk their lives by going public? Many of the participants would know only a small part of the picture. But all of them would have a keen sense of the immensely powerful and sinister forces they would be up against were they to become too talkative. In fact, a good number of those who agreed to cooperate with investigators met untimely deaths. Finally, what credible direct evidence was ever offered to prove that Oswald was the assassin?

Chomsky is able to maintain his criticism that no credible evidence has come to light only by remaining determinedly unacquainted with the mountain of evidence that has been uncovered.

There has even been a decision in a U.S. court of law, *Hunt vs. Liberty Lobby*, in which a jury found that President Kennedy had indeed been murdered by a conspiracy involving, in part, CIA operatives E. Howard Hunt and Frank Sturgis, and FBI informant Jack Ruby.[4]

Nixon advisor H. R. Haldeman admits in his memoir: "After Kennedy was killed, the CIA launched a fantastic coverup." And "In a chilling parallel to their coverup at Watergate, the CIA literally erased any connection between Kennedy's assassination and the CIA."

Indeed, if there was no conspiracy, why so much secrecy and so much cover-up? If Oswald did it, what is there to hide and why do the CIA and FBI still resist a full undoctored disclosure of the hundreds of thousands of pertinent documents? Would they not be eager to reveal everything and thereby put to rest doubts about Oswald's guilt and suspicions about their own culpability?

The remarkable thing about Erwin Knoll, Noam Chomsky, Alexander Cockburn, and others on the Left who attack the Kennedy conspiracy findings is they remain invincibly ignorant of the critical investigations that have been carried out. I have repeatedly pointed this out in exchanges with them and they never deny it. They have not read any of the many studies by independent researchers who implicate the CIA in a conspiracy to kill the president and in the even more protracted and extensive conspiracy to cover up the murder. But this does not prevent them from dismissing the conspiracy charge in the most general and unsubstantiated terms.

---

[4] See Mark Lane, *Plausible Denial; Was the CIA Involved in the Assassination of JFK?* (New York: Thunder's Mouth Press, 1991). For testimony of another participant see Robert Morrow, *First Hand Knowledge: How I Participated in the CIA-Mafia Murder of President Kennedy* (New York: S.P.I. Books, 1992).

Let's Hear It for Structuralism

When pressed on the matter, left critics like Cockburn and Chomsky allow that some conspiracies do exist but they usually are of minor importance, a distraction from the real problems of institutional and structural power. A structural analysis, as I understand it, maintains that events are determined by the larger configurations of power and interest and not by the whims of happenstance or the connivance of a few incidental political actors. There is no denying that larger structural trends impose limits on policy and exert strong pressures on leaders. But this does not mean that all important policy is predetermined. Short of betraying fundamental class interests, different leaders can pursue different courses, the effects of which are not inconsequential to the lives of millions of people. Thus, it was not foreordained that the B-52 carpet bombing of Cambodia and Laos conducted by Nixon would have happened if Kennedy, or even Johnson or Humphrey, had been president. If left critics think these things make no difference in the long run, they better not tell that to the millions of Indochinese who grieve for their lost ones and for their own shattered lives.

It is an either-or world for those on the Left who harbor an aversion for any kind of conspiracy investigation: either you are a structuralist in your approach to politics or a "conspiracist" who reduces historical developments to the machinations of secret cabals, thereby causing us to lose sight of the larger systemic forces. As Chomsky notes: "However unpleasant and difficult it may be, there is no escape from the need to confront the reality of institutions and the policies and actions they largely shape." (*Z Magazine,* 10/92)

I trust that one of the institutions he has in mind is the CIA. In most of its operations, the CIA is by definition a conspiracy, using covert actions and secret plans, many of which are of the most unsavory kind. What are covert operations if not conspiracies? At the same time, the CIA is an institution, a structural part of the national security state. In sum, the agency is an institutionalized conspiracy.

As I pointed out in published exchanges with Cockburn and Chomsky (neither of whom responded to the argument), conspiracy and structure are not mutually exclusive dynamics. A structural analysis that a priori rules out conspiracy runs the risk of not looking at the whole picture. Conspiracies are a component of the national security political system, not deviations from it. Ruling elites use both conspiratorial covert actions and overtly legitimating procedures at home and abroad. They finance everything from electoral campaigns and publishing houses to mobsters and death squads. They utilize every conceivable stratagem, including killing one of their own if they perceive him to be a barrier to their larger agenda of making the world safe for those who own it.

The conspiracy findings in regard to the JFK assassination, which the movie *JFK* brought before a mass audience, made many people realize what kind of a gangster state we have in this country and what it does around the world. In investigating the JFK conspiracy, researchers are not looking for an "escape" from something "unpleasant and difficult," as Chomsky would have it, rather they are raising grave questions about the nature of state power in what is supposed to be a democracy.

A structuralist position should not discount the role of human agency in history. Institutions are not self-generating reified forces. The "great continuities of corporate and class interest" (Cockburn's phrase) are not disembodied things that just happen of their own accord. Neither empires nor national security institutions come into existence in a fit of absent-mindedness. They are actualized not only by broad conditional causes but by the conscious efforts of live people. Evidence for this can be found in the very existence of a national security state whose conscious function is to recreate the conditions of politico-economic hegemony.

Having spent much of my life writing books that utilize a structuralist approach, I find it ironic to hear about the importance of structuralism from those who themselves do little or no structural analysis of the U.S. political system and show little theoretical grasp of the structural approach. Aside from a few Marxist journals, one finds little systemic or structural analysis in left periodicals including ones that carry Chomsky and Cockburn. Most of these publications focus on particular issues and events—most of which usually are of far lesser magnitude than the Kennedy assassination.

Left publications have given much attention to conspiracies such as Watergate, the FBI Cointelpro, Iran-Contra, Iraq-gate, CIA drugs-for-guns trade, BCCI, and savings-and-loans scandals. It is never explained why these conspiracies are important while the JFK assassination is not. Chip Berlet repeatedly denounces conspiracy investigations while himself spending a good deal of time investigating Lyndon LaRouche's fraudulent financial dealings, conspiracies for which LaRouche went to prison. Berlet never explains why the LaRouche conspiracy is a subject worthy of investigation but not the JFK conspiracy.

G. William Domhoff points out: "If 'conspiracy' means that these [ruling class] men are aware of their interests, know each other personally, meet together privately and off the record, and try to hammer out a consensus on how to anticipate and react to events and issues, then there is some conspiring that goes on in CFR [the Council for Foreign Relations], not to mention the

Committee for Economic Development, the Business Council, the National Security Council, and the Central Intelligence Agency." After providing this useful description of institutional conspiracy, Domhoff then conjures up a caricature that often clouds the issue: "We all have a tremendous tendency to want to get caught up in believing that there's some secret evil cause for all of the obvious ills of the world." Conspiracy theories "encourage a belief that if we get rid of a few bad people, everything will be well in the world."

To this simplistic notion Peter Dale Scott responds: "I believe that a true understanding of the Kennedy assassination will lead not to a few bad people but to the institutional and parapolitical arrangements which constitute the way we are systematically governed." In sum, national security state conspiracies are components of our political structure, not deviations from it.

Why Care About JFK?

The left critics argue that people who are concerned about the JFK assassination are romanticizing Kennedy and squandering valuable energy. Chomsky claims that the Nazi-like appeals of rightist propagandists have a counterpart on the Left: "It's the conspiracy business. Hang around California, for example, and the left has just been torn to shreds because they see CIA conspiracies . . . secret governments [behind] the Kennedy assassination. This kind of stuff has just wiped out a large part of the left" (*Against the Current* 56, 1993). Chomsky offers no evidence to support this bizarre statement.

The left critics fear that people will be distracted or misled into thinking well of Kennedy. Cockburn argues that Kennedy was nothing more than a servant of the corporate class, so who cares how he was killed (*Nation* (3/9/92 and 5/18/92). The left critics' hatred of Kennedy clouds their judgment about the political significance of his murder. They mistake the low political value of the victim with the high political importance of the assassination, its implications for democracy, and the way it exposes the gangster nature of the state.

In 1894 Captain Alfred Dreyfus was a conservative militarist. Clemenceau once conjectured that if the man's name had not been Dreyfus, he would have been an anti-Dreyfusard. Does that mean that the political struggle waged around *l'affaire Dreyfus* was a waste of time? The issue quickly became larger than Dreyfus, drawn between Right and Left, between those who stood with the army and the anti-Semites and those who stood with the republic and justice.

Likewise Benigno Aquino, a member of the privileged class in the Philippines, promised no great structural changes, being even more conservative than Kennedy. Does this mean the Filipino people should have dismissed the conspiracy that led to his assassination as an event of no great moment, an internal ruling-class affair? Instead, they used it as ammunition to expose the hated Marcos regime.

Archbishop Romero of El Salvador was a member of the Salvadoran aristocracy. He could not have risen to the top of the church hierarchy otherwise. But after he began voicing critical remarks about the war and concerned comments about the poor, he was assassinated. If he had not been murdered, I doubt that Salvadoran history would have been much different. Does this mean that solidarity groups in this country and El Salvador should not have tried to make his murder an issue that revealed the homicidal gangster nature of the Salvadoran state? (I posed these questions to Chomsky in an exchange in *Z Magazine*, but in his response he did not address them.)

Instead of seizing the opportunity, some left writers condescendingly ascribe a host of emotional needs to those who are
concerned about the assassination cover-up. According to Max
Holland, a scribe who seems to be on special assignment to repu-
diate the JFK conspiracy: "The nation is gripped by a myth . . .
divorced from reality," and "Americans refuse to accept their own
history." In *Z Magazine* (10/92) Chomsky argued that "at times of
general malaise and social breakdown, it is not uncommon for
millenarian movements to arise." He saw two such movements in
1992: the response to Ross Perot and what he called the "Kennedy
revival" or "Camelot revival." Though recognizing that the audiences differ, he lumps them together as "the JFK-Perot enthusi-
asms." Public interest in the JFK assassination, he says, stems from
a "Camelot yearning" and the "yearning for a lost Messiah."

I, for one, witnessed evidence of a Perot movement involving
millions of people but I saw no evidence of a Kennedy revival, certainly no millenarian longing for Camelot or a "lost Messiah."
However, there has been a revived interest in the Kennedy *assassination*, which is something else. Throughout the debate,
Chomsky repeatedly assumes that those who have been troubled
about the assassination must be admirers of Kennedy. In fact,
some are, but many are not. Kennedy was killed in 1963; people
who today are in their teens, twenties, thirties, and forties—most
Americans—were not old enough to have developed a political
attachment to him.

The left critics psychologize about our illusions, our false
dreams, our longings for Messiahs and father figures, our inabil-
ity to face unpleasant realities the way they can. They deliver
patronizing admonitions about our "conspiracy captivation" and
"Camelot yearnings." They urge us not to escape into fantasy.

They are the cognoscenti who guide us and out-left us on the JFK assassination, a subject about which they know next to nothing and whose significance they have been unable to grasp. Having never read the investigative literature, they dismiss the investigators as irrelevant or irrational. To cloak their own position with intellectual respectability, they fall back on an unpracticed structuralism.

It is neither "Kennedy worship" nor "Camelot yearnings" that motivates our inquiry, but a desire to fight back against manipulative and malignant institutions so that we might begin to develop a system of accountable rule worthy of the name of democracy.

THE WONDERFUL LIFE AND STRANGE DEATH OF WALTER REUTHER[1]

(co-authored with Peggy Noton)

In recent decades, organized labor has endured a serious battering from conservative interests in both government and the corporate world. As progressives in the AFL-CIO try to rally their forces, they would do well to remember those few especially dedicated and gifted union leaders who understood the broader social and political dimensions of the labor struggle. Among such leaders looms the great figure of Walter Reuther. Rising from the ranks to spearhead the creation of the United Auto Workers (UAW), Reuther brought a special blend of unfaltering progressivism and efficacy to the U.S. political scene. For this he earned the wrath of powerful corporate and political interests.

On the evening of May 9, 1970, Reuther, along with his wife, two close UAW associates, and the plane's two-man crew, were

---

[1] Our thanks to William J. Gallagher, news investigator at WJBK-TV, Detroit, for sharing his extensive files on Reuther.

killed when their chartered Lear jet crashed near the Emmet County Airport in northern Michigan. The brief flight had originated in Detroit and was coming in through the mist on an instrument landing when it plowed into the treetops and burst into flames. There were no survivors. A year and a half earlier, in October 1968, Reuther and his brother Victor had barely escaped death in a remarkably similar incident while flying into Dulles Airport, again in a small private plane. On that night the sky was clear enough for the pilots to realize that their altimeter was malfunctioning, and at the last moment they managed a crash landing that smashed a wing of the plane but left no one seriously injured.

Years later, Victor Reuther told us: "I and other family members were convinced that both the fatal crash and the near-fatal one in 1968 were not accidental." Any number of highly placed persons might have wanted Walter Reuther out of the way. Indeed, as we shall see, there was evidence of foul play against him through much of his public life and evidence of sabotage relating to the fatal crash itself.

The Early Struggle

Eight months before his death, Reuther reflected on the broader dimensions of labor's struggle: "The labor movement is about changing society. . . . What good is a dollar an hour more in wages if your neighborhood is burning down? What good is another week's vacation if the lake you used to go to, where you've got a cottage, is polluted and you can't swim in it and the kids can't play in it? What good is another $100 pension if the world goes up in atomic smoke?" Reuther was the kind of labor leader who unsettled the higher circles: militant, incorruptible, and dedicated both to the rank-and-file and a broad class agenda.

The son of a German immigrant who was a lifelong socialist and labor organizer, Reuther devoted his life to the labor struggle. In 1932, after being fired from his job at a Ford plant because of his unionizing efforts, he departed with his brother Victor on a three-year trip around the world. Their itinerary included a prolonged stint as workers in a Ford plant in the Soviet Union. Writing to a friend back in the states, Victor described Soviet society in enthusiastic terms. The letter, which he signed "Vic and Wal," later was doctored in a number of places. Most notably, its closing comment, "Carry on the fight" was changed to "Carry on the fight for a Soviet America." The FBI possessed the original letter in its internal files but circulated only the forged one to political leaders, corporate heads, and rival unionists in an attempt to show that the Reuthers were communist tools.

Returning to Detroit in late 1935, Walter and Victor emerged as leaders in the often bloody struggle against the automotive bosses, winning landmark victories against Chrysler, GM, and Ford. In May of 1937, during a major leafleting effort, Reuther and dozens of other UAW organizers were brutally assaulted by Ford's thugs. Testifying at a federal hearing, Reuther described how he and his fellow organizers were repeatedly punched, kicked, and slammed against the concrete floor, then thrown down several flights of stairs—while the police stood by doing nothing.

Murder Attempts

In April 1938, two masked gunmen forced their way into Reuther's Detroit home during a party and attempted to abduct him. While they were trying to beat Reuther into submission, one guest managed to flee and summoned help. The assailants were eventually arrested, but their trial proved to be a sham. Facing a jury packed with Ford sympathizers, the defense argued that Walter had staged the whole event as a publicity stunt. The state prosecutor conveniently neglected to mention that Reuther's organizing activities had made him a target at Ford and that both of the accused recently had been working for Ford's security chief Harry Bennett. The jury acquitted them.

No one could claim that the attack ten years later was staged. In April 1948, Reuther was nearly killed by a shotgun blast fired through his kitchen window. He suffered chest and arm wounds and never recovered the full use of his right arm and hand.

In 1949, an attempt on Victor Reuther's life suggests outright complicity by law enforcers. Victor began receiving calls from the Detroit police telling him that neighbors (whom the police refused to name) were complaining about his dog's barking. In fact, the dog had occasionally barked at night. When Victor went to see why, he would see a parked car start up and speed away. After the police issued a "final warning," the family reluctantly gave their pet to some friends. The very next evening Victor was shot in the head as he sat reading in his home. The bullet took out his right eye and parts of his jaw. A neighbor who volunteered a detailed description of the assailants to the police was never contacted for follow-up questioning and began receiving anonymous phone calls warning him to shut up.[2]

Two days after Victor was shot, the U.S. Senate, in an unprecedented move, unanimously adopted a resolution requesting the FBI to investigate both attacks. U.S. Attorney General Tom Clark, the governor of Michigan, and the UAW itself also demanded an investigation. Although Attorney General Clark—FBI chief

---

[2] In December 1957, Ralph Winstead's body was recovered from Lake St. Clair. Winstead had been investigating the Reuther shootings for the UAW for eight years and, according to Victor, was the greatest source of worthwhile information on the case. His death was declared "accidental" and no investigation was made.

J. Edgar Hoover's putative superior—pointed out that there were possible violations of the Fugitive Felon Act and several other federal statutes, Hoover refused to move, claiming a lack of jurisdiction because no federal laws had been broken.[3]

Neither the FBI nor the Detroit police followed any of the leads uncovered by UAW investigators. Nor did they come up with any of their own. No corporate officials were ever questioned. Ford strongman Harry Bennett, who had been implicated in the 1938 attempt against Walter, was never interrogated. In fact, Bennett was Hoover's golfing buddy and was considered a valuable ally who gave the FBI access to his files on "communist" activity, consisting mostly of dossiers on labor activists.

At the end of 1949, an attempt to bomb UAW headquarters in Detroit was foiled by an anonymous call to a *Detroit Times* reporter. According to the caller, the explosive was "planted when the big guy [Walter] was in the building." Needless to say, investigations conducted by the police and the FBI led nowhere.

On the National Scene

By the 1950s Reuther and the UAW had reached an uneasy modus vivendi with the auto bosses. According to Victor Reuther, the relationship was marked by an absence of rancor in the last years of Walter's life. Under Walter's leadership, the UAW not only grew into the largest union in the Western world with 1.2 million members but became a powerful political organization. By 1952, as president of both the UAW and the entire CIO, Reuther had

---

[3] Clark told UAW attorney Joseph Rauh, "Edgar says no. He says he's not going to get involved every time some nigger woman gets raped": Elizabeth Reuther Dickmeyer, *Reuther: A Daughter Strikes* (Southfield, Mich.: Spelman, 1989), 9; also Hoover to Tolson, Ladd and Harbo, memorandum May 26, 1949, FBI archives, 61-9556. On the demands for an investigation, see FBI archives 61-9556, section 4, passim).

become, in the opinion of many, the most influential labor figure in the country.

Reuther used his position to promote progressive stances on a wide range of domestic and foreign policy issues. UAW locals around the country formed political action committees that lobbied lawmakers and helped elect candidates friendly to organized labor. At the same time, Walter and his brother Roy were building alliances between labor, church, and civic groups and ethnic minorities.

Throughout the sixties, the UAW lent financial and moral support to the civil rights movement. Reuther worked closely with Martin Luther King Jr., joining him in all the great civil rights marches and serving as a longtime member of the NAACP's board of directors—whose meetings the FBI routinely bugged.

Reuther sparked the creation of a Citizen's Board of Inquiry into Hunger and Malnutrition. The board's findings that millions of Americans were not getting enough to eat spurred Congress into enacting reforms. The UAW leader pioneered a variety of innovative programs, including employer-funded health and pension plans, cost-of-living allowances, and a guaranteed annual wage. He fought for federally funded affordable housing, nationalized health care, government ownership of monopolistic industries, worker participation in economic planning, and other proposals for redistributing power and wealth, all of which were taken as threats to ruling-class interests—as indeed they were.

Under Walter and Victor's leadership, the UAW became one of the strongest proponents of the 1963 Nuclear Test Ban Treaty. UAW members marched in peace demonstrations and voted funds to support antiwar campaigns. Abroad, Reuther was the USA's best-known and best-liked labor leader in a number of nonaligned countries. In India, he told an appreciative audience that U.S. foreign policy in Asia placed undue emphasis on military power and "doubtful military allies" to the neglect of "reliable democratic friends."

By the 1950s because of these kinds of activities, Reuther had earned a number of powerful political enemies on the national scene. During the 1956 presidential campaign, Vice President Richard Nixon told Republican stalwarts that the UAW leader, not Democratic presidential candidate Adlai Stevenson, was "the man to beat" because of his organizing power and "big money." In 1958, at a GOP fundraiser, Senator Barry Goldwater declared that "Walter Reuther and the UAW-CIO are a more dangerous menace than . . . anything Soviet Russia might do to America." Other members of Congress warned of Reuther's "dream of establishing a Socialist labor government in the United States." A two-page ad in the *Wall Street Journal* (9/22/58) ran an inch-high headline: "WILL YOU LET REUTHER GET AWAY WITH IT?" The ad warned: "Walter Reuther is already within reach of controlling your Congress. The American Labor movement has now become a political movement with the objective of establishing a socialist labor government in control of the economic and social life of this nation." For his activities at home and abroad, as Victor recalled, "the right wing never lost its violent bitter taste against Walter."

Hoover's Vendetta

FBI chief J. Edgar Hoover certainly never lost his violent bitter taste, stalking Walter for some forty years, using undercover informants and illegal bugging equipment. Reuther was on friendly terms with several Democratic presidents who submitted his name for positions on presidential boards and commissions. In each instance, Hoover successfully blocked Reuther's appointment by secretly circulating disinformation packets to the White

House and members of Congress, featuring the doctored "For a Soviet America" letter and testimony by individuals falsely accusing Walter of communist affiliations.

Both the CIA and the FBI monitored Reuther's foreign travel, taking note of public comments of his that "might be construed as contrary to the foreign policy of the United States." During World War II, Hoover made preparations to put all three Reuther brothers in custodial detention. He was ultimately dissuaded from doing so by John Bugas, chief FBI agent in Detroit.

In his early Detroit days, Walter had formed an alliance with communists within the union in order to combat conservative labor factions and company bosses. In 1938 he severed this association and some years later, after gaining control of the UAW board, he launched a purge of dedicated UAW organizers who were communists or close to the party. In 1949, he played a key role in the expulsion of eleven unions accused of being communist-led.

Over the years, Reuther denounced communism at every opportunity, seeking thereby to legitimate his own status as a loyal American. Like so many on the Left then and now, he did not realize that those who fight for social change on behalf of the less-privileged elements of society are abhorred by conservative elites whether they be communists or not. For the industrialists, financiers, and leading politicos, it made little difference whether their wealth and power was challenged by "communist subversives" or "loyal Americans." The communist label was used in attempts to smear and delegitimate Reuther. But it was not an obsession with communism that caused them to hate and fear Reuther but an obsession with maintaining their privileged place in the politico-economic status quo.

At the same time, Reuther was critical of right-wing radicalism. In 1961, Attorney General Robert Kennedy asked him, Victor, and Joseph Rauh, an attorney for the UAW, to investigate the ultra-Right. (Reuther was a close friend and advisor to the Kennedys.) The resulting report warned of radical right elements inside the military and urged the president to dismiss generals and admirals who engaged in rightist political activities. The report also faulted J. Edgar Hoover for exaggerating "the domestic Communist menace at every turn" thus contributing "to the public's frame of mind upon which the radical right feeds."

Though initially confidential, the report later became public. One can imagine the negative impact it had on Hoover and top circles in the Pentagon.

Final Break

From the first days of the AFL-CIO merger in 1955, irreconcilable political differences existed between Reuther and AFL-CIO president George Meany, a cold-war hawk. Under Meany, the AFL-CIO entered into an unholy alliance with the CIA in order to bolster conservative, anticommunist unions in other countries. These unions, as Victor Reuther describes them, were run by people who were "well soaked with both U.S. corporate and CIA juices. It was, in effect, an exercise in trade union colonialism."

In early 1968 the UAW withdrew from the AFL-CIO and joined forces with the Teamsters and two smaller unions to form the Alliance for Labor Action (ALA), with a membership totalling over four million. The Teamsters gave Reuther a free hand on political and social issues. With Nixon in the White House and the bombings in Indochina escalating to unprecedented levels, Reuther ran ads in the national media and appeared before congressional committees to denounce the war and call for drastic cuts in the military budget. While the AFL-CIO was proclaiming its support for Nixon's escalation of the war and his anti-ballistic missile program, the ALA was lobbying hard against both.

Nixon's invasion of Cambodia and the killing of four students at Kent State University prompted Reuther—the day before his death—to send a telegram to the White House condemning the war, the invasion, and "the bankruptcy of our policy of force and violence in Vietnam." By 1970, Reuther was seen more than ever as a threat to the dominant political agenda, earning him top place on Nixon's enemy list.

The Fatal Crash: Some Disturbing Evidence

The struggles of Walter Reuther's life should cause us to give more than cursory attention to the questionable circumstances of his death. Here are some things to consider:

First, as president of the largest union in the country, Reuther had the resources for advancing his causes on the national scene as did few others. He was an extraordinarily effective proponent of socio-economic equality and an outspoken critic of the military-industrial complex, the arms race, the CIA, the national security state, and the Vietnam war. For these things he earned the enmity of people in high places.

Second, in the years before the fatal crash there had been assassination attempts against Walter and Victor. (Victor believes the attempt against him was intended as a message to Walter.) In each of these instances, state and federal law-enforcement agencies showed themselves at best lackadaisical in their investigative efforts, suggesting the possibility of official collusion or at least tolerance for the criminal deeds.

(In this context, it might be noted that in January 1970, only three months before the fatal plane crash, the Nixon White House

requested Reuther's FBI file. The call came from Egil Krogh, a
Nixon staff member who was later arrested as a Watergate burglar.
The file documented Reuther's leadership role in progressive and
antiwar organizations. In 1985, when Detroit newsman William
Gallagher asked why Nixon had wanted the file, Krogh was eva-
sive, claiming a lack of memory.)

Third, like the suspicious near-crash that occurred the previous year, the fatal crash also involved a faulty altimeter in a small
plane. It is a remarkable coincidence that Reuther would have
been in two planes with the exact same malfunctioning in that
brief time frame.

Fourth, the investigation conducted by the National
Transportation Safety Board (NTSB) of the fatal crash of May
1970 turned up some disturbing evidence, to say the least. When
the investigators disassembled the captain's altimeter, they found
no fewer than seven abnormalities.

Most significantly, they discovered a brass screw lying loose in the
instrument case. The report notes that with a loosened screw, "the
altimeter would have read high by 225 to 250 feet." The screw "locks
the movable aluminum calibration arm in place when the instrument is calibrated. The threads within the screw hole were torn and
ragged. Deposits of aluminum particles were observed on the
threads of the screw. . . . Examination of the X-rays revealed that the
locking screw was in place prior to disassembly."[4] The report does
not speculate as to who or what might have loosened the screw.

Testing to see if the heat of the crash might have disassembled
the screw, investigators placed a similar calibration arm mecha-

---

[4] National Transportation Safety Board, *Aircraft Accident Report, Executive Jet
Aviation, Inc. Lear Jet L23A N434EJ Near the Emmet County Airport, Pellston,
Michigan, May 9, 1970* Adopted: December 22, 1970, Report no. NTSB-AAR-71-
3), Washington, D.C. All subsequent materials and quotations relating directly to
the crash are from this report, unless otherwise indicated.

nism in an oven and heated it for two hours at 1,100 degrees F. "This screw was found to be tight when examined." When the test screw was removed, "aluminum deposits were found on its threads. The hole from which it was removed displayed torn and broken threads similar to those of the accident calibration arm," suggesting that the loose screw in Reuther's plane had not been disassembled by the heat of the crash but had been removed or loosened by deliberate human effort.

Further examination revealed six other unusual defects in the altimeter:

　　　—An incorrect pivot was installed in one end of a rocking shaft.

　　　—An end stone was missing from the opposite end of the rocking shaft.

　　　—A ring jewel within the mechanism was installed off center.

　　　—A second rocking shaft rear support pivot was incorrect.

　　　—The wrong kind of link pin, which holds a spring clip in place at the pneumatic capsule, was installed.

　　　—An end stone, which supports a shaft within the mechanism, was installed upside down.

That these many abnormalities could accidentally and coincidentally appear in a single altimeter are close to impossible. With notable understatement, the investigators concluded that "such conditions undoubtedly caused excessive friction [in the altimeter mechanism]. . . . The board believes that while the evidence is not conclusive, the captain's altimeter was probably reading inaccurately."

There were other problems. The pilots chose runway 5, the only approach that was lit. But it lacked both runway end identifier lights and a visual approach path indicator (VAPI). The VAPI gives pilots their proper flight angle and helps them determine whether they are too high or too low. The principal approach, runway 23, was equipped with a VAPI, but one of the runway lights was out. Normally, pilots are given notification if a light is out on the main runway. This was not done, suggesting that perhaps the light had been broken close to landing time. Why did runway 5 lack identifier lights and a VAPI? Why was such a deficient approach the only one that was lit, inviting the pilots to chose it? Why was the light on runway 23 not operating and why was no notice sent out? The NTSB report neither asks nor answers these questions.

In its opening synopsis, the NTSB report emphasized the "lack of visual cues" as a cause of the accident. The body of the report, however, placed more emphasis on the faulty altimeter, noting that in the absence of sufficient visual cues "use of the altimeter is a necessity." An "altimeter which read too high" could have caused the pilot mistakenly to think he had sufficient altitude for a safe landing. "In view of the condition of the captain's altimeter, such a situation is highly possible."

Aside from the altimeter, the report found no other defects in the aircraft. The Lear jet "was properly certificated and airworthy" and "there was no malfunction of the aircraft prior to the accident."

Nor was there evidence of crew incapacity or error. Previous medical records and post mortem examination of the pilot and first officer did not reveal any disease or physical disability that would have affected their performance. Captain George Evans had logged more than 2,000 hours of flight time on Lear jets, and more than 140 hours in the previous three months. And both pilots had flown into Pellston Airport many times under far worse conditions.

An Associated Press story carried in the *New York Times* (7/16/ 1970) under the headline, "NO SABOTAGE FOUND IN REUTHER CRASH," stated that the NTSB "said today that it had found no indication of sabotage to explain the jet air taxi crash." The *Times* story is seriously misleading. In fact, the final NTSB report utters not a word about sabotage one way or the other. It notes how numerous unusual defects in the altimeter may have caused a malfunction, but it says nothing about what caused the defects themselves (except to rule out heat as a factor in disassembling the locking screw). The report never questions whether the altimeter was tampered with—yet it proffers a good deal of evidence to suggest that it was. In effect, the investigators ignored their own findings, leaving it for the press to announce there were no suspicious findings.

Earlier on the day of the fatal crash, the same ill-fated Lear jet, carrying popular singer and outspoken right-winger Glen Campbell, had flown into Detroit with no report of a faulty altimeter. Victor Reuther noted that there was sufficient time between flights for tampering with the altimeter. He also pointed out that because they have so many clients and different pilots, rental planes are inspected with unusual care and frequency. The pilots demand as much. In a July 27, 1995, interview, a spokesperson for the Aircraft Owners and Pilots Association stated that civil aircraft used for commercial purposes undergo rigorous mandatory inspection programs. In sum, it is inconceivable that an altimeter with seven defects would have gone undetected if properly inspected before the flight.

Was there such an inspection? If so, by whom? If not, why not? The NTSB report never asks these questions. It makes no inquiry about when the altimeter had been last inspected. Victor Reuther commented: "I was never convinced that there had been a thor-

ough investigation by federal authorities. . . . There had been too
many direct attempts on [Walter's] life and there was too much
evidence of tampering with the rental plane."[5]

In a follow-up interview with us, Victor further noted:

> Animosity from government had been present for some
> time [before the fatal crash]. It was not only Walter's stand on
> Vietnam and Cambodia that angered Nixon, but also I had
> exposed some CIA elements inside labor, and this was also
> associated with Walter. . . . There is a fine line between the mob
> and the CIA. There is a lot of crossover. Throughout the entire
> history of labor relations there is a sordid history of industry in
> league with Hoover and the mafia. . . . You need to check into
> right-wing corporate groups and their links to the national
> security system.

Checking into such things is no easy task. The FBI still refuses to
turn over nearly 200 pages of documents regarding Reuther's
death, including the copious correspondence between field offices
and Hoover. And many of the released documents—some of them
forty years old—are totally inked out. It is hard to fathom what
national security concern is involved or why the FBI and CIA still
keep so many secrets about Walter Reuther's life and death.

Reuther's demise appears as part of a truncation of liberal and
radical leadership that included the deaths of four national figures:
President John Kennedy, Malcolm X, Martin Luther King, and
Senator Robert Kennedy, and dozens of leaders in the Black Panther
Party and in various community organizations. Whether Reuther's
death was part of a broader agenda to decapitate and demoralize the
mass movements of that day, or whether such an agenda existed at
all, are questions that go beyond the scope of our inquiry.

---

[5] Victor Reuther, interview, January 30, 1992.

Suffice it to say that Victor's belief, shared by Walter's daughter Elizabeth Reuther Dickmeyer and other members of the family, that the crash was no accident sounds disturbingly plausible. Despite the limited investigation, there is enough evidence to suggest that foul play was involved. The untimely death of this dedicated and effective progressive labor leader raises disquieting questions about the criminal nature of state power in what purports to be a democracy.

4 POLITICAL THEORY AND CONSCIOUSNESS

FALSE CONSCIOUSNESS

Some observers hold that whatever people define as being in their interest at any given time must be taken as such. To postulate that individuals may often pursue goals that do not really serve their personal, group, or class interest is to presume to know better than they what is best for them. Thus, in order to avoid superimposing one's ideological perspectives or expectations on others, the neutral observer should take people's identification of their interest as the only actually existing interest—so the argument goes.

This "neutral" position, however, rests on an unrealistic and deliberately crude view of the way people arrive at their beliefs. It denies the incontrovertible fact that people's awareness of issues and events is often subject to social control. In judging what is in their interest they are influenced by many factors, including the impact of social forces greater than themselves. In C. Wright Mill's words: "What people are interested in is not always what is to their interest; the troubles they are aware of are not always the ones that beset them. . . . It is not only that [people] can be unconscious of their situations; they are often falsely conscious of them."

For example, if the U.S. public manifests no mobilized opposition to the existing social order or some major aspect of it, this is treated as evidence of a freely developed national consensus. What is ruled out a priori is the possibility of a manipulated consensus, a controlled communication universe in which certain opinions are given generous play and others—such as many of the ones found in this book—are systematically ignored, suppressed, or misrepresented.

To deny the possibility of false consciousness is to assume there has been no indoctrination, no socialization to conservative values, no control of information and commentary, no limitation of the topics to be considered in the national debate, no predetermination of issue agendas, and that a whole array of powers have not helped prestructure how we see and define our own interests and options.

In fact, if no overt conflict exists between rulers and ruled, this may be because of one or more of the following reasons:

> *Consensus satisfaction:* Citizens are content with things because their interests are being served.
>
> *Apathy and lack of perception:* People are indifferent to political matters. Preoccupied with other things, they do not see the link between issues of the polity and their own well-being.
>
> *Discouragement and fear:* People are dissatisfied but acquiesce reluctantly because they do not see the possibility of change or they fear that change will only make things worse or they fear the repression that will be delivered upon them if they become active.
>
> *False consciousness:* People accept the status quo out of lack of awareness that viable alternatives exist and out of ignorance as to how their rulers are violating their professed

interests or out of ignorance of how they themselves are being harmed by what they think are their interests.

Those who are enamored with the existing order of things would have us believe that of the above possibilities only the first three, relating to consensus, apathy, and fear, are conditions of consciousness that can be empirically studied because they are supposedly the only ones that exist.

In fact, there exist two kinds of false consciousness. First, there are the instances in which people pursue policy preferences that are actually at odds with their interests—as they themselves define those interests. For instance, there are low-income citizens who want to maximize their disposable income but then favor a regressive sales tax over a progressive income tax because of a mistaken understanding of the relative effects of each type on their pocketbooks. The sales tax actually costs them more. A limited level of information or a certain amount of misinformation leads people to pursue policy choices that go directly against their self-defined interests.[1]

In the second instance of false consciousness, the way people define their interests may itself work against their well-being. Thus, they may think that supporting the actions of U.S. troops in Vietnam or Panama or Iraq may be furthering their interest in maintaining the United States as the world's leading superpower. But the superpower nation-state, with its huge arms expenditures, heavy taxes, gigantic national debt, neglected domestic services, and economic military conscription, may actually be

---

[1] Public support for term limits is an example of false consciousness. People perceive correctly that many of their political leaders do not serve them. This perception is manipulated by conservatives, who have no interest in serving them, to induce people to get rid of some of those who do try to represent their interests. See "Term Limits: Trick or Treat?" p. 91.

lowering rather than enhancing the security and quality of their lives and the nation's vitality.

It is possible to demonstrate that many people support positions or candidates that violate their own *professed* interests and that many people profess interests that violate their actual well-being.

We who believe that false consciousness is a reality argue that people's preferences may be themselves a product of a socio-political system that works against their interests, and that their interests can only be legitimately identified when they are fully aware of their vital choices and free and able to choose.

The rejection of false consciousness as being an "ideological" (read: "Marxist") superimposition leads mainstream social scientists and other opinion makers to the conclusion that no distinction should be made between *perceptions* of interest and what might be called *real* or *objective* interest.

If we accept the view that a preference expressed by any individual must be accepted as his or her real interest, then there is no distinction to be made between our perceived interests (which might be ill-informed and self-defeating) and our real interests (which might be difficult to perceive because of a lack of accurate, honest, and readily accessible information). Thus the development of one's own interests and political consciousness in general may be stunted or distorted by misinformation, disinformation, and a narrow but highly visible mainstream political agenda that rules out feasible alternatives. The reduction of interest to a subjective state of mind leads us not to a more rigorous empiricism but to a tautology: "people act in their own interest" becomes "people act as they are motivated to act." Whatever individuals are motivated to do and believe, or not do and not believe, is taken as being in their interest because, by definition, their interest *is* their motivational condition.

The point, then, is that without making judgments about people's beliefs we can still inquire as to how they came to their preferences rather than treat these preferences as an irreducible and unchallengeable given. For instance, Americans are not congenitally endowed with loyalty to a particular order of competitiveness, consumerism, militarism, economic inequality, and environmental devastation. The definition they give to their interests is shaped in large measure by the social forces determining their life chances. And their life chances may be limited by all sorts of still larger forces acting well beyond their awareness, especially when the so-called impartial information being circulated is actually profoundly biased and manipulative in favor of corporate power and conservative values.

One can see instances of false consciousness all about us. There are people with legitimate grievances as employees, taxpayers, and consumers who direct their wrath against welfare mothers but not against corporate welfarism, against the inner city poor not the outer city rich, against human services that are needed by the community rather than regressive tax systems that favor the affluent. They support defense budgets that fatten the militarists and their corporate contractors and dislike those who protest the pollution more than they dislike the polluters.

In their confusion they are ably assisted by conservative commentators and hate-talk mongers who provide ready-made explanations for their real problems, who attack victims instead of victimizers, denouncing feminists and minorities rather than sexists and racists, denouncing the poor — rather than the rapacious corporate rich who create poverty. So the poor are defined as "the poverty problem." The effects of the problem are taken as the problem itself. The victims of the problem are seen as the cause, while the perptrators are depicted as innocent or even beneficial.

Does false consciousness exist? It certainly does and in mass marketed quantities. It is the mainstay of the conservative reactionism of the 1980s and 1990s. Without it, those at the top, who profess a devotion to our interests while serving themselves, would be in serious trouble indeed.

DIVIDENDS ARE NOT ROYALTIES

It has been frequently noted that IQ examinations, while professing to measure innate intelligence, are riddled with racial, gender, and class biases. Thus a low-income, inner-city youth, confronting a seemingly innocuous phrase like "behind the sofa" on an IQ test, may find it unfathomable, not realizing that it is simply a middle-class way of saying "in back of the couch."

Along with IQ exams, the Scholastic Aptitude Test (SAT) has come under fire. Going through my file, I came across a story, clipped years ago from the *Washington Post* (4/28/89), noting that the Center for Women Policy Studies found that the SAT was biased against women. The center reported that about one out of every seven questions favored males over females, specifically questions about sports, science, war, and business. A more recent story in the *New York Times* (5/26/93) reiterated the charge of gender bias.

One claim made for the SAT is that it is designed to predict a student's college performance. Not true. Men consistently outscore women on the SAT, yet women earn higher grades both in high school and college. But, because of the gap in SAT scores, women are less likely to win scholarships or gain entry to certain schools and programs.

While agreeing that there is gender bias in the SAT, we might also wonder about the test's unexamined politico-economic bias. What caught my eye was an example offered in the *Post* article of the questions that favored males. Males are more likely to answer correctly the comparison: "Dividends is to stock as royalties is to writer." According to the SAT, the correct answer is "true." Presumably, both dividends and royalties are seen as income, while stock and writer are the respective income producers.

Wait a minute, I thought. What is so correct about that parallel? It is just such thinking that leads some people to accuse me of being a "capitalist" because I earn royalties on my books. But income accrued from stock ownership is something apart from salary or wages or royalties earned from hard work. ("Royalties" are analogous to dividends only when they refer to profits on land, oil, and mineral rights that go to the landowners, something quite different from the royalties that go to writers.)

Dividends from stock represent profits from capital investment, money you make without having to work. The author of a book does not make profits on his or her book. She or he earns an income from the labor of writing it, proportionately much less than the sum going to those who own the publishing house and who do none of the writing. Likewise, those who do the other necessary labor of editing, proofing, printing, and marketing the book do not receive profits. They are paid a portion of the money that the book will make and, like the writer, that portion will be less than the value added to the book by their labor.

The sum going to the *owners* is profits, the dividends on the stock they own in the publishing house. It is a portion of the value added to the commodity by the labor power of others. It is what federal tax forms used to call "unearned income" and with good reason. Again — it cannot be said too often — profits are what you make when *not* working. This explains why, in most instances, the secret to getting rich is not to work hard but to get others to work hard for you.

While corporations are often called "producers," the truth is they produce nothing. They are organizational devices for the expropriation of labor and for the accumulation of capital. The real producers are those who apply their brains, brawn, and talents to the creation of goods and services. Capitalists like to say that they are "putting their money to work," but money as such cannot create more wealth. Of itself, not all the money in the world can build a house or harvest a crop. Even in regard to what is called "productive capital," machines and other mechanisms and technologies cannot of themselves produce anything. They need human labor to become productive and are themselves the products of previous human labor.

What capitalists really mean when they talk about "putting their money to work" is that they are putting human labor to work, paying workers less in wages and salaries than they produce in value, thereby siphoning off the surplus for themselves. "Surplus value" is not only a Marxist concept but a reality of life — so much so that the capitalists themselves talk about "value added," meaning more or less the same thing as surplus value: the value that the workers add to the product over and above the wages they are paid and other costs of production.

This expropriation of the value created by labor is the biggest rip-off that working people (including writers) endure. While it is easy for all of us to see the money taken from us by the government, in the form of taxes deducted from our paychecks, it is less easy to see the far greater wealth taken from us in the form of the value created by our efforts and pocketed by those who do not work.

Typically, in an eight-hour workday, the value of the products that workers create in the first two hours of labor will equal their wages. For the remaining six hours, they are performing surplus labor time, creating surplus value that is taken in by the shareholders, bondholders, and others who do not work. It is from this surplus value (or "added value" as management would say) that the corporate capitalists make their profits, after paying off overhead costs, interest on loans, advertising fees, and what little taxes they sometimes pay.

Consider the U.S. Census Bureau's *Census of Manufacturers,* which reported that in 1987 workers in twenty manufacturing industries produced an average $95,519 worth of product per worker a year, or $1,837 a week. Yet the wage paid averaged only $394 a week. So the $64 subsequently taken from the worker's paycheck in taxes was far less than the $1,443 in surplus value pocketed by the owners. This constant and massive transfer of wealth from those who produce it to those who pocket it explains why the net assets of the four hundred richest Americans is $300 billion, while the net assets of the one hundred fifty million poorest Americans is zero.

This process of expropriation of value explains why the owners of big commercial publishers of books, newspapers, and other publications enjoy such immense wealth while most of their writers live at the subsistence level. In 1975, when I published an op-ed piece in the *New York Times,* I was paid $150. Eight years later I published another in the *Times* and, despite the intervening inflation, I again was paid only $150. Today, almost two decades since I first appeared in that illustrious publication, the fee is still

$150. I got the same munificent sum for an Op-ed piece I published in the *Los Angeles Times*. Furthermore, neither of these newspapers—nor most other major publications—pay permission fees or reprint fees to authors. That means the piece might get picked up by various other newspapers who then pay a fee to the *Times*—but the author sees not a penny of it. Some of the major magazines, known as the "big slicks," not only have frozen their fees but have reduced them over the years. Forget about trying to keep up with inflation; freelance writers are not even keeping up with the nominal earnings of the 1970s—even without accounting for inflation.

To get an idea of how poorly paid writers are, consider the following. At a meeting of the Washington, D.C. chapter of the National Writers Union, the chair asked for a show of hands of those who had earned over $5,000 from their writing in the previous year. Of about thirty persons, I was the only one who raised his hand—and that's only because I had a textbook that had enjoyed some college course adoptions.

Writers will tell you about their many grievances, about publishers who lie about sales figures and withhold royalties, about manuscripts accepted then never published, about book publication dates that are postponed for as much as three or four years, about books that are published only to have their distribution deliberately and completely aborted— "privished" it is called— usually because the publisher decides the book is politically unacceptable. Writers will tell you about payments and kill fees never collected, about articles completely rewritten and distorted by clunky-styled editors, about having no say regarding framing, titling, headlining, and rewrite. And they will tell you about major magazines and big publishing houses that have grown rich off their labor.

So a correct analogy would be: "Dividends is to stock as profits is to publisher." Leave the writer out of it, unless you want to say: "Wages is to workers as royalties is to writers." To repeat: Authors make money off their own hard work, and usually not all that much. Unlike the publisher, they make nothing from the capital investment on their books because they don't have any capital invested. Like the proofreaders, editors, printers, and sales representatives, writers create value through the direct application of their mental and physical labor. A portion of the value they create goes to them. The rest goes to the investors.

What the *Washington Post* article and the study it reported on both missed was the political and class bias in that particular SAT question. The "correct" answer is true only if we accept the capitalist ideological presumption that treats the pocketing of value by investors as identical to the creation of value by writers. Both investor and writer supposedly are "working" in partnership to create "earnings." Tell it to Forbes, not to us underpaid scribes.

The *Post* quotes a New York state judge: "After a careful review of the evidence, this court concludes that SAT scores capture a student's academic achievement no more than a student's yearbook photograph captures the full range of her experience in high school." Well said. All I would like to add is that at least one of the SAT questions captures the ideological biases and disinformation of a capitalist system all too well, biases that are so thoroughly ingrained as to go undetected and unchallenged in the very investigations that purport to expose bias.

POLITICAL SCIENCE FICTION

Science is something more (and less) than the dispassionate pursuit of knowledge. How scientific information is shaped is often predetermined by the prevailing ideological climate. For centuries scientists have paid dearly for maintaining iconoclastic views. Their oppressors often have been other scientists working in tandem with the established powers of society.

Likewise with the study of politics and society, established views preempt the field of discourse, pushing alternative perspectives to the margins, thereby allowing important scientific questions to remain unexamined or be settled by injunction rather than by a free exchange of evidence and ideas. To be sure, orthodoxy has not gone unchallenged. In the house of political science, for instance, there are many windows. But some of them are easier to open than others. And those dissident political scientists who have sought an aggiornamento have had to struggle.

Today there exists more diverse fields of study in political science than ever before—which isn't saying much. For if orthodoxy no longer goes unchallenged, it still rules. What follows is my understanding of the major disputes that have emerged in political science. Much of what is said here also holds for sociology, economics, psychology, and other social sciences.

Looking Backward: From Traditionalism to Behavioralism

In the period before World War II, the predominant orientation in political science, and to a lesser extent other social science disciplines, might be described as nontheoretical and nonsystematic. Concepts were seldom operationalized, and methods and data were rather haphazardly treated. The goal of the research was often left unclear. Generally, the burden of one's research was descriptive and informational rather than abstracted and theoretical. The focus usually was on specific institutions rather than on processes that cut across them. For this reason, the practitioners of this approach were sometimes described as "institutionalists."

Political scientists studied particular political leaders, events, issues, and policies with little thought to constructing theories of leadership, decision making, or other generalizable subjects. Similarly in sociology and anthropology, or in the earlier ethnology, one usually studied a group or tribe with the hope of reporting something interesting about its ways, usually with little attention afforded the broader social relations or culture. In short, the major focus was on the ideographic, that is, the concrete and particular, rather than on the nomothetic, the generalizable phenomena, the kind that modern science is supposed to uncover in order to advance our theoretical understanding and our ability to generalize and predict.

To be sure, more than half a century ago there were scholars like political scientists Arthur Bentley and Charles Merriam and sociologist W. I. Thomas who by word and example showed colleagues how to be empirical in approach and theoretical in intent. But they were the exceptions. In the prewar era, as behavioralist critics would later claim, the theorists were of the armchair kind, their game being "theory spinning" rather than theory building.

The Eisenhower era of the 1950s witnessed the emergence and rather swift triumph of what has been called the "behavioralist" approach in political and social science. The emphasis was now on moving from the ideographic to the nomothetic, from description to systematic analysis and theory building. Political and social phenomena were to be studied not primarily for their intrinsic interest but for the purpose of extracting scientific hypotheses and theories that might be useful for further research and for an overall understanding of political phenomenon. Cross-disciplinary approaches were encouraged, and political scientists learned to draw from other fields and place greater emphasis on quantification and on the rigorous testing of hypotheses so that subjective impressions might be minimized.

Behavioralists were to avoid making value judgments about their subjects. Their task was not to judge or criticize the world but to study it. Outstanding traditionalist political scientists like James MacGregor Burns and E. E. Schattschneider could still write books entitled, respectively, *Congress on Trial* and *The Semi-Sovereign People,* but behavioral studies of Congress and interest groups would contain no such muckraking overtones and would concentrate on a systematic delineation of process as such. Questions about the normative worth of the phenomena studied were to be left to the moral philosophers. Behavioral scientists might wish to speak out on these subjects but they could do so only as private citizens and not in their capacity as scientists.

Behavioralism's impact was soon to be felt throughout the profession. In the academic journals, plodding exegeses written, as if with patience and quill pen gave way to schematized, quantified, formula-ridden studies produced by computerized research teams. The same trend could be observed in sociology. If in the 1940s a study of a Boston street gang was entitled—as was William Foote Whyte's book—*Street Corner Society,* now an investigation of street gangs was more apt to be called: "Net Theory, Interactional Patterns, Status Resolution and Role Accession Conflicts: The Case of the Street Gang as a Small Group Paradigm."

By the early sixties the behavioralists came to occupy the high ground in the discipline. In short time it seemed every political science department had to have a "quantifier." It would be wrong to assume that this ascension was achieved purely by intellectual means. Many factors having nothing to do with scholarly dialogue exercised a decisive effect, most notably the enormous financial support given to the behavioral persuasion by foundations, government, corporations, and other interests who saw the behavioral sciences as useful to them.

By the early 1960s the Pentagon alone was spending about $25 million a year on what it designated as "social science research." About $14 million went to such defense think tanks as the Rand Corporation, the Institute for Defense Analysis, and the Research Analysis Corporation. Another $10 million went each year to the universities and their related research organizations. And approximately $500,000 went to the "social science" sectors maintained by industrial firms. Added to this were the millions given by the foundations and the lesser but still substantial sums that came directly from university sources, individual donors, and private business.

Spurred by this largesse, a vast array of "centers," "institutes," "projects," "councils," and "programs" arose, offering the kind of research money the lonely traditionalist scholar had never envisioned. The money went to cross-disciplinary teams of behavioralists who produced elaborate studies on such subjects as the American soldier, voting behavior at home and abroad, community decision making, the lures of communism, social deviancy, student protestors, urban riots, management systems, savings bond sales campaigns, military recruitment campaigns, lobbying techniques, cultural systems of Southeast Asia, and insurgency and counterinsurgency at home and abroad.

Whether it was a question of developing new techniques for making the tax burden less visible, or consumers more responsive, or assembly-line workers, inner-city residents, and Latin American villagers more compliant, the social science teams—with behavioralist political scientists among them—were there with bright and often ruthless ideas, never challenging the ideological premises and interests of their patrons but always serving the objectives desired by those who paid so well for their talents. Their task was not to change the world but to help those in power control it. As the Advisory Committee on Government Programs in the Behavioral Sciences proudly reported in 1968: "The behavioral sciences are an important source of information, analysis and explanation about group and individual behavior, and thus an essential and increasingly relevant instrument of modern government."

Writing in *PS* (spring 1983), one of the house journals of the American Political Science Association (APSA), Joseph LaPalombara, a Yale political scientist, noted that academics could be useful to banks and corporations, helping them determine how political conditions in foreign lands might affect the safety and profitability of their investments. "The day is past when banks and corporations operating abroad could call on their national governments, on their diplomats and/or gunboats to keep the restless natives in line," he wrote. Now they must deal with "the restless natives" on a "well informed basis," hence the burgeoning field of "political risk analysis." If political scientists were to be of use to those whom LaPalombara described admiringly as "intelligent, harried bankers and corporate managers," they must be prepared to apply their theories about political upheaval, stability, and policy implementation in ways that served the profit needs of the transnationals. For such services big business was willing "to spend hard cash." "It is a heady challenge," LaPalombara breathlessly announced.

Corporations and banks were not the only ones interested in the technical skills of behavioralist analysis. In the January 1983 APSA *Personnel Service Newsletter,* the CIA advertised for "analysts to work in the areas of political change in the Third World. . . . They should have an interest in social change, revolutionary organizations and regime responsiveness and capabilities."

While composing less than a majority of the profession, the behavioralists were the ones who, with their research, outside funding, advisory council positions, and control over graduate training and over the APSA's offices and journals, defined the direction of the profession, its subject matter, implicit ideological limits, and standards of professional success.

The "Post-Behavioralist" Challenge

In the late 1960s, a time of political ferment, dissident political scientists began complaining that important happenings were being ignored by the discipline. The more active of the "post-behavioral" critics, as David Easton called them, organized themselves into the Caucus for a New Political Science. Some of them wanted the behavioral sciences to be used as an instrument of the poor and powerless rather than the rich and powerful. Others were simply Luddites who wanted to smash the fancy new research computers and statistical jargon and return to plain English. Some complained that political scientists should give serious attention to value questions. Others felt that the behavioral sciences were already too riddled with hidden values, and conservative ones at that. The following are what I consider some of the more important criticisms of behavioralism made by the post-behavioralists.

First, in their search for the nomothetic, behavioralists tend to place undue emphasis on process and show a disregard for the content of political events and systems. Processes abstracted from their content tend to be treated in an ahistorical reductionist fashion. Hence, it may be true that both Napoleon and his valet engaged in the decision-making process, one for the Empire and the other for the Emperor's household. Both organized staffs, set priorities, allocated scarce resources, and saw that things got done. Perhaps one might come up with a model that could apply to the activities of both, but in doing so one would obscure differences in historical substance that were of far greater significance than the generalizable patterns of process. A theory of decision making abstracted in this fashion would be a somewhat meaningless accomplishment. Indeed, there is a question of whether the process itself is being properly understood when so utterly divorced from the context of interest and power, purpose, and substantive policy.

Second, as the behavioral methodologies became increasingly elaborate and complex, the problems studied seemed to get ever more narrow and insignificant. The very demand for precision of method imposed limits on the kinds of subjects that could be dealt with. So it seemed that the methodological mountain brought forth an intellectual mouse, a proliferation of what in graduate school we used to call "the-greater-the-turnout, the-larger-the-vote" studies.

Third, having adopted the accoutrements of science, behavioralists leave the impression that their approach is more rigorous than it actually is. Anyone who has worked with statistical models and other such materials should appreciate the often ambiguous, elastic, and inconclusive quality of most "hard data." The precision and objectivity of behavioralism is more an appearance than a reality.

Fourth, in their desire to maintain the appearance of scientific neutrality, the behavioralists often have selected neutral, noncontroversial subjects to study. If politics, as Marx said, is concerned with "the Furies of private interest," we would never guess it from the kinds of dreary articles published in what are supposed to be the leading academic journals. Instead of neutralizing the investigator, the behavioralists succeeded in neutralizing their subject matter. Highly abstracted jargon leaves the impression that the observer is detached and neutral when, in fact, it is the subject matter that has been diluted, often at a cost to its indigenous meaning.

Fifth, the emphasis on process causes behavioralists to overlook the social effects of many policies. Frequently they think of outputs as inviting value judgments of a kind they say they do not wish to make. But most of their critics have not been asking them for evaluations but for systematic descriptions of policy repercussions: Who benefits and who pays? Why and how? What does this say about the distribution of power and the functioning of democracy? What is the relationship of economic to political power, of democracy to capitalism, and other such questions. There is, after all, a difference between making value judgments about empirical phenomena and studying value-laden political activities in an empirical way. The desire to avoid the first should not lead us to neglect the second.

Sixth, there are in fact all sorts of value judgments hidden in behavioralist research. Much of their literature assumes that the overall political system is a benign one. A smoothly functioning system therefore is presumed to be desirable. The eagerness of behavioralists to put their science at the service of government, military, and business rests on this unexamined assumption. Anything that increases the system's ability to predict and control social behavior that is troublesome for ruling interests becomes a plus.

The behavioralist persuasion, then, is anything but value free. This unacknowledged acceptance of the presumably beneficial qualities of our politic-economic system allows the behavioralist to dismiss important kinds of critical empirical investigations as ideological departures from science.

Radicals versus Centrists

Not long after the Caucus for a New Political Science was formed, it became clear that the post-behavioral critique was really a radical one, directed less at a particular research mode than at the orthodox ideology shared by many behavioralists and traditionalists alike. It was not the behavioral methodology that prevented political scientists from studying the undemocratic and plutocratic features of the U.S. polity (although, as already noted, certain behavioralist techniques did encourage a narrow and, in effect, conservative research approach). Rather it was the unexamined centrist political persuasion of those who applied the methodology. Statistical methods should not be discredited but why were they used only for questions that fit within the confines of the centrist ideology? Case studies were useful but why were only certain kinds of cases studied? A cross-disciplinary approach was helpful but why draw so much from psychology while ignoring economics? Why leave political economy to centrist economists who in turn relegated that subject to the realm of politics? The net effect was that essential questions in both politics and economics—especially those relating to class power—remained untouched.

Today centrist ideological preconceptions still prefigure the research agenda of the social sciences. In foreign policy analysis, the assumptions about the benevolent intent of U.S. interventions remain largely unquestioned. It is assumed that "democratic capitalism" has an actual empirical referent and is not an ideological or propaganda term. Most features of the politico-economic social order are taken as neutral givens, having no relation to the realities of class power.

The radicals do not complain that the centrists are evading the important value questions but that their work is riddled with unexamined values that are treated as empirical truths, while the empirical hypotheses introduced by radicals that discomfort the centrists are dismissed as polemics or value judgments.

The centrists claim to be nonpartisan and nonpolitical. But the determination of what is nonpartisan is itself a highly partisan matter. Radicals argue that mainstream political scientists are "nonpartisan" only in that their ideological commitment to liberal capitalism and to their own self-interested position within that system are seldom explicated. Indeed, their ideological interests are best served by denying the existence of such interests.

In turn, the centrists charge the leftists with failing to maintain a proper distance from political affairs and with being motivated by partisan concerns. In truth, the centrists themselves have been up to their ears in partisan affairs. We already noted LaPalombara's unapologetic invitation to political scientists to help big business investors deal with troublesome overseas situations. For years, eminent members of the profession boasted about how political scientists served the interests of the high and mighty. At ceremonies for the Pi Sigma Alpha Award—given to political scientists who make significant contributions "to strengthening the relationship between political science and public service" —speakers proudly list the many colleagues who occupy public office, work for political campaigns, or occupy other such positions of responsibility. It seems there is nothing wrong with political activism as long as it is the mainstream variety rather than the critical kind.

The centrists never bother to justify this double standard. They also never explain how they themselves are able to avoid injecting politics into their science while so assiduously and proudly injecting their science into politics. What they fail to acknowledge is that working to maintain the status quo is as activist and partisan a position as working to alter it.

Radicals would not deny that they want to change the world. Social research of any importance is rarely neutral in its effects. Either it challenges or supports the status quo. But they also want to study the world. That is why they became scholars rather than community organizers. In any case, it can be argued that activism can often furnish insights and experience that will enrich scholarly work, and that ideology in itself is not a bad thing, only unexamined ideology. It is important to have research of a wider ideological scope so as to open unexamined questions and put the centrist orthodoxy to the test. Indeed, the times demand it. One does not have to be a Marxist to know there is something very wrong with this society. Neither mainstream economists nor political scientists will come up with new answers until they start asking new questions.

Scholars with dissenting viewpoints may have their blind spots but they also are likely to be free from conventional blind spots. It is no accident that it is Marxist scholars who are giving us studies of the relationship between capitalism and the political system, a subject left largely untouched by centrists. It is no accident that feminist social scientists are uncovering women's contributions to culture and history and are exploring gender-related issues that their male counterparts never imagined were fit subjects for study. It is no accident that African American scholars see much of history, power, and social reality as defined from a white perspective, while their white colleagues have preferred to think of such subjects as colorless. In sum, a critical ideology can awaken us to things overlooked by the established orthodoxy.

Radical scholars, especially Marxist ones, have been keenly interested in theoretical questions, notably the kind that deal with political oppression and systemic conflict, and with the relationship of wealth to power and class to democracy. Marxists are interested both in current political issues and in the underlying forces that give coherence and generality to seemingly disparate phenomena. This is certainly a genuine scientific dedication. Yet most mainstream political scientists judge Marxism as beyond the pale of scientific scholarship, so much so that they feel little obligation to sound like scholars themselves when criticizing Marxism. Our academic literature, book reviews, and discussions are cluttered with facile swipes at unspecified "Marxists" who supposedly say things I have never heard Marxists utter. Such forays are usually unburdened by any first-hand familiarity with the subject that is being disparaged.

Marxism is dismissed but not for a moment is it forgotten.

Declared "simplistic," "dogmatic," and "irrelevant," it remains very much on the minds of the centrists. It is the other great paradigm that haunts the bourgeois scholarly world like a specter, repeatedly acknowledged in gratuitous asides that seek to contain it without having to confront it.

The competition of ideas between centrists and leftists, as with most class-related ideational conflicts, is greatly influenced by underlying material factors. It is the centrists who control most of the foundations, funds, professional journals, fellowships, graduate programs, faculty appointments, and promotions. The result is that there are only a handful of colleges with more than one or two Marxists on their faculties—if that. And it is common for leftist scholars to encounter serious difficulties when seeking employment or tenure.[1] In the last two decades, financial exigencies have provided a convenient opportunity to purge younger and more heterodox scholars, although they have not been the only victims.

There are many who prefer the sedative of orthodoxy to the stimulant of heterodoxy, relying on position to settle questions of science. Meanwhile, from beyond the confines of the ivory tower, politico-economic realities threaten to intrude rudely upon academic paradigms. Virulent forces put democracy and the environment itself at risk. Time is running out. The scientistic pretenders fiddle while the planet burns.

---

[1] See "Struggles in Academe," p. 235, for a detailed account of my own case.

STRUGGLES IN ACADEME: A PERSONAL ACCOUNT

Amidst the cornfields of central Illinois there stands that congestion of graceless brick buildings known as the University of Illinois, Champaign-Urbana (UI). This story begins in the spring of 1970, during the Vietnam War, when I was a visiting associate professor at the UI campus.

Repression in Illinois

Save for a few peace marches, there had been little antiwar activity at UI until one day in early March 1970 when some two hundred people demonstrated against a General Electric recruitment team that was conducting job interviews on campus. Several of the protesters were beaten and arrested by the police while attempting to force their way into the building. A few hours later it was announced that the board of trustees had voted in an emergency session to bar William Kunstler, one of the defense attorneys at the Chicago 7 conspiracy trial, from speaking on the campus.

In the eyes of many students, the university was revealing the true nature of its commitments. A corporation like GE with its extensive involvement in the war machine was being granted privileged access to the campus for recruitment purposes, while Kunstler and his audience were denied their rights to an open forum. Angered by the actions of the police and the trustees, a crowd of more than one thousand took to the streets that evening, blocking traffic, stoning the windows of several of the more over-priced and unpopular campus stores, as well as the windows of the administration building and the armory buildings where ROTC was housed. This was followed by two more nights of demonstrations, rallies, and minor trashing.

A curfew was enforced with numerous arrests and much unnecessary police brutality. Students caught in the streets after curfew were chased and clubbed by police in what looked at times like a primitive rabbit hunt. From the window of a campus build-ing, I witnessed a young woman beaten over the head and then dragged, apparently unconscious, to a police car. In the days to follow, it was a cause of dismay to some of us that UI Chancellor Jack Peltason (later to serve the powers that be as President of the University of California) issued statements of praise for the police, undiluted by a single critical or restraining word.

For the next two months, the administration weeded out the activist students, many of whom had not been arrested in the March disturbances but who were known to be radicals. In viola-tion of the university's own procedure, the chancellor bypassed the faculty-student committee that had been established to deal with disciplinary cases and invited a prominent Illinois lawyer (whose firm was on retainer with the university) to preside as an ostensibly disinterested investigator over suspension hearings involving some forty students.

Other measures were taken in the name of security. The campus police, notoriously inept at protecting students from the many robberies, assaults, and rapes that plagued the campus community, devoted their main efforts to protecting the UI administration from its own populace. Elaborate and detailed dossiers were kept on hundreds of students and scores of faculty members. News clippings in which one's name appeared in association with a controversial issue, statements one made at public or organizational meetings as reported by police agents, photographs documenting one's presence at a rally, teach-in, or demonstration — such were the kinds of things to be found in an individual's campus security file.

The campus police knew the names and faces of the "troublemakers" and of many others who would have been surprised to discover themselves deserving such attention. For weeks after the March events, university police were busy taking snapshots of people on campus, issuing suspension warrants and filing complaints in criminal court. Scores of students were arrested, held for bail, then released. In most cases, charges were dropped months later for lack of evidence, indicating that the purpose of the arrest was intimidation, not prosecution. After being released, some students were arrested a second and third time in their homes or dormitories on vaguely stated charges.

A Killing and a Beating

Not long after this reign of repression seemed to have run its course, President Nixon invaded Cambodia. National Guardsmen killed four Kent State students. And a day later, a local Champaign police officer killed an African American man named Edgar Hoults. From all evidence, Hoults, a bookstore employee, was

innocent of any crime except driving without a license—and
DWB (Driving While Black). Hoults made the mistake of taking
flight when police approached his car and was shot in the back
without warning. The culpable officer was indicted for voluntary
manslaughter, later reduced to involuntary manslaughter,
released on $5,000 bond and eventually found "not guilty" by an
all-white middle-American jury.

On the evening after the Hoults murder and the Kent State kill-
ngs, a crowd of more than three thousand attended a rally called
by student leaders. Several students and faculty, including myself,
spoke in support of an immediate strike to protest Cambodia,
Kent State, the Hoults murder, police brutality, and the presence
of ROTC and the Illiac IV Pentagon supercomputer on campus.
The next day, May 6, 1970, the strike gathered momentum.
Pickets appeared in front of the major buildings and thousands of
students boycotted classes.

That afternoon, I joined a group of students and faculty who
were standing in a service driveway arguing with campus police.
It seemed the police had ordered a garbage truck to be backed
into a crowd of striking students without making any effort to
clear the driveway. Luckily no one had been hurt. The exchange
ended when approximately fifty club-swinging state troopers
charged the crowd without warning. Several students were
knocked down. Others were pushed into the shrubbery. One had
his front teeth bashed out by a police club. I was clubbed full force
over my left eye and on the back of my head. After being knocked
to the ground, I was clubbed on the legs and kicked and beaten on
the back, chest, and neck by state troopers. A colleague and close
friend of mine, the late Philip Meranto, raced into the knot of
police surrounding me, shouting at them to leave me alone.
Professor Meranto threw himself on me in a courageous attempt

to absorb some of the punishment, only to be dragged off, kicked, and held face down in the driveway. While the crowd was restrained by troopers and university police, Meranto and I were handcuffed and driven to the campus police station along with several students arrested in the same incident.

I was held without medical care for approximately an hour, my face, head, and neck soaked with my own blood. Outside the station, a crowd of about one thousand angry students faced a ring of police armed with shotguns. In the adjacent hallway, I heard an officer say, "If I had gotten a clean first lick on that fella [me], he'd be a dead man now." Three men in plainclothes, standing more directly in my view, began a conversation in low but audible tones. I heard one remark excitedly, "That's Parenti, the one who made the speech last night. Now the chancellor will want us to throw the book at him."

A moment later, a man entered the room to examine my wounds. He began questioning me while making a great show of friendly concern. His inquiries invited inquiries of my own, and he eventually admitted that he was not a doctor but an FBI agent. In response to my refusal to provide him with any details, he made a point of saying, "That's okay, we know all about you, Michael John." The use of my middle name doubtless was intended to impress me with the intimacy of his knowledge.

Eventually, I was taken to the hospital where I received twelve stitches on my face and head and X-rays for internal injuries. I was then transported to a state jail, booked, fingerprinted, and held in a cell for some thirty sleepless hours with my head burning and my body shivering, without knowledge of the charges against me, and having been denied repeated requests to see a doctor. I was released the next day on a $10,000 bond—by the same judge who had placed only a $5,000 bond on the policeman who had killed

Edgar Hoults. Much to my surprise, I was charged with five counts including aggravated battery. A state trooper testified during my preliminary hearing that I had chipped his tooth with my "hand." Earlier he had reported to university officials that I had struck him with a "hard object." On a later occasion he said he was hit by a "fist." Whatever his claims, I and other eyewitnesses knew his story to be either a fabrication or a case of mistaken identity.

Professor Meranto, who had been arrested with me, was arrested again the next day while appearing in court for his arraignment. The same state trooper told the court that Meranto's knee had "brushed against" his leg. A complaint of aggravated battery was filed against Meranto, and he, too, was released under a $10,000 bond by the same judge.

Needless to say, Chancellor Jack Peltason offered no assistance to the two of us who had been beaten, kicked, arrested, and falsely charged. He did not call for an investigation of the incident to ascertain whether justice had been done. He made no effort to determine whether his security officers were dangerous fools in ordering the garbage truck to back into the crowd of students. In fact, it was his office that filed the complaints against Meranto and me. On the day of our release, Peltason announced to the press that the status of our positions at the university was under review. In glowing terms, he voiced confidence in the security officer who had so determinedly protected the rights of a garbage truck. Students were demanding that the officer be fired.

Rallies and Purges

The beating and arrests further galvanized the students. As at Columbia, Harvard, and elsewhere, great numbers seemed ready to set aside their political differences and close ranks when their own people were being attacked by police. In response to the beatings and arrests, some ten thousand students, faculty, and community people rallied the next day. Most seemed intent upon violating that evening's curfew, despite the presence of a National Guard contingent, an act of defiance that moved civil authorities to lift the curfew. The strike, now involving the great majority of the students, continued for the next week or so, replete with pickets, demonstrations, "liberated classes," and over one hundred more arrests and numerous beatings by the club-happy, lawless forces of law and order.

During the strike, fifteen political scientists formed a "Faculty for Resistance" and promulgated a statement condemning President Nixon, the Cambodian invasion, the Vietnam War, the Kent State killings, the systematic murder of black militants, and the increasing repression of dissent. They vowed to devote their time to teaching students how to "intellectually arm" and protect themselves from "the encroachments of a criminal regime."

These events were followed by the usual threats and retributions. Some graduate students who had been active in the strike found themselves faced with loss of fellowships and teaching assistantships. At least two teaching assistants were dismissed outright. Philip Meranto, who previously had been assured of tenure and promotion because of his teaching abilities and publications, and whose only crimes were being an outspoken radical critic and trying to protect a colleague from physical harm, was informed that he would be wise to begin searching for a new position. At the same time, young instructors in various departments were informed that any future "strike activities" would be grounds for cancellation of contract. Chancellor Peltason sent a letter asking all department heads to have their faculty account for their time during the week of the strike.

In a letter to me, Peltason stated that the "allegations" against me (which he assumed to be true) were grounds for dismissal, but that since I was soon departing anyway, he decided that a report of the entire matter was to be placed in my "permanent record file," and made available to any university, public agency, or prospective employer wanting information on me. He also informed me that for the duration of my stay he would see that I "be reassigned to the extent necessary to eliminate any further interaction with students in [my] teaching or research functions." In response, I informed him that I disliked being judged guilty on a matter pending before the courts, that the threat to make a dossier available to other prospective employers savored of black-listing, and that any attempt to interfere with my interaction with students would further infringe on my civil liberties.

In the weeks after the strike, I found myself undergoing a trial by newspaper and radio. One local talk show kept referring to "that violent Professor Parenti" who "stuffed a brick in a policemen's face" and who "stirred up the students to riot." Meranto and I were informed by a sympathetic news reporter that we were on an "elim-ination list" compiled by a coterie of local police and that we had better take precautions. Two students also reported separate con-versations they had with campus police who spoke of their intent to "get Parenti." Another student reported that a campus cop had told him that "Parenti has a Swiss bank account" containing secret funds from the Russians and Chinese. Facing possible imprisonment because of a marijuana charge, one student reluctantly had accepted the FBI's offer to monitor all my campus speaking engagements in exchange for having the charges against him dropped. Troubled by the whole thing, he later asked his roommate to tell me about it.

For the first two weeks after the strike, whenever Meranto and I were either driving or walking together, we found ourselves tailed by police. One evening during the strike, a patrol car followed me home and then staked out directly in front of my house for the entire night. I left via a backyard path under the cover of darkness and spent several days at a friend's house. The mother of a friend of mine was visited at her Chicago residence by FBI agents who unsettled her with the information that her daughter was in the company of a "dangerous revolutionary," who was being kept "under constant surveillance." They volunteered speculations about the nature of her daughter's relationship with me.

The political scientists who signed the "Faculty of Resistance" statement in the spring of 1970 did not fare too well. A *Chicago Tribune* editorial called for their dismissal, accusing them of being "academic vipers," guilty of "unprofessional and unethical conduct and academic incompetence." Soon afterward, a state senator took up the cry and the UI board of trustees demanded that the fifteen retract their statement or face further action. One board member suggested that their classes be monitored. Two of the original signers wrote a fawningly conciliatory letter that the trustees were pleased to accept.

The remaining thirteen sent a clarifying but uncompromising response, and the trustees voted unanimously to rebuke them for using such terms in their original statement as "official racism," "present societal madness," the "systematic elimination of black militants," and "a criminal regime." One trustee called it "anarchist language." All agreed that the thirteen were guilty of descriptions of this country that did not reflect "the standards of scholarly and professional expression." Thus did the business executives, corporate lawyers, and successful speculators and investors who composed the UI board of trustees become self-appointed arbiters of what the faculty could say about sociopolitical conditions in the United States.

Repressive measures extended beyond the boundaries of the University of Illinois. One of the thirteen signers, considered too "controversial," was turned down for a job at Purdue University. One UI political science graduate student, applying for a teaching position at an Indiana state college, was informed by the department chair that the school's administration already had rejected two applicants because of their "radical propensities" and that no interviews could be arranged with any "radical or SDS types." Another graduate student provided me with a written account of his job-hunting experience. I quote from his letter:

> From first to last the item of highest priority was student issues, the complaints they were raising and the trouble they caused. Of much less importance were my qualifications for the position. Since I generally found myself at odds with my questioners about the major topics at hand, and since I wanted the job, I tried to balance diplomacy and honesty, with little success. Feigning ignorance of the facts or little concern about the problem partially accomplished the former; trying to show empathy (as opposed to agreement) with the students partly accomplished the latter. Naturally, the result of all this was an unsettling feeling that I had sold out, but not enough.

Another job seeker reflected on his experiences: "At one place I was asked a continuous barrage of questions about student disorders and Black militants. Perhaps my interviewers never realized they were administering a loyalty test." A colleague of senior rank comments: "[One school] refused me because they felt my recent involvement with political issues showed a lack of scholarly detachment, even though my past work was quite scholarly. . . ." The experiences of people at Illinois are representative of what was happening to teachers at colleges and universities around the country.

Kangaroo Court

In September 1970, I arrived at the University of Vermont (UVM) to begin a new teaching job only to discover that the events in Illinois were already being widely publicized in sensationalist fashion by the local right-wing newspaper, the *Burlington Free Press,* which regularly branded me a "violent agitator" and ran letters from readers who called me "un-American" and a "Red propagandist."

The following October, I returned to Illinois to stand trial for aggravated battery, disorderly conduct, and resisting arrest. Given the climate of opinion in Champaign County, my lawyer advised that I waive my right to a jury trial and settle for a bench trial. I reluctantly agreed, thinking that he knew better than I. The presiding judge, a reputed arch-conservative named Birch Morgen, heard the testimony of two state troopers, both of whom gave widely contradictory accounts of what transpired. The trooper with the chipped tooth testified that he was struck by an open hand. On cross-examination he admitted he never saw the blow struck, but was sure I had done it while I was attempting to rise from a sitting position, a remarkable if not impossible way of throwing a punch. The trooper who clubbed me described me as standing upright, toe-to-toe with the "injured" officer, delivering a succession of blows upon him with clenched fists while he stood motionless and helpless, wearing his helmet and face visor and holding his riot baton. (At six-foot-three the trooper with the chipped tooth loomed almost a head taller than I.)

My lawyer presented six witnesses who described in detail my actions of that day. All of them testified that I struck no one and that I at no time resisted arrest. At the close of the trial, friends who had watched the proceedings were confident that the state had not made a case.

The following day, Judge Morgen delivered a most remarkable opinion. He ignored all the conflicts in the trooper's testimonies, as well as the consistencies in the testimonies of defense witnesses. Without benefit of evidence, he implied that I must have been the instigator of the entire garbage truck incident. He observed that I had "no business being there in the first place." By focusing on a few minor discrepancies in their testimony (such as whether the garbage truck was facing north or south), Morgen concluded that defense witnesses were hopelessly confused. He asserted that the most credible testimony was that of the troopers: "I can't believe a state trooper would hit anyone for no reason." It seems the beating they administered to me was prima facie proof of my culpability. The trial, then, was merely a formality.

Having proclaimed the infallibility of law enforcement agents, the judge found me "guilty beyond a reasonable doubt" on all three counts. Many students and faculty who followed the trial closely felt that I was tried and convicted because of my highly visible political activities. I left Illinois and went to the University of Vermont to resume my teaching postion.

In June 1971 I returned to Illinois for sentencing. Because I was already employed outside the state and because a host of academic lights from around the country had sent in appeals on my behalf, I was saved from having to do time. Instead, I was given two years probation, a fine, and ordered to pay court costs. In the interim, Meranto was tried, found guilty of disorderly conduct and sentenced to one year probation and court costs.

In early 1972 at the University of Vermont, my department voted unanimously to renew my contract as did the faculty senate committee on promotion and tenure, the council of deans, the vice president and the president of the university. But as I predicted, the UVM board of trustees, composed of affluent, conservative businesspeople—as are almost all university and college boards—and a few conservative state legislators, voted fifteen to four against me, citing as evidence of "unprofessional conduct" my continued antiwar activities, the Illinois conviction, and the fact I had been seen carrying a "Vietcong" flag at a peace march in Vermont. Despite strong faculty and student support on my behalf, the Vermont trustees refused to renew my contract.

Lawless Guardians

Regarding the events described above, several observations are in order. First, while the established authorities expect others to treat regulations and procedures as inviolate, they themselves are not above playing fast and loose with the rules. Witness the many unlawful acts of brutality committed by the police and the willingness of adminstrators like Peltason to overlook them. Then there was Peltason's bypassing of the student-faculty disciplinary committee at UI in favor of a hand-picked hearing officer; the treatment meted out to Meranto who, according to the rules, qualified for promotion because of his exceptional capabilities as scholar and teacher; the suspension of teaching assistant contracts and the bypassing of qualified but politically bothersome graduate students; and the many other politically motivated hiring and firing practices encountered throughout the profession.

There were other things. Not long after radical students at UI won control of the student government in an election against two competing slates and on an openly professed radical platform, student government found certain of its supplies and funds cut off. When some UI students attempted to establish a nondisruptive dialogue with workers by leafleting in front of the Magnovox factory in Urbana—and received a surprisingly sympathetic

response from employees passing through the gate—they were
run off the street by police under threat of arrest for "disorderly
conduct" and "disrupting traffic." Thus peaceful and orderly
activities, as well as disruptive ones, were suppressed.

Students stopped delivery trucks approaching the UI campus
and, in the best tradition of trade unionism, persuaded the first
two incoming truck drivers to honor the picket line. They then
were forcibly dispersed, clubbed, and arrested by police, who follow their own traditions in such matters. At no time did the striking students seek to block any other student from going to class.
Pickets, teach-ins, "liberation classes," and spontaneous discussions were the various means utilized by radical activists to reach
their fellow students—and with much success. The coercion
came from the other side, from police who constantly resorted to
excessive and unnecessary force, from unsympathetic faculty who
deliberately scheduled examinations during the strike and threatened absent students with failure, and from administrators who
suspended and expelled strike leaders and gave the police carte
blanche to be as brutal as they chose.

Dialogue, persuasion, and appealing to the minds of others,
then, are all very well until such tactics begin to generate real support for the dissenters—which brings us back to what I call my
"iron law of bourgeois politics": When change threatens to rule,
then the rules are changed.

How do we get the guardians to abide by the law and order they
profess to uphold? In a widely publicized book that celebrated
obedience to the law and won the kudos of mainstream critics,
Abe Fortas wrote in one neglected passage that, like everyone else,
the police "are subject to the rule of law, and if they exceeded the
authorized bounds of firmness and self-protection and needlessly
assaulted the people whom they encountered, they should be dis-

ciplined, tried, and convicted. It is a deplorable truth that because they are officers of the state they frequently escape the penalty for their lawlessness."

They escape the penalty because the institutional elites whose rule they buttress are not only uncritical of police abuse but seemingly supportive of it. Indeed, as Peltason demonstrated, they can be downright congratulatory.

Those who are quiescent and conformist in their political views and actions, yet fear they might have their liberties taken away by a "backlash" repression, have a mistaken notion of how repression works. They will almost always be left unhampered when enunciating ideologically safe opinions and theories and remaining inconspicuously inactive. Contrary to Orwell's *1984*, a book that long enjoyed an undeserved authority on this question, the state has no interest in hounding obedient, compliant citizens. If acquiesence to injustice is the freedom some people seek, they will always be free.

They suffer no repression because they repress themselves, refusing to sign protest statements or join controversial organizations or get involved in any manner, except to accept whatever is handed to them. They never dream of marching in a picket line or demonstrating, or engaging in a sit-in, or burning their draft cards, or refusing to pay taxes. And they are careful that none of their opinions might get them into difficulties with future employers or public authorities.

Unsurprisingly, from the Vietnam era to the present, those academics most fearfully anticipating the backlash of tomorrow have tended to give less than adequate attention to the repression of today. They counsel that the best way to preserve our freedom of movement is to be still. But the freedoms of speech and protest are best secured when most vigorously utilized by masses of people. The freedom of quietude is no freedom at all. Yet, in all periods of political struggle there are those who urge that self-policing is the best way to "remain free." It is certainly a good way to remain in one's profession.

Aftermath

In the years after Illinois and Vermont, I was unable to procure a regular teaching position—except for a two-year stint in an experimental program with a leftist bent at the State University of New York, Albany, which was obliterated because of "fiscal exigencies." Much is made in academia of research and scholarship. "Publish or perish" is the academy's slogan. For me and other dissenting scholars a new catagory applied: publish *and* perish. I have published ten books and about 150 articles, a number of them in leading political science journals. I have a Ph.D. from Yale, glowing recommendations from two former presidents of the American Political Science Association and from other prominent members of the profession, and top evaluations as a classroom teacher. Yet, over the next twenty years I was turned down for positions at over one hundred colleges and universities, passed over in many instances in favor of less qualified, but politically safe, inactive candidates—often by departments whose entire membership collectively had not published as much as I.

Time and again I heard from sympathetic associates who were privy to recruitment procedures in their departments that I was rejected because of my leftist views and political activism. On several occasions, when a particular department manifested interest in making an offer, my candidacy was squelched by administrators. A notable instance occurred at Virginia Commonwealth University, where the political science department unanimously supported me to be chair, only to be overruled by a newly appointed dean, Elske Smith, who summarily informed them that having a leftist for an assistant professor was one thing but having a leftist for chairperson was unacceptable. She did not explain to her stunned colleagues why that was so.

In 1985-86, I was invited to teach political science for a year at Brooklyn College, CUNY. The department chair, Morton Berkowitz, and most of the other department members, were enthusiastic about having me stay on as a permanent faculty member. But their efforts were to no avail. The administration refused to renew my contract even though a budgetary line was available. During this time, a close associate of mine, Professor John Lombardi, a chemist who was teaching at City College, CUNY, happened to meet a dean from Brooklyn College at a party. When Lombardi asked him why his school had chosen not to retain me, the man responded, "We found out about him." Since I had spent the entire academic year at Brooklyn College on good terms with my colleagues and students, I presume that what the administration "found out" was of a political nature.

The very last academic position I ever applied for was almost comical in its aspects. In June 1993, after I moved to Berkeley, California, an acquaintance associated with the Institute for the Study of Social Change at the University of California suggested that I apply for affiliation. In my letter I pointed out that I was requesting neither salary nor office space and that I just wanted a link with scholars with whom I could occasionally share ideas and information. As its name indicates, this particular institute had a reputation for progressive views. But would they take on someone who was so visibly engaged in ideological combat with the powers that be? It was not until ten weeks later that I received a reply from the institute's director, Troy Duster. Because of the continued budgetary crisis, he wrote, there were no "support resources" available for additional affiliates. He conveniently overlooked the fact that I had requested an affiliation that would have cost the institute nothing in support resources. To ask for almost nothing and get not even that—such was my last attempt at landing a "position" in academia.

The experiences I have described above are hardly personal to me. There are scores of other highly qualified teachers and scholars who could write autobiographical case histories of political discrimination. They are part of a larger pattern of purges conducted in the "free and open" academy by those who profess a dedication to democracy and academic freedom while practicing political repression.[1]

In the end I created a career of my own, concentrating on my writing and lecturing, reaching larger audiences than I would had I ended up with tenure and a full teaching load. It was Virginia Wolfe who said that it is terrible to be frozen out of a sacred tradition—but even more terrible to be frozen into it.

---

[1] For an analysis of other instances, see my *Against Empire* (San Francisco: City Lights Books, 1995), chap. 10.

LA FAMIGLIA:
AN ETHNO-CLASS EXPERIENCE

Decades ago in the northeast corner of Manhattan, in what is still known as East Harlem, there existed a congestion of dingy tenements and brownstones wherein resided one of the largest Italian working-class populations outside of Italy itself. The back-yards were a forest of clotheslines, poles, and fences. The cellars, with their rickety wooden steps and iron banisters, opened directly onto the sidewalks. On warm days the streets were a focus of lively activity, with people coming and going or lounging on stoops and chatting. Small groups of men engaged in animated discussions, while children played ball in the streets or raced about wildly.

On certain days horse-drawn carts offered a lush variety of fruits and vegetables trucked in from Jersey and Long Island farms. The cries of the vendors were of a Southern Italian cadence unspoiled by almost a half-century in the new land. Women sat at window sills with elbows planted on pillows, occasionally calling down to acquaintances or yelling at the children. There was always something of interest going on in the streets but rarely anything of special importance except life itself.

It was in this East Harlem of 1933 that I made a fitful entrance into the world. My birth was a Caesarean because, as my mother explained years later: "You didn't want to come out. You were stubborn even then." Since she suffered from a congenital disease called "enlarged heart," there was some question as to whether both of us would survive the blessed event. At the last minute the hospital asked my father to grant written permission to have my life sacrificed were it to prove necessary to save his wife.

In those days during a dangerous birth, a doctor might crush the baby's head in order to remove it from the womb and avoid fatal injury to the mother, a procedure the Catholic Church strenuously opposed. The Church's position was to let nature take its course and make no deliberate sacrifice of life. This sometimes meant that the baby came out alive but the mother died, or sometimes both perished. Obeying his heart instead of the Church, my father agreed to give the doctors a free hand. As it turned out, they decided on a Caesarean, a risky operation in 1933 for a woman with a heart condition. Happily both of us came through.

To talk of my family I would have to begin with my grandparents who came from the impoverished lands of Southern Italy (as did most of the Italians in America), bringing with them all the strengths and limitations of their people. They were frugal, hardworking, biologically fertile—and distrustful of anyone who lived more than a few doors away.

One grandmother had thirteen children of whom only seven survived, and the other had fourteen, also with only seven survivors. This was the traditional pattern of high fertility and high mortality carried over from the old country. Given the burdens of repeated childbirth, both my grandmothers died years before my grandfathers. Their children, however, adopted the American style of small families. The image of the large Italian family is an anachronism that hardened into a stereotype. By the 1930s and 1940s, Italian Americans—having discovered birth control and urban living—were rarely having more than two or three children.

My father's mother, Grandma Marietta, was a living portrait of her generation: a short squat woman who toiled endlessly in the home. She shared the common lot of Italian peasant women: endless cooking, cleaning, and tending to the family, with a fatalistic submergence of self. *"Che pu fare?"* ("What can you do?") was the common expression of the elderly women. Given their domestic confinement, they learned but a few words of English even after decades of living in New York. They accepted suffering as a daily experience, rather than as something extraordinary. They suffered while mending and washing clothes in their kitchens, or standing over hot stoves; they suffered while climbing tenement stairs, or tending to the children or sitting alone at the windows; and they suffered while praying to their saints in church and burying their dead. Most of them went through life dressed in black in an uninterrupted state of mourning for one or another kin.

Marietta often cast her eyes up toward the kitchen ceiling and muttered supplications to Saint Anthony of the Light Fixture. She lived in fear of *u mal'occhio,* the evil eye. When younger members of the family were sick, it was because someone had given them *u mal'occhio.* Like a high priestess she would sit by my sickbed and drive away the evil eye, making signs of the cross on my forehead, mixing oil and water in a small dish and uttering incantations that were a combination of witchcraft and Catholicism. Witchcraft was once the people's religion, having been in Southern Italy centuries before Catholicism and having never quite left. The incantations seemed to work, for sooner or later I always recovered.

Some of the first-generation Italians were extreme in their preoccupation with *u mal'occhio*. I remember as late as the 1950s a few of the postwar immigrants would put an open pair of scissors (with one blade broken) on top of the television set so that no one appearing on the screen could send *u mal'occhio* into their living rooms. In this way the magic of medieval times protected them from the technological evils of the modern era, although, as we now know, the contaminations of television are not warded off that easily.

My mother's mother, Grandma Concetta, was something of an exception to this picture of the Italian woman. Endowed with a strong personality and a vital intelligence, she turned to the only respectable profession open to rural Italian women in the late nineteenth century: she became a midwife, a skill she learned in Italy and brought with her to New York. In those days midwives did more than deliver babies. They advised families on the care of children, diagnosed and treated illnesses with herbs, dietary prescriptions, heat applications, and other natural remedies that were said to work with far less destruction and sometimes more efficacy than the expensive chemicalized remedies pushed by the medical and drug industries of today.

My father spoke of Concetta, his mother-in-law, with a reverence he seldom expressed toward his own parents. She died at the age of sixty, a few years before I was born. I knew her only from the testimony of others and from a few faded photographs of a woman who gazed into the camera with a friendliness and gentle strength that made me miss her even though I had never known her.

The men of my grandfathers' generation, like the women, were beset by forces greater than themselves. In the old country they had toiled like beasts of burden, trapped in a grinding poverty, victimized by landlords, tax collectors, and military press gangs. Having fled to the crowded tenements of New York, they found they had a little more to live on but sometimes less to live for. My mother's father, Vincenzo, came to the United States from Calabria in 1887. He spent his working days in East Harlem carrying 100-pound bags of coal up tenement stairs, a profession that left him permanently stooped over. My father's father, Giuseppe, arrived in 1909. A landless peasant who had worked for one of the great estates outside Bari, he was fleeing military conscription. Like many of the immigrant men, Giuseppe worked as a ditchdigger and day laborer in New York, managing to raise an enormous family on subsistence wages.

These immigrant laborers were the paragons of the humble, thrifty toilers whom some people like to point to when lecturing the poor on how to suffer in silence and survive on almost nothing. In truth, the immigrants were not all that compliant—at least not originally. In fact, they had taken the extraordinary measure of uprooting themselves from their homelands in order to escape the dreadful oppression of the Old World. Rather than suffer in silence, they voted with their feet. We may think of them as the virtuous poor (although in their day they were denounced as the swarthy hordes), but they saw themselves as lifelong victims who were somewhat less victimized in the new land than in the old. Now they worked only twelve hours a day instead of fourteen and were better able to feed their children.

Still, in their hearts, most of the first-generation immigrant men nursed a sentimental attachment to Italy. Many of them, like Grandpa Giuseppe, never quite accepted their economic exile in the new land. And as the years wore on they idealized the past and "the old country" all the more. Italy became Paradise Lost. It was not uncommon to hear the old men curse America. To them the new land could be heartless, money-mad, and filled with the kind of lures and corruptions that turned children against parents. They felt little patriotic devotion. What kept them in the United States were the loaves and fishes, not the stars and stripes.

The immigrant men drank wine made in their own cellars, and smoked those deliciously sweet and strong Italian stogies (to which I became temporarily addicted in my adulthood). They congregated in neighborhood clubs, barber shops, and the back-rooms of stores to play cards, drink, and converse. They exercised a dominant presence in the home, yet left most domestic affairs including all the toil of child rearing to the women who exercised a greater day-to-day influence over the children and over the domestic scene in general.

Religion was also left to the women. The immigrant males might feel some sort of attachment to the saints and the church but few attended mass regularly and some openly disliked the priests. In the literal sense of the word, they were "anticlerical," suspicious of clergymen who did not work for a living but lived off other people's labor and who did not marry but spent all their time around women and children in church.

The Italians who came to the United States during the great migrations at the turn of the century, like other groups before and since, were treated as unwelcome strangers. Considered incapable of becoming properly Americanized, they endured various forms of discrimination and harassment. Huddled on the margin of American society, they often looked to Italy for solace. For many of them, Mussolini appeared on the world stage in 1922 as some-

thing of a redeemer. This was certainly the view reflected in the
U.S. press throughout the 1920s and early 1930s. Through his ex-
ploits in Africa and by "standing up" to other European powers,
Mussolini won "respect" for Italy and for Italians everywhere—
or so many of the immigrant men believed.

"When Mussolini came along," an elderly Italian once told me,
"they stopped calling us 'wop.'" The statement is pathetically inac-
curate. The admiration expressed by the U.S. establishment for
Mussolini did not generate a new respect for Italians in America.
If anything it bespoke a low regard for them. The U.S. plutocrats
thought no better of ordinary Italians than they did of their own
American workers. To them, the Italian was a vice-ridden ne'er-
do-well, a disorderly bumpkin lacking in Calvinist virtues, just the
sort of person most in need of a dictator's firm hand.

Like many other ethnic groups that have felt the sting of discrimination, many of the immigrants developed a late-blooming
compensatory nationalism. Many became more nationalistic
regarding Italy when they were in the new country than when
they had lived in Italy. Certainly that was true of Grandpa
Giuseppe.

The second generation, that is, the American-born children of
the immigrants, usually spoke of Mussolini with scorn and deri-
sion, especially after the United States entered World War II. I
recall bitter arguments in my grandfather's house between the
older and younger men. (The women rarely voiced opinions on
such matters.) As the war progressed and Mussolini showed himself to be nothing more than Hitler's acolyte, the old men tended
to grow silent about him. But in their hearts, I believe, they never
bore him any ill-feelings.

The military performance of Italy's legions in the war proved
something of an embarrassment to those who had been antici-

pating Benito's version of the Second Coming of the Roman
Empire. The ordinary recruits in the Italian army had no desire to
fight Il Duce's battles. Rather they manifested a decided inclination to flee or surrender the moment they realized the other side
was using live ammunition. One of my uncles gleefully told the
story of how the entire Italian army landed one evening in
Brooklyn to invade the Navy Yard, only to be routed and driven
into the sea by the nightshift maintenance crew. Grandpa was not
amused by that story. When Italy switched sides and joined the
Allies in the middle of the war, there was much relief and satis-
faction among the American-born and probably even among
many of the immigrants.

Contrary to what we have heard, the immigrant Italians were
not particularly loving toward their children. They sent their
young ones to work at an early age and expropriated their earnings. For most of the adults there was little opportunity to face the
world with ease and tenderness. Of course, infants and toddlers
were hugged, kissed, fondled, and loved profusely, but as the children got older it would have been an embarrassment, and in any
case was not the custom, to treat them with much overt affection.
Besides, there were so many of them, so many living and so many
dead, and after a while each new child was either an additional
burden or an early tragedy but seldom an unmitigated joy.

"*La famiglia, la famiglia,*" was the incantation of the old
Italians. The family, always the family: be loyal to it, obey it, stick
with it. This intense attachment to the family was not peculiar to
Italians but was, and still is, a common characteristic of almost
any poor rural people—be it in the Philippines, Nigeria, India, or
Appalachia—where the family has an important survival function. More than anything the family was one's defense against

starvation, the *padrone,* the magistrates, strangers, and rival families. As in any survival unit, its strictures were often severe and its loyalties intense. And betrayals were not easily forgiven.

The Italian family could also be a terrible battleground. "Nobody can hate like brothers," the saying goes, especially brothers (and sisters) who had hard childhoods ruled over by immigrant parents who themselves saw life as a series of impending catastrophes. I remember the many squabbles, grudges, and hurt feelings that passed between my father, his brothers and sisters, and their respective spouses. The series of shifting alliances and realignments among them resembled the Balkan politics of an earlier era. Years later, as the siblings put the deprivations and insecurities of the immigrant family behind them and mellowed with time and prosperity and the advent of children and grandchildren of their own, they tended to get along much better with each other.

I enjoyed the nourishing embrace of the big family gatherings, the outings at the beach, the picnics, parties, and holiday dinners. The Italian holiday feast was a celebration of abundance with its platters of antipasto, pasta, the variety of seasoned meats, the bowls of thick tasty soups, the green salads seasoned in garlic and olive oil, the crisp crusty bread, fresh fruits, roasted nuts, rum pastries, and the endless bottles of homemade wine. I wonder if those feasts were a kind of ritual performed by people who had lived too long in the shadows of want and hunger, a way of telling themselves that at least on certain days the good life was theirs. Whether or not there was any larger meaning to them, the dinners were enjoyed for themselves.

I have an especially fond memory of my maternal grandfather, Vincenzo, a stooped, toothless, unimposing old man who was my closest ally in early life. During his last years, finding himself relegated to the edges of the adult world, he entered wholeheartedly into my world, playing cards with me, taking me for walks around the block, watching with undisguised delight as I acted out my highly dramatized cowboy-and-Indian games. He always took my side and despite his infirmity was sometimes able to rescue me from the discipline of my parents—which is the God-given function of grandparents.

Years before, when Vincenzo was still a youngster of seventy-five or so, and a widower, he was discovered to have a girlfriend, a woman of about fifty-five. She would steal into the house when no one was home and climb into bed with him. The discovery of this tryst plunged the family into a state of panic and rage. My relatives denounced the woman as a whore of the worse sort, whose intent was to drive Grandpa to an early grave by overexerting his heart. (He died at age eighty-seven.) Under the threat of collective family reprisal, the poor lonely woman dared not see Vincenzo anymore. And my poor grandfather, after being scolded like a child, was kept under a sort of house arrest. In those days the idea that elderly parents might have sexual desires caused a furious embarrassment among their grown children.

Italian grandfathers were frequently made captives by their families after passing a certain age, as the sons, daughters, older nieces and nephews competed to put the old man under their protective custody. If a car came too close for comfort while the grandfather was crossing the street, as might happen to any pedestrian, the family would try to keep him from taking unaccompanied strolls, convinced that he could no longer judge traffic. If he misplaced his hat or scarf, as might anyone, he would be judged no longer able to care for his personal articles. At the beach, if an Italian grandfather waded into the water much above his knees, one or another of his self-appointed guardians could be seen jumping up and down on the shore, waving frantically at him and shouting: "Papa's gonna drown! Somebody get him!" I read somewhere that this phenomenon of grandfather captivity still exists in parts of Italy.

I saw the protective custody game repeated with my paternal grandfather, Giuseppe, who in his later years presided in silence at the head of the table during holiday meals, a titular chieftain whose power had slipped away to his sons and sons-in-law, those who now earned the money and commanded their own households. While a certain deference was still paid him because of his age, more often he found himself, much to his annoyance, a victim of overprotection—which was a sure sign of powerlessness.

Years later in 1956, when an adult, I had occasion to have a few long talks with him and discovered that he was a most intelligent and engaging man—although he did have a number of opinions that were strange for that time, namely that country air was better for one's health than city air, canned and packaged foods were of less nutritional value than fresh foods, and physical exertion was better than sitting around doing nothing. Giuseppe also believed that doctors and hospitals could be dangerous to one's survival, automobiles were the ruination of cities, and too much emphasis was placed on money and material things. We treated such views as quaintly old-fashioned, having no idea that Grandpa was merely ahead of his time.

After my birth the doctors warned my mother that another pregnancy would be fatal. So I went through life as an only child. My mother tended to spoil me, for which she was criticized by her older sisters. More than once she mentioned how sorry she was that I had no brothers and sisters to play with, and she encouraged my playmates to come spend as much time as they wanted at our house. But I entertained no regrets about being an only child, for why would I want to share my lovely mother with some other little brat? My father played a more distant parental role than my mother, as was the usual way in Italian working-class families—and in just about any other family where the division of labor is drawn along gender lines. He labored long hours for meager sums, sometimes two jobs at a time. Born in Italy, he was transported to this country at the age of five. He did poorly in school mostly because of the burdens the immigrant family imposes on its first-born son. When he was only ten years old, his day went something like this: up at 6 a.m., work on his father's ice truck until 8 a.m., then to school, then back to work from 3 p.m. to 7 p.m. to complete a thirteen-hour day. On Saturdays he worked from 6 a.m. to midnight, an eighteen-hour day. On Sunday he labored eight hours, from 6 a.m. to 2 p.m.—that was supposed to be a half-day.

My father understandably blamed his poor academic performance on his work burdens. As he put it: "I was too damn tired to learn to read and write." His fatigue often overcame him and he would fall asleep in class. On one such occasion a teacher dumped water on him. He retaliated by taking the inkwell out of the desk and throwing it at her. After that the teachers labeled him "a bad kid." Kicked out of school at age fourteen, he went to work full time.

Almost sixty years later, shortly before his death, I talked to him about his youthful days and recorded his thoughts. The things he remembered most were the toil, the humiliation of not being able to speak English, and the abuse he received from teachers. There was one bright spot, as he tells it:

> The only teacher that cared about me was Miss Booth because she saw me carry ice a few times on 110th Street and

she asked, "How come you're carrying ice at your age?" I said, "I got to work. My father can't afford a man. There's seven of us at home to feed." So she saw I wasn't really a bad kid. She saw I was no good in school really on account of I had to work. That Miss Booth, she got me to wash the blackboard. Anything she wanted, I did because she showed she cared about me.

In his adult life, my father's friends were all men. Cross-gender friendships were not a common thing in those days. The women in a man's life consisted of his mother, his wife, his sisters, and other female relatives. He might know various women in the neighborhood and stop and chat with them briefly but there was no occasion for sustained socializing. It would have been considered inappropriate.

To illustrate the patriarchal mentality of my father's world I might recall the time he informed me in troubled tones that Uncle Americo, while drunk one night, had started beating his wife, Aunt Fanny (my mother's sister). Americo's son, my cousin Eddy, forcibly intervened and wrestled his father to the floor. What shocked my father was not Americo's behavior but Eddy's. "I don't care what happens," he concluded, "a son should never raise a hand to his father"—a pronouncement that left me wondering what I would have done if I had been in Eddy's place.

Hovering over us was the Great Depression, a mysterious but palpable phenomenon that explained why there was never enough money, why my father was away working all the time, why I couldn't have this or that new toy. I remember during one unusually difficult period my mother bought a small steak and cooked it for me as a special treat. She sat watching as every morsel disappeared into my mouth. When I offered her a piece

she declined, saying she wasn't hungry. Only years later did I realize with a pang that she very much would have wanted some.

None of my relatives talked of "careers"; I don't think the word
was in vogue among us. But everyone talked about jobs—or the
fear of being without one. A high-school education was considered an unusual accomplishment, and the one uncle who had
graduated high school was considered something of a celebrity.
My mother's dream was that I would someday get a high-school
diploma, for then all doors would be open to me. As she said, I
would be able to "dress nice every day not just Sundays" and
"work in an office," a fate that sounded more like death than salvation to a spirited street boy.

Toward the end of World War II things improved for my family. My father got steady work driving his uncle's bread truck and
my mother found a job in a neighborhood dress shop, sitting at a
machine all day sewing buttons on children's clothes. I pledged to
her that someday I would earn lots of money so that she would
never have to set foot in that sweatshop again, a vow that heart-
ened her more because of its expression of concern than because
she believed she would live to see the day. As it happened, when I
was seventeen she died, at age forty-three, still employed by the
same shop.

From time to time during my childhood, I would wonder
about the world outside East Harlem, about the strange American
people who inhabited parts of Manhattan we passed through on
rare occasions, the tall, pink-faced, Anglo-Protestants who pronounced all their r's, patronized the Broadway theater, and went
to Europe for purposes other than to locate relatives. I would
think of other equally strange peoples and unexplored worlds
with anticipation. This "intoxication of experiences yet to come"

left me with the feeling that East Harlem was not my final destiny in life, a feeling that would grow with time.

When I was about twelve or thirteen I chanced upon a copy of *Life* magazine that contained an article describing East Harlem as "a slum inhabited by beggar-poor Negroes, Puerto Ricans, and Italians," a sentence that stung me enough to remain in my memory. Slum or not, most of the Italians, including all my relatives, abandoned East Harlem in the late 1950s, moving to what sociologists call "second settlement areas," leaving the old neighborhood to the growing numbers of more recently arrived Puerto Rican immigrants. The money they had saved during the relatively prosperous war years and postwar period became the down-payment passage to the mass-produced housing tracts of Long Island, Staten Island, and New Jersey, where as proud homeowners they could settle down to a life that better resembled the one in the movies.

The few surviving old immigrants were taken along in this exodus, often reluctantly, now in the isolation of suburbia to regret the loss of both Italy and East Harlem. For Grandpa Giuseppe, who spent his last few years in Lindenhurst, Long Island, not even the magnificent vegetable garden he grew in the back of his daughter's house could compensate for the sense of double displacement he now endured.

The new prosperity and lifestyle took its toll of the second generation, too. One uncle, who used to have huge parties for friends and relatives in his home on Third Avenue complete with mandolins, accordions, and popular and operatic songs—drawn from the amateur talents of the guests themselves—now discovered that no one came to visit him on the outer edge of Queens. An aunt of mine, who had lived all her life within shouting distance of at least three of her sisters, tearfully told my mother how lonely she was way out in Staten Island.

In time, I went off to graduate school and saw far less of my extended family, as they did of each other. Years later in 1968 I got a call from my cousin Anthony asking me to attend a family reunion. It took place in Anthony's home in Queens, a crowd of cousins and their fourth-generation children, the latter being youngsters whom I was meeting for the first time and for whom East Harlem was nothing more than a geographical expression, if that.

Time had brought its changes. The women wore coiffured hairdos and stylish clothes, and the men looked heavier. There was much talk about recent vacations and a slide show of Anthony's travels to Europe, also a magnificent buffet of Italian foods that made the slide show worth sitting through. And there were a lot of invitations to "come visit us." Much to my disappointment the older surviving aunts and uncles had decided to stay away because this was an affair for the younger people, an act of age segregation that would have been unthinkable in earlier times. In all, we spent a pleasant evening joking and catching up on things. It was decided we should get together more often. But we never did have another reunion.

In the late 1970s I began to have recurring dreams, one every couple of months or so, continuing for a period of years. Unlike the recurring dreams portrayed in movies (in which the exact same footage is run and rerun) the particulars and fixtures of each dream in real life—or real sleep—differ, but the underlying theme is the same. In each dream I found myself living in a lovely newly done apartment; sometimes it had spiral stairwells and bare brick walls and sometimes lavish wood panelling and fireplaces, but it always turned out to be a renovation of 304 East 118th Street, the old brownstone in East Harlem where I had spent most of my early life.

We might think of recurring dreams as nightmarish, but these were accompanied by sensations of relief and yearning. The life past was being recaptured and renovated by the life now accomplished. The slum was being gentrified. The working-class Italian youth and the professional-class American academic were to live under the same roof. I had come home to two worlds apart. Never quite at home in either, I would now have the best of both. Once I understood the message, the dreams stopped.

THE BLESSINGS OF
PRIVATE ENTERPRISE

Years ago, my father drove a delivery truck for the Italian bakery owned by his uncle Torino. When Zi Torino returned to Italy in 1956, my father took over the entire business. The bread he made was the same bread that had been made in Gravina, Italy, for generations. After a whole day standing, it was fresh as ever, the crust having grown hard and crisp while the inside remained soft, solid, and moist. People used to say that our bread was a meal in itself.

The secret of the bread had been brought by my Zi Torino all the way from the Mediterranean to Manhattan, down into the tenement basement where he had installed wooden vats and tables. The bakers were two dark wiry men, *paisani* from Gravina, who rhythmically and endlessly pounded their powdery white hands into the dough, molding the bread with strength and finesse. Zi Torino and then my father after him, used time and care in preparing their bread, letting it sit and rise naturally, turning it over twice a night, using no chemicals and only the best quality unbleached flour. The bread was baked slowly and perfectly in an old brick oven built into the basement wall by Zi Torino in 1907, an oven that had secrets of its own.

Often during my college days, I would assist my father in loading up the bread truck at 5:00 a.m. on Saturday mornings. We delivered in the Bronx to Italian families whose appreciation for good bread was one of the satisfactions of our labor. My father's business remained small but steady. Customers, acquired slowly by word of mouth, remained with us forever. He would engage them in friendly conversations as he went along his route, taking nine hours to do seven hours of work. He could tell me more than I wanted to know about their family histories.

In time, some groceries, restaurants, and supermarkets started placing orders with us, causing us to expand our production. My father seemed pleased by the growth in his business, but I felt a vague uneasiness about making commercial deliveries to such unconsecrated places as the Jerome Avenue Supermarket. I began to wonder where it would all lead.

Some months after my father had begun to build his new clientele, as if to confirm my worst qualms, the Jerome Avenue Supermarket manager informed him that one of the big companies, Wonder Bread, was going into the "specialty line" and was offering to take over the Italian bread account. As an inducement to the supermarket, Wonder Bread was promising a free introductory offer of two hundred loaves. With that peculiar kind of generosity often found in merchants and bosses, the supermarket manager offered to reject the bid and keep our account if only we would match Wonder Bread's offer at least in part, say a hundred loaves.

"Their bread is paper compared to mine," my father protested. Indeed, our joke was: the reason they call it Wonder Bread is because after tasting it, you wonder if it's bread. But his artisan's pride proved no match for the merchant's manipulations, and he agreed to deliver a hundred free loaves, twenty-five a day, in order to keep the supermarket account, all the while cursing the manager under his breath. In the business world, this arrangement is referred to as a "deal" or an "agreement." To us it seemed more like extortion.

In response to "deals" of this sort, my father developed certain tricks of his own. By artfully flashing his hands across the tops of the delivery boxes he would short-count loaves right under the noses of the store managers: "Five and five across, that's twenty-five, Pete," he would point out, when in fact it was only twenty-three. We would load 550 loaves for the morning run, and he would sell 575. Not since the Sermon on the Mount had the loaves so increased.

"Pop," I said to him after one of his more daring performances, "You're becoming a thief."

"Kid," he said, "It's no sin to steal from them that steal from you." [*Individual competition in the pursuit of private gain brings out the best of our creative energies and thereby maximizes our productive contributions and advances the well being of the entire society.* Economics 101]

I left for a few years to go to graduate school, only to return home in 1959 without a penny in my pocket. I asked my father to support me for a semester so that I could finish writing my dissertation. In return, I offered to work a few days a week on the bread truck. My father agreed to this but he wondered how he would explain to friends and neighbors that his son was twenty-five years old and still without full-time employment.

"Kid, how long can you keep going to school and what for?" he asked. "All those books," he would warn me, "are bad for your eyes and bad for your mind."

Well," I said, "I'm getting a Ph.D." To this he made no response. So I put in a few days a week of hard labor on the truck. Nor did he complain. In fact, he needed the help and liked having me around (as he told my stepmother who told me).

When the bakers asked him how come, at the age of twenty-five, I was working only part-time, he said: "He's getting a Ph.D." From then on they called me "professor," a term that was applied with playful sarcasm. It was their way of indicating that they were not as impressed with my intellectual efforts as some people might be.

On the day my dissertation was accepted and I knew I was to receive my Ph.D., I proudly informed my father. He nodded and said, "That's good." Then he asked me if I wanted to become a full-time partner in the bread business working with him on the truck every day. With all the education out of the way, now maybe I would be ready to do some real work.

I almost said yes.

One day the health inspectors came by and insisted we could not leave the bread naked in the store aisles in open display boxes, exposed to passers-by who might wish to touch or fondle the loaves with their germ-ridden fingers. No telling what kind of infected people might chance into a supermarket to fondle the loaves. So my father and I were required to seal each loaf in a plastic bag, thus increasing our production costs, adding hours to our labor, and causing us to handle the bread twice as much with our germ-carrying fingers. But now it looked and tasted like modern bread because the bags kept the moisture in, and the loaves would get gummy in their own humidity inside their antiseptic plastic skins instead of forming a crisp, tasty crust in the open air.

Then some of the bigger companies began in earnest to challenge our restaurant and store trade, underselling us with an inferior quality "Italian bread." At about this time, the price of flour went up and the son of the landlord from whom Zi Torino had first rented the bakery premises a half century before raised our rent substantially.

"When it rains it pours," my father said. So he tried to reduce costs by giving the dough more air and water and spending less time on the preparation. The bakers shook their heads and went on making the imitation product for the plastic bags.

"Pop," I complained, "the bread doesn't taste as good as it used to. It's more like what the Americans make."

"What's the difference? They still eat it, don't they?" he said with a tight face.

But no matter what he did, things became more difficult. Some of our old family customers complained about the change in the quality of the bread and began to drop their accounts. And a couple of the big stores decided it was more profitable to carry the commercial brands.

Not long after, my father closed the bakery and went to work driving a cab for one of the big taxi fleets in New York City. In all the years that followed, he never mentioned the bread business again.

SPEAK TRUTH TO POWER,
MY LOVE

Speak truth to power, my love,
and watch their sleek smiles disappear.
The gatekeeper's face hardens
from the unaccustomed exposure
and those who should feel only shame
are filled with righteous puffery.

Meanwhile, the loyal oppositionists and labor dealers,
academic acolytes and kept scribes
all sniff the wind and test the *Times*,
trimming their sails, ready about!

With elaborate casualness,
they flash their ideological credentials.
With earnest asides,
they counsel self-censorship,

urging you to a smaller voice
to gain a bigger audience,
as they twist themselves in a tighter circle,
twisting for their credibility.

They know how to show courage
against easy targets.
Waiting for an approving glance,
they demand faultless standards
from besieged infant revolutions.
A critical distance they keep
when victims fight back and win.
They do mainstream imitations
Responsible Critics from Pragmatics, Inc.
and flash their anti-Menace pose
as they seek entry through the reception gate.

But you, my love, standing outside
under the chill glare of mean eyes,
you just speak truth to power
and feel your power rise.
Your life itself an unsung testimony
to fightback and fightforward
against their steel and gossamer.

Moving quietly in a raucous history,
the trickle becomes a tide
until one day the soldiers
look the other way or melt into the crowd,
drawn by the padding of a million footsteps.

M'lords squawk urgent commands
to stop the insolent dance.
M'lords sit in their bayonet temples,
calling upon the Furies of private interest
hurling their incantations.

And you,
you stand there like a thousand legions
and speak truth,
remembering how the tides
can break down walls.

YOUNG PEOPLE ARE DIFFERENT

Young people are different.
Hostages in their own homes,
kept alive by the telephone,
fully animated only when taking flight
    in rough formation.

They rebel
so better to submit
    to their totalitarian peerage.

Worshipping stereophonic gods
spirits gyrating to an endless beat
from Memphis to Moscow
from Tokyo to Tanzania
moving in unison
regiments of youth

bonded to their cassette cults
beeped to each other
wanting it both ways.

Stacey, Tracey, Buffy, and Tiffy
Kevin, Brian, Ryan, and Jamie
Dione, Tyrone, Dawne, and Fawne
incorporated for angst
with a genius for unhappy crisis
giggling at every mishap
a passion for the irrelevant
green hair and evasive eyes.

Worse still,
unwilling to drink from your fountain
with no loyalty to your struggles
no applause for your past glories
not terribly impressed by your words
seeing you only in the present
the sacrifices of yesterday mean little
    against the opportunities of today.

Don't be too harsh on them
for they have struggles of their own
and sacrifices for our planet's dwindling legacy.
Our young people, Yuri Andropov said, are not bad
only different.
Would we could say as much
    about the world we leave them.

TO MY SON
AS I CONTEMPLATE MY DEATH

Upon my departure
grieve not too fiercely,
for casting across that spaceless light
like Saturn's orbit dimmed by distance,
waiting to touch you,
I shall be transformed—
    only that.

After a life answering its call,
fretting over shadows on the cave wall
for vain promises not really desired,
yet with sense enough to pit a middling talent
    against majestic goals,
a small walk-on part for a better world.

Now to find beyond the dark passage
a world of luminous wonder and joyful comprehension

of things you and I pondered
when you were scarcely ten years old,
surmising that the personality cannot capture the soul,
but the joyful soul remembers the personality.

I'll not hesitate to re-enter
but shall move in another time,
urging your guardians to perfect diligence,
cheering you on from across a mute universe.

Yet grieve a little,
for who knows what deposit of love
can survive that distance?
When even the prodigy of your metaphysics
and the protective ferocity of a father's heart
cannot produce certitude,
when one's composition is immolated by time,
    never to recompose,
never again these hands, these eyes,
a dreadful certitude that creates the pain of doubt.

So I ask you, in your later years,
in a quiet moment,
to keep the memory of our company and our struggle,
and the loyal unfinished love,
each for the other.

Ciao bambino

In the fading cosmic light
two little boys embrace good night.

About the Author

MICHAEL PARENTI is considered one of the nation's leading progressive thinkers. He received his Ph.D. in political science from Yale University in 1962, and has taught at a number of colleges and universities. His writings have been featured in scholarly journals, popular periodicals, and newspapers. Dr. Parenti lectures around the country on college campuses and before religious, labor, community, peace, and public interest groups. He has appeared on radio and television to discuss current issues or ideas from his published works. Tapes of his talks have played on numerous radio stations to enthusiastic audiences. Audio and video tapes of his talks are sold on a not-for-profit basis; for a listing, contact People's Video, P.O. Box 99514, Seattle WA 98199; tel. 206 789-5371. Dr. Parenti lives in Berkeley, California.

CITY LIGHTS PUBLICATIONS

Mrabet, Mohammed. LOVE WITH A FEW HAIRS
Mrabet, Mohammed. M'HASHISH
Murguía, A. & B. Paschke, eds. VOLCAN: Poems from Central America
Murillo, Rosario. ANGEL IN THE DELUGE
Nadir, Shams. THE ASTROLABE OF THE SEA
Parenti, Michael. AGAINST EMPIRE
Parenti, Michael. DIRTY TRUTHS
Pasolini, Pier Paolo. ROMAN POEMS
Pessoa, Fernando. ALWAYS ASTONISHED
Peters, Nancy J., ed. WAR AFTER WAR (City Lights Review #5)
Poe, Edgar Allan. THE UNKNOWN POE
Porta, Antonio. KISSES FROM ANOTHER DREAM
Prévert, Jacques. PAROLES
Purdy, James. THE CANDLES OF YOUR EYES
Purdy, James. GARMENTS THE LIVING WEAR
Purdy, James. IN A SHALLOW GRAVE
Purdy, James. OUT WITH THE STARS
Rachlin, Nahid. THE HEART'S DESIRE
Rachlin, Nahid. MARRIED TO A STRANGER
Rachlin, Nahid. VEILS: SHORT STORIES
Reed, Jeremy. DELIRIUM: An Interpretation of Arthur Rimbaud
Reed, Jeremy. RED-HAIRED ANDROID
Rey Rosa, Rodrigo. THE BEGGAR'S KNIFE
Rey Rosa, Rodrigo. DUST ON HER TONGUE
Rigaud, Milo. SECRETS OF VOODOO
Ross, Dorien. RETURNING TO A
Ruy Sánchez, Alberto. MOGADOR
Saadawi, Nawal El. MEMOIRS OF A WOMAN DOCTOR
Sawyer-Lauçanno, Christopher, transl. THE DESTRUCTION OF THE JAGUAR
Scholder, Amy, ed. CRITICAL CONDITION: Women on the Edge of Violence
Sclauzero, Mariarosa. MARLENE
Serge, Victor. RESISTANCE
Shepard, Sam. MOTEL CHRONICLES
Shepard, Sam. FOOL FOR LOVE & THE SAD LAMENT OF PECOS BILL
Smith, Michael. IT A COME
Snyder, Gary. THE OLD WAYS
Solnit, Rebecca. SECRET EXHIBITION: Six California Artists
Sussler, Betsy, ed. BOMB: INTERVIEWS
Takahashi, Mutsuo. SLEEPING SINNING FALLING
Turyn, Anne, ed. TOP TOP STORIES
Tutuola, Amos. FEATHER WOMAN OF THE JUNGLE
Tutuola, Amos. SIMBI & THE SATYR OF THE DARK JUNGLE
Valaoritis, Nanos. MY AFTERLIFE GUARANTEED
Veltri, George. NICE BOY
Waldman, Anne. FAST SPEAKING WOMAN
Wilson, Colin. POETRY AND MYSTICISM
Wilson, Peter Lamborn. SACRED DRIFT
Wynne, John. THE OTHER WORLD
Zamora, Daisy. RIVERBED OF MEMORY